DISCARD

Designed in Germany
Since 1949

Designed in Germany

Since 1949

Edited by Michael Erlhoff
for the Rat für Formgebung / German Design Council
Editorial Supervisor: Bernd Busch

With contributions by
Bernd Busch, Michael Erlhoff, Dieter Rams,
Gwendolyn Ristant, and Brigitte Wolf

Prestel

This book was published in conjunction with the exhibition "Designed in Germany Since 1949" organized by the Rat für Formgebung, the German Design Council, Frankfurt/Main in 1990 and shown in several cities in the United States.

Translations from the German by Jeremy Gaines

On the cover: ET 66 Pocket calculator, Braun AG
Frontispiece: Kardan bi system 9×12 camera, Linhof Nikolaus Karpf KG

Published by Prestel-Verlag, Mandlstrasse 26, D-8000 Munich 40, Federal Republic of Germany.
Tel. (89) 38 17 09 0, Telefax (89) 38 17 09 35

Distributed in continental Europe and Japan by Prestel-Verlag, Verlegerdienst München GmbH & Co KG, Gutenbergstrasse 1, D-8031 Gilching, Federal Republic of Germany
Tel. (81 05) 21 10, Telefax (81 05) 55 20

Distributed in the USA and Canada by te Neues Publishing Company, 15 East 76th Street, New York, NY 10021, USA. Tel. (212) 288 0265, Telefax (212) 570 23 73

Distributed in the United Kingdom, Ireland and all other countries by Thames & Hudson Limited, 30–34 Bloomsbury Street, London WC1B 3QP, England,
Tel. (1) 636 54 88, Telefax (1) 636 47 99

Typeset by Utesch Satztechnik GmbH, Hamburg
Color separations by Fotolito Longo, Frangart, Italy
Printed and bound by Druckerei Kösel, Kempten

Printed in Germany
ISBN 3-7913-1079-8 (German edition)
Softcover edition not available to the trade
ISBN 3-7913-1067-4 (English edition)

Preface

This volume appears during sensational times. It is perhaps an expression of this ferment and the utopia intrinsic to it; for even though the book deals mainly with history, it is a part of the present and the future.

It seems that suddenly everything has been set in motion. Borders are shifting, blocs are crumbling, walls are becoming transparent, and received patterns of order are being subverted. Fixed spaces and containing structures are disintegrating into mobile elements or are becoming fluid. All at once, everything has a new shine to it, is no longer what it used to be, and standards are revealing themselves to be paper tigers.

This is not only the result of microelectronics and telecommunications, which have been changing the world for some time now, generating new styles and a new dynamism which have affected both the human imagination and, in particular, objects themselves – an exciting enough development, which has occasionally turned the logic of design upside down, setting completely new tasks and stimulating new approaches thereto. But also – at least in Europe – it is now the political and possibly even the geographical structures and circumstances that are being shaken. And the upheaval is all the greater given that late 1989 saw the abrupt opening of the frontiers to Eastern Europe, long before the planned realization of a Single European Market in 1992. We should not forget that the Single European Market in itself entails tremendous changes, which will largely remove the borders between the countries of the European Community (the United Kingdom, France, Italy, Ireland, Denmark, Spain, Belgium, Holland, Luxembourg, Greece, Portugal, and the Federal Republic of Germany) and thus facilitate transport, free trade, and the freedom to move and settle anywhere within the Community. This will create completely new social and economic coordinates and forms of cooperation and will lead to the emergence of idiosyncratic structures no longer dictated by national frontiers.

The current changes in Eastern Europe have, however, pre-empted all such reorientations and will continue in the long term to shake all static forms of thinking to their very foundations. The geographic and economic hub of Europe has suddenly been shifted eastwards and has raised hitherto marginal areas to the status of centers. Moreover, the basis is crumbling away for traditional images of who and what constitutes the enemy, revealing new vistas of a pan-European network such as has never been dreamed of before. And all of this will have a highly tangible impact, particularly on all questions concerning organization and form, and thus on design. Amidst these transformation processes, in other words, one history is ending in order that a new history may begin, developing new criteria, posing new challenges, and calling for new solutions.

At the same time, however, particularly in this phase of upheaval, history can once again be experienced as history, as transcience and preservation, as the source of forward-looking thought and action. History appears as the form in which the particular present encounters itself and fulfills its promise. For history is the place in which the future is thinkable. What is more, it becomes apparent in such turbulent times that history is not some rigid edifice, that it does not exist of itself, but rather intrinsically reflects the process of the present, appears full of cracks and in need of interpretation. Not only the present, but also history itself have of late become obscure. Monuments have collapsed, the rigid adherence to "universal" values has proved to be dishonest, and a wealth of new possibilities for learning from history – especially from its contradictions – are starting to emerge.

When viewed in this light, history becomes wonderful again, and manifold reasons arise for presenting history in new ways – in particular, the history of materialized forms and shapes, those designs and objectifications which were an early attempt to encapsulate what life and work were and always pointed beyond their own historicity. For history reveals itself in design in all its complexity, occurs as something that has gelled, i.e., is thing-like and yet transitory. In this respect, the present volume consistently attempts to explore the two sides of the subject: on the one hand, following the changing perspectives, presenting the designs that were considered important in their own time; and on the other hand, looking back from the standpoint of today and highlighting those phenomena which might still surprise us as anticipatory "patterns of possible worlds."

The present volume takes this approach with regard to design in the Federal Republic of Germany, which is summarized here under the title "Designed in Germany" and which could therefore to a certain extent be understood as an updated version of the universal trade mark "Made in Germany," which from 1949 onwards undoubtedly referred to the Federal Republic of Germany, thus equating "Germany" with "the Federal Republic." Given that both Germanies are particularly affected by the current changes in Europe and that no one can predict how the relationship between them will develop in the future, the present book takes on a special significance. For it appears at a time when the forty years of profound dispute between the German Democratic Republic and the Federal Republic of Germany are coming to an end. This confrontation was indeed so comprehensive at all levels of society that fundamentally divergent forms and structures evolved, superimposing themselves on all the preceding common historical roots. Despite German design's traditional wish to have an international outlook, the great differences in the political, cultural, and economic forms of the two German states also resulted in differences in matters of design and, above all, in their practical realization, so that only partial correspondences were possible. After all, it was only recently that official East German design policy came to accept the Bauhaus as a historical heritage, and to recognize the existence of Otto Haesler, the German architect who was treated with contempt by both Germanies. Once an associate of the Bauhaus, he consciously chose to live in the GDR after 1949 – his work was, in consequence, rejected in West Germany and yet, because he continued to uphold the ideas of the Bauhaus, it was also ignored in East Germany.

So, despite the existence both of a common design history prior to 1945 and of some links between designers in East and West Germany, there is every justification for the publication of a book on design in the Federal Republic of Germany, especially when one considers that it offers the first comprehensive review of the field. It may also mark the conclusion of a forty-year historical period, for the future may well bring a new dimension to German design, and will certainly entail a new cooperative element.

For all its topical relevance, this book was unfortunately subject to the usual restrictions, namely of having to confine its subject-matter within a limited number of pages. A sometimes almost despairing selection had to be made from over 60,000 possible and no doubt significant designs; criteria of taste were bound to influence us, although we always tried to be objective. The selection presented is, we hope, fairly representative; though we are aware that this or the other omission may well be noted with regret by some readers.

Designed in Germany Since 1949 is published in conjunction with the exhibition of German design staged by the German Design Council in Los Angeles and other cities in the United States and Canada. I would like to take this opportunity to thank the benefactors, board of trustees, and managing committee of the German Design Council, who have sponsored the exhibition and lent their support in matters of content. In connection with this book, I would particularly like to thank not only the authors, but also Bernd Busch, who did all the editing and coordinating work. I would also like to express my special thanks to Helge Aszmoneit, the German Design Council's librarian, Ursula Wenzel and Stephan Ott, who are in charge of the Council's archive of photographic material, and Uta Brandes for her extensive assistance in planning and compiling this publication, not to mention GDC staff members Brigitte Lareche, Alfred Guck, Julia Lang, Anne Dombrowski, Gerda Mikosch, and Christel Berchem, and the staff of the Prestel publishing house, all of whom made an often out-of-the-ordinary contribution to the creation of this book.

The result of so much work is a book that is hopefully as surprising as it is analytical and descriptive, and, not least, a book that expresses the high quality and the unique character of "Designed in Germany."

Michael Erlhoff
Frankfurt, February 1990

Contents

Design as a Form of Social Organization
An Attempted Topography of West German Design
Michael Erlhoff   9

Design in Daily Life
Brigitte Wolf   15

Ulm
Gwendolyn Ristant   21

Other Manifestations of the Fifties
Gwendolyn Ristant   47

Good Form
Gwendolyn Ristant   101

Product Design in the Sixties
Dieter Rams   131

The Seventies
Bernd Busch   145

Corporate Identity
Gwendolyn Ristant   189

Contemporary Design Trends
Gwendolyn Ristant   207

Design-Orientated Companies in the FRG   245

Appendix   272
  Designers
  Design Institutions
  Design Awards
  Design Periodicals
  Selected Bibliography
  Picture Credits
  Index

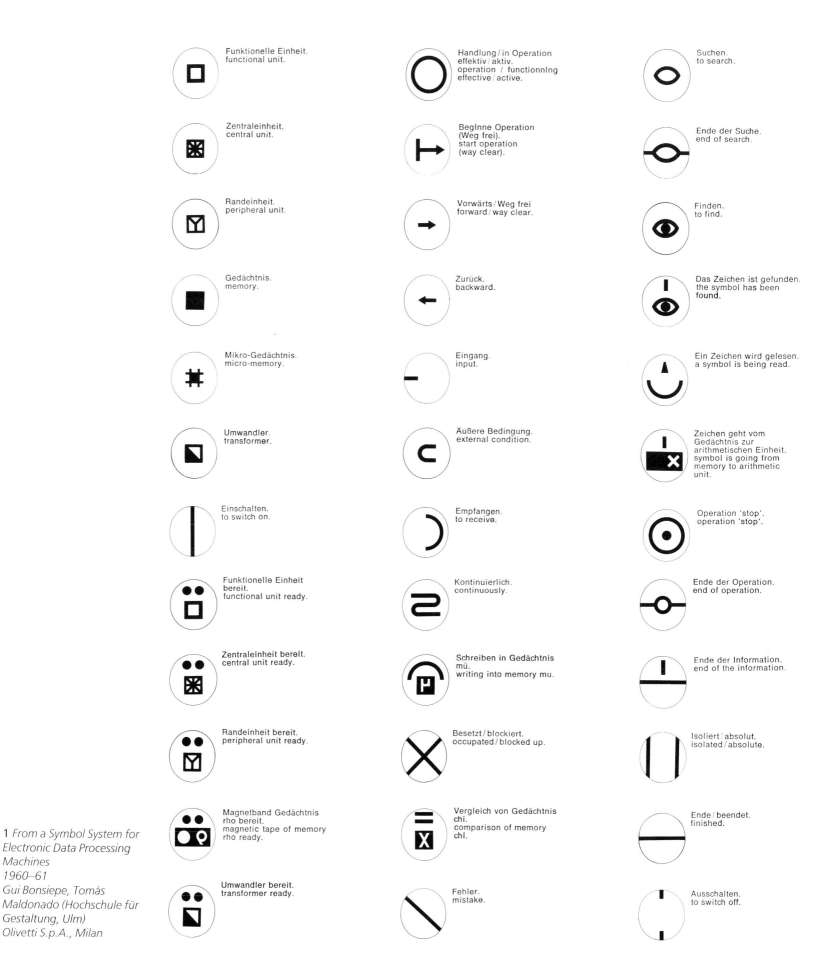

Funktionelle Einheit.
functional unit.

Zentraleinheit.
central unit.

Randeinheit.
peripheral unit.

Gedächtnis.
memory.

Mikro-Gedächtnis.
micro-memory.

Umwandler.
transformer.

Einschalten.
to switch on.

Funktionelle Einheit
bereit.
functional unit ready.

Zentraleinheit bereit.
central unit ready.

Randeinheit bereit.
peripheral unit ready.

Magnetband Gedächtnis
rho bereit.
magnetic tape of memory
rho ready.

Umwandler bereit.
transformer ready.

Handlung / in Operation
effektiv / aktiv.
operation / functionning
effective / active.

Beginne Operation
(Weg frei).
start operation
(way clear).

Vorwärts / Weg frei
forward / way clear.

Zurück.
backward.

Eingang.
input.

Äußere Bedingung.
external condition.

Empfangen.
to receive.

Kontinuierlich.
continuously.

Schreiben in Gedächtnis
mü.
writing into memory mu.

Besetzt / blockiert.
occupied / blocked up.

Vergleich von Gedächtnis
chi.
comparison of memory
chi.

Fehler.
mistake.

Suchen.
to search.

Ende der Suche.
end of search.

Finden.
to find.

Das Zeichen ist gefunden.
the symbol has been
found.

Ein Zeichen wird gelesen.
a symbol is being read.

Zeichen geht vom
Gedächtnis zur
arithmetischen Einheit.
symbol is going from
memory to arithmetic
unit.

Operation 'stop'.
operation 'stop'.

Ende der Operation.
end of operation.

Ende der Information.
end of the information.

Isoliert / absolut.
isolated / absolute.

Ende / beendet.
finished.

Ausschalten.
to switch off.

1 *From a Symbol System for
Electronic Data Processing
Machines
1960–61
Gui Bonsiepe, Tomás
Maldonado (Hochschule für
Gestaltung, Ulm)
Olivetti S.p.A., Milan*

Michael Erlhoff

Design as a Form of Social Organization

An Attempted Topography of West German Design

1. Design as Reconstruction

In German, the word "design" is translated as *Form-gebung* ("giving form") or *Gestaltung* ("giving shape"). Where the English term contains a static element, the German denotes the dynamic category, emphasizing the work-process, the active element. A further difference is that whereas "design," which is related to *dessin*, implicitly contains the sense of drawing, sketching, outlining, the words *Gestaltung* and *Formgebung* point toward a far more complex state of affairs. *Formgebung*, in particular, suggests the possibility of intervening extensively in all kinds of processes, or of triggering them off.

"Design" in other words seeks to clothe and possibly to qualify something which has always existed or has been manufactured – by engineers, economists, and others – and is thus inextricably linked to the empirically visible existence of things. By contrast, *Formgebung* has always connoted the true force, the alpha and omega of objects, the center to be generated from within, thereby bringing objects into relation with one another and with human beings. All this might be mere hair-splitting, of no particular interest, especially since everyday usage with its tendency to obscure nuances has long since established the word "Design" in German: it is used even in such contexts as *Forschungs-Design* ("research design") or the "design" of bread-rolls. However, the distinction between the two concepts does in fact reveal tangible, concrete differences between American and British design, excessively governed by empiricism, the continually spatially and culturally oriented design of the Latin countries, and German design, which has always sought to formulate social and educational intentions. For despite all processes of international assimilation, the remnants of cultural, economic and political traditions make themselves felt all over the world as idiosyncratic characteristics which for the sake of convenience are termed "national" or "regional" features – and this is also true of German design. Thus it is indeed possible to talk of "Designed in Germany," something that often takes a more concrete form – even in the cliché that outsiders still tend to regard the overall reality of German interior decoration as *gemütlich* and admire German design for being "rectangular and reliable."

Certainly, all individuality has its roots in a particular history. For example, in the history of a Germany that became a nation-state only at a comparatively late date – in the 19th century – and German political thinking hinged on concrete notions with an aversion to empirical existence. Or take the philosophical debate in which eighteenth century German Enlightenment gathered behind the banner of metaphysics, dismissing Anglo-Saxon empiricism – that trust in sound common sense and the tangible or visible – as short-sighted. Again, German economic structure was very late in accepting industrialization; even today it is still based on the ideas of medium-scale industry, and often feels the need to find social justification for its existence. Similarly, we cannot expect to understand German design without tracing the idiosyncratic historical evolution of some of its present-day features.

2. Design as History

All these developmental currents – and doubtless many more that cannot be taken into consideration here – led to a curious public awareness in Germany that demanded not only of design, but even to a certain extent of industry and technology, that they should justify themselves in social terms or at least be capable of providing such a justification, be forced to accept social responsibility. Thus it was quite early on that many companies built housing-estates for their employees or organized cultural programs for them. Design in Germany always had a socio-political side to it, or tried to establish such, positing the healthy relationship between subject and object as the source of the dream of identity; yet at the same time it implicitly accorded priority to the objects themselves. For in the final analysis, even German Enlightenment had already shifted the principles of life away from the randomness of the person as subject in the direction of a hope placed in objectifiability. It was seen that objects were the basis of experience and action, while human beings made the experiences and carried out the actions. It was then up to design either to adopt the latent didactic thrust of this conception or develop one of its own. Certainly, this claim to a social role cannot be regarded without ambivalence, for dictates, and educational measures imposed from above, always veil the true nature and the manifestations of social conflicts; they tend in fact to give rise to ideology, blinkeredness, and appeasement. At the same time, however, it is always possible to generalize the claim to social responsibility and thus to keep it alive. Incidentally, this social and didactic component of German design is often viewed with incredulity and enthusiasm by non-Germans.

The development of German design was marked by this sense of social commitment from the outset and even nurtured on it. An early embodiment of this attitude was the Werkbund, an association of architects, artists and craftsmen founded in Munich in 1907. Its aim was to formulate a humane culture of everyday life as opposed to high-culture, which had been a prerogative of the elite. Members endeavored to enhance the quality of working and living conditions by improving the use value of objects by means of design. This involved combating the rigid social structures of the late nineteenth century and seeking unconventional ways to establish solidarity between human beings and to further their common interests, while wresting benefit for the people from the process of industrialization. Efforts focussed particularly on architecture and town planning (culminating in 1926 in the building of the Weissenhof Estate in Stuttgart), and on establishing new communally based modes of life and production. For example, in certain factories, where the workers had a say in the shaping of work routines, communal gymnastics and callisthenics sessions were introduced for the workforce.

These endeavors were inspired by the wish to modernize everyday culture, to reconcile it with the idea of modernity. In anticipation, as it were, of present-day concepts of corporate identity and corporate culture, people were, for example, supposed to work and act collectively and happily together; indeed, like the products of their labor, they were supposed to radiate from within. In other words, the body, which also consisted of shapes and surfaces, was reduced to being an expression of the soul. This was to be accomplished by means of a sort of idealistic self-realization, because what was introduced from the outside — a didacticism that extended to the very heart of the objects — was then supposed to develop a brilliant radiance from within.

The Werkbund still remained faithful to this concept even when it was explicitly cooperating with German industry. The overall desire was to form an industrial culture and basically amounted to the attempt to adjust the everyday character of work and life to modernism. An exemplary figure in this movement was Peter Behrens, who originally came from the fine arts and played an important role in Art Nouveau (a movement that had in Germany at times been accompanied by strong moral overtones); for the AEG electrical combine he then proceeded to design not only posters, advertising, and other forms of presentation, but also the products themselves (lamps, fans, switchboxes), and even the architecture. This was the sort of complex system of interconnections and combinations that has only recently, in the course of the discussion surrounding corporate identity, been rediscovered as an outstanding quality of design.

Behrens's work was based on the concept of design as the kingpin of social and economic life; precisely as a social deed and as a structure that bore the hallmarks of society as a whole. With the Werkbund was founded the tradition of sociopolitical legitimateness for design that is still strong today and has itself almost always been considered part of the socially critical spectrum. Most German designers have adhered to some extent to the idea of social commitment in the search for new aesthetic and organizational forms.

Constructivism was inspired by similar ideas, as was Dadaism, at least in its Berlin variant (particularly as espoused by Raoul Hausmann). The same is true of the work of Kurt Schwitters from Hannover, who not only created collages, assemblages, reliefs, poetry, and his Merz art-form, but was also co-founder of the *Ring Deutscher Werbegestalter* (Circle of German Advertising Designers). Furthermore, together with architect Otto Haesler from Celle, he designed chairs and tables (*Celler Volksmöbel*), wrote critiques of architecture, and collaborated with Walter Gropius.

Indeed, it was Walter Gropius who in 1919 founded the Bauhaus, which probably embodied the most famous educational and design concept in the history of German architecture and design. It is symptomatic of the development of German design theories and practices that here, too, innovation in design was accompanied by educational concepts: in other words, it took place in a school. It taught the importance of social and political awareness, and aimed like in the Werkbund to relate art and life in design on the basis of a vernacular culture.

There was perhaps a strain of rigidly idyllic Romanticism at the Bauhaus (cf. the re-introduction of the title "master craftsman"), which at times was taken to the point of an ossified idyll. It played a dominant role in this concept and also in the initial organization of the Bauhaus, but this serves only to demonstrate a crystallization in the 1920s of the essence of the previous two centuries attempts to impose a new order on the chaos that was society and to restore human reason to its pristine purity. Furthermore, the Bauhaus saw itself as something of an international movement.

Particularly in Germany there were additional reasons for this international outlook. A didactic design movement which believed itself to possess, or to have recognized and be implementing, justifiable principles and which considered itself capable of rational action, necessarily and obviously had to lay claim to international significance — what was true must surely be true everywhere. Of course, the ambivalence of metaphysics (especially a metaphysics that has not been comprehensively elaborated) immediately reveals itself here, namely in the tendency to turn dogmatic somersaults and proclaim itself to be unshakably objective. Since this internationalism also fitted neatly in with the expansion of German industry and its conquest of world markets, one cannot help but conclude that the Bauhaus, be it ingeniously or deliberately, also produced ideology. This is also apparent from some of the designs themselves, which betray the Bauhaus ideal of pure function and pure use-value in the name of superficial gloss.

Nevertheless, the Bauhaus is undeniably a monument, and an impressive demonstration of the quality of German design. The Nazis lost no time in closing it down when they came to power, even though some Bauhaus professors naively believed that they could cooperate with the new architects of a "Thousand-Year Reich." In fact, the way was paved for social chaos, bringing the history of democratic design to a temporary halt; its place was taken by irrational, purely abstract, merely violent, authoritarian gestures that purported to be form. The real differences between thought and action, and between empiricism and reason, were now forcibly and fictitiously reconciled by the fascist and power principle, and the erstwhile dream of a "total design" or a *Gesamtkunstwerk* was now, after 1933, realized in the destructive form of isolation and extermination.

3. Design as Construct

The beginnings of the Federal Republic of Germany after 1949 can be seen as an attempt at social reorganization and reconstruction – and, right from the start, this involved design.

In order to understand the events fully, it is necessary to consider the situation. In 1948 the currency reform was effected in the zones controlled by the Western Allies – and Germany was divided into two nations. In 1949, the Federal Republic was founded, a constitution was drawn up, the first elections were held, and the Federal Parliament convened for the first time. This all took place in a Germany that – not just in physical terms – lay in ruins, that had worshiped German fascism, started the war, and lost it.

The mounds of debris reflected the psychological misery of a people that had wanted to proclaim themselves masters and to this end had betrayed and derided all notions of morality, society and internationalism. It was the misery of a people in the morass of an arrogant and fictitious, inhuman and enforced order that had finally revealed itself to be chaos. The Germans had dutifully adhered to a social order that had substituted force for all legitimation and had dismissed any debate as mere "hot air." They had lost their roots even before the war, before 1945 – but this did not become evident until after the Allies had declared an end to fascism and the war.

This prompted the Allies, following their victory, to establish a German society organized according to a different conception and a different set of principles. Of course, they had only their own criteria of order, which they simply tried to superimpose on the chaos they found. This was how the West German political and educational system came into being, how the economy and the legal system were organized, and was also the basis for postwar German architecture, musical fantasy and silver-screen worlds, and other manifestations of everyday culture.

Not all of this, however, was accepted without question. The opposition came not so much from those who had been such keen supporters of fascism – they tried desperately to save their skins and their capital – rather, it was those who had worked for the resistance and had been incarcerated or forced into exile. At any rate, different political factions existed in post-1945 Germany, and some of these were represented in the first Federal Parliament in 1949; these people were convinced that the creation of a society involves questions of form, and that thought and dissension on these issues needed to be encouraged.

Remarkably enough, the year 1949 spawned not just one but two processes that were of equal importance both for the new democratic consciousness in Germany and for design. Firstly, not long after the war's end, Inge Scholl had founded an adult education center in Ulm in memory of her brother and sister, who had been murdered by the Nazis. With the support of Otl Aicher and Carl Zuckmayer, she invited intellectuals whose integrity was still intact to speak and lead discussions on democracy and democratization. It goes without saying that in this context all approaches were accepted, the philosophical, just as much as the explicitly political, or those based on poetic notions or visual art. In 1949, Inge Scholl embarked on the task of forging a college of higher education from these rudimentary beginnings. Initially, it was to be a comprehensive College of Democracy in the broadest sense, but then, under the influence of Otl Aicher, who nevertheless shared the same underlying intentions, it became a college of design. These were the origins of the famous HfG Ulm, which was founded in 1953 with considerable support from a few enlightened and reputable Americans.

The second event that also occurred in 1949 was the parliamentary introduction by the Social Democrats of a bill proposing the initiation of a "Rat für Formgebung," a German Design Council.

This move was evidently inspired by members of the Werkbund, which had been so important for design in the early twentieth century. It constituted a remarkably far-sighted attempt to focus political discussion on precisely those objectives which were imperative: namely, to investigate and provide justification for the potential of form and the multiplicity of forms – and to expand the concept of design in a wonderful and future-oriented manner so that it should cover all shaping of form, in other words, organization, grammar, syntax, and order, for democracy is indeed a problem of form.

In 1953, the year in which the HfG was opened, the Federal Parliament approved the establishment of the Rat für Formgebung foundation, which was assigned the task of ensuring the good form of German products and of mediating on behalf of design among the various interest-groups involved. It was recommended that the Federal Minister for Economic Affairs should provide the required support, and the Council soon became, quite idealistically, an agency representing good taste. Its mission was to formulate standards and, in equal measure, to promote and propagate the qualities of German design. In this context, the already familiar didactic intentions were once again to be linked very directly with economic interests; thus the economic element in form was regarded as one of the social objectives – which design, after all, had to provide for in the first place – or the social benefit for all was held to be a primary component of economic development. As a result, it was not long before the term "social free-market economy" was coined, a formulation practically unique to West Germany. Education was, incidentally, always a fundamental principle of the HfG, too, in terms of both its internal didactic program and its aim to educate the public about objects and their meaning. In this respect, both the Rat für Formgebung and the HfG remained steeped in the German design tradition, although there was an explicit difference between the two in that the Rat für Formgebung was always embedded in the national promotion of design, whereas from the very beginning the HfG had an internationalist orientation and was the workplace for many overseas students and lecturers.

4. Design and Orientation

Now the agenda henceforth also included, besides the explicitly political and the administrative reorganization and the restructuring of the economy, the reorganization of everyday culture. For the intention was that the externally imposed new order of a democratic Germany should find an expression that would be disseminated and communicated. And design was to play an active role precisely here.

Admittedly, many other domains were involved in this reshaping of everyday culture, Fashion designers were called upon to create new clothes for the new society, dance schools opened and did good business all over the country imparting new styles and a new conviviality, and the fifties saw the remarkable success of books that aimed to teach the Germans good behavior. A certain Frau von Pappritz cut a particularly awe-inspiring figure in this context; she was employed by the government to hammer the military heel-clicking out of its politicians and to drill them in etiquette instead. This resulted, among other things, in a searching public debate on the question of whether politicians should wear long or short underpants. (The debate apparently ended in favor of the long-legged variety, which, however, should not be visible.)

Emphasis was placed on the question of behavior and bearing (the German word *Geisteshaltung* involves both, meaning "intellectual bearing" or "attitude"). In addition, encyclopedias offered a wealth of useful knowledge, for now education counted for something again and could be accepted as being antibarbarian per se. An institution was founded to which Germans like to refer as "the nation's school," namely the German army, now termed the *Bundeswehr* as distinct from the earlier *Wehrmacht*. This not only pandered to the general remilitarization of the dawning "Cold War" era but also helped to ease West Germany's entry into the Western Alliance and thus NATO; above all, the concept of the army, as part of the goal of establishing political order, fitted in with the general education and reordering of a nation. It lent this nation prestige, order, style, and self-confidence.

In this respect, the gulf dividing the HfG or the Rat für Formgebung on the one hand and the Bundeswehr on the other well illustrates the differences in and the overall coherence of the driving desire of the day to find a new (or newish) form, to attempt to reshape society and place at its disposal the means necessary to put this reorganization into practice. However, leaving aside the fundamental qualitative differences between the respective ideas of form involved – and these should really have rendered any comparison between design and the military obsolete – all these didactic measures failed to take account of the most relevant factor: empirical beings. For at the level of social reality, these educational approaches came up against what was a very heterogeneous resistance. Instead of design, what spread throughout the country was the usual kitsch, once again filling nice German living-rooms (and doubtless certain sectors of the economy profited from this) with the set pieces of imaginary affluence, such as radiograms, oak furniture, smoking-room furnishings, and the like. And good behavior did not last long either, particularly in the increasingly heavy traffic, where drivers made a habit of gesturing that their fellow travelers were crazy. On the other hand, voices were raised against remilitarization, and the Easter Marches began to advocate pacifism and disarmament. Thus, an extraparliamentary opposition developed, engaging in vehement conflicts with what had recently become the iron hand of the state. Some also sounded off against the exaggerated or perhaps dishonest rationality that was now constantly being preached; many reactionaries or "incorrigibles" gathered in a *gemütlich* atmosphere to enjoy "old comrades'" reunions, demonstrating that re-education could not be achieved as easily as many had thought. On the other hand, teenagers began to rebel against the new ordinances, and rock 'n' roll gained real fans in the young Federal Republic. For the educationalists in all the parliamentary parties, this was just as much chaos incarnate as was the existentialism suddenly in vogue among young intellectuals.

Thus, whereas "good form" was obviously unable directly to fulfill its educational task of bringing rational and well-designed products home to everyone on a broad scale, it nonetheless strengthened the designers' cause and encouraged companies to pay careful attention to form and to experiment – whereby it was the larger firms who in turn gave a boost to "good form." Here again, the dividing-line between commercial and ethical considerations was often blurred.

During this period the foundation of outstanding design was laid for the second time; it has visibly shaped the image of West German design – which is usually associated with the names of a few companies. And its influence has extended as far as technical equipment and capital goods, for in these sectors, too, design enhances the respectability of a company, as it were, and has always improved the quality of the products. However, as was the case in other countries, most German companies in the sixties and seventies subordinated design to technological progress, frequently regarding it as a mere dogsbody for the engineers. All the same, a number of technical inventions, such as the rotary magazine for slide projectors, developed by Hans Gugelot, were even at that time the work of designers who, thanks to their multidisciplinary skills, have always had a good nose for original, pioneering developments.

In the late sixties, in connexion with the largely student-based protest movement, West German design finally acquired the explicit political impact it had so long desired, for now the question of social form was once again being raised, indeed being raised in a very fundamental and public manner. What official policymakers and broad sections of the population had treated all too summarily while rebuilding Germany in the fifties, namely the question as to how society could be reorganized within democratic parameters, was now being asked again in a highly public manner. Some design colleges, most notably the HfG (which the authorities then promptly closed in 1968), participated directly in this protest movement, which at the beginning had predominantly had its base in the universities. Design, with all the demands it made of objects and creative work, was easily able to identify with and feel at home amidst this politicization of the sciences and everyday life as well as the concomitant radical reflection on how and where one lived and worked.

This led to design – particularly as a course of study – temporarily turning its back on the immediate world of commodities as such and concentrating more on subjects like ergonomics, the shaping of the public domain (including the development of public design) and on questions of social benefit or ecology, thus reflecting upon and affirming the foundations of an extended concept of design.

The 1968 protest movement, which had been born of an attitude that had cast into question society as a whole (it was for this reason alone that it met with so much response and was in fact able to bring about some real changes), at the same time marked the end of an unbroken faith in technology and progress. It also heralded the beginning of new reflections on our environment and our lifeworld, and on the material nature of objects. All dogmas were called into question and, at long last, society itself came to be regarded as a process, namely as the history of an inner dynamic which moved in a rational direction only if it was halted by enlightened individuals the minute it veered off that path.

This very general increase in the level of reflection and awareness at least intensified people's attentiveness and sensitivity to social processes, to forms of coexistence, and also to the forms of objects. We should, of course, be wary of oversimplified generalizations here, but it is nevertheless possible to classify this phenomenon – not least because of a demand for education triggered off among the majority of the population at the time – as a social trend that necessarily influenced design or debates about form. Furthermore, given that West Germany was gradually moving into a position where it could offer many people greater affluence (which was achieved, as usual, at the price of exceptional poverty for some others), the demands of the people (generally referred to as "consumers") began to rise. At the same time, there was intensified activity on the part of design and design-oriented companies. This has in turn led to the present-day situation in which the only objects that have a chance on the market are the ones whose "design" is clearly evident; today, everyone is talking about design, and everyone wants to acquire and possess design.

One could be forgiven for thinking that the socially oriented didactic thrust of German design has borne fruit and thus found fulfillment. Yet nothing of the sort has happened, for despite the attempts of designers to convey a sense of form and function per se and win acceptance for this, design suddenly became caught up in the current of a compulsive desire for self-presentation on the part of consumers and indeed of many a company. This time around, in other words, design does not have to compensate for the technical shortcomings of the products (which they since no longer have), but rather for the psychological shortcomings of human beings or of society itself. Nowadays, beholders or users demand of objects that they display qualities they cannot possibly have: identity, individuality, the meaning of life, the fulfillment of the widest range of wishes and cravings. The concept of function has suddenly undergone boundless expansion – and this at a time when developments in microelectronics and telecommunications are virtually abolishing the concrete reality of objects. That is why design is now called on to supply an imaginary objectivity, to fill the world of commodities with sensations and give life, action, work, and enjoyment a new meaning.

Design as a consequence runs the risk of becoming just another illusionary attempt to improve the world, of collaborating in the production of mere glossy appearance. This, as we have seen, would contradict the principles of German design.

5. Design as Concept

The vexed issue of empiricism versus a quest for objectifiable forms is still unsolved today, not least in design. German design is no exception, often allowing itself to be beguiled by the abstractions of market research and to adapt to meet the immediate desires of the consumers. Occasionally, young designers even demand this explicitly and put it into practice in their work, abhorrence of all didacticism and of what they see as loftiness on the part of design, prompting them to subordinate themselves and pander to the *volonté de tous*, to the quantifiable will of all, or at least of individual groups. This led to a brief revolt against the traditions of German design, but also, in a certain sense, to a broadening of the spectrum thereof.

Nevertheless, German design has largely continued to be imbued with the ideal that social commitment and educational thrust must go hand in hand. Today, most of the conferences and symposia on design seldom deal with marketing and marketing strategies, and yet at some point still address design's responsibility and its social mission. The latter must indeed be given priority, if only for the simple reason that design is then always discussed in the context of a multifaceted complex of moral and ethical questions, and – alongside economics – is always seen in a future-oriented perspective, both thus being accorded a utopian moment. For society does not now appear as an entity that has always existed, but rather as a concept, which thus allows for the possibility of conceiving and causing change and intervention. This way of thinking is also anticipatory in that it has been able at an early stage to adjust to the increasing immaterialization of objects and their transformation by the mass media, thus unshackling design from an existence as concrete objects.

This is evident, for example, in the fact that West German design was quick to recognize the existence of corporate identity and corporate culture. (This process was already familiar to the lecturers at the HfG, and their systematic thought and practice ensured that design was not swallowed up as a facet of corporate identity but instead played an active part in shaping it.) What is more, this state of reflective thought has enabled West German design to secure its due place in an industrial framework which is becoming more and more service-oriented.

Thus, design now finds itself, if anything, closer to the center of economic and social planning and – thanks to the competent organizational abilities of designers – is in a position to act as the source of concepts for a rational life in the future.

These are concepts which no longer focus on the presentation of an individual object, but rather concentrate on discovering new objects and interconnections between objects or providing fundamental solutions to problems.

It is thus common practice in West Germany today for a corporation to commission a design agency to organize conferences or to investigate the question of storage, to plan new ways of making purchases and payments (for example, abolishing the tills in department stores), to evaluate forms of transportation, and to propose changes in forms of communication. In this manner, design is transforming itself, in accordance with the spirit of the age, from hardware to software, and may be taking on social responsibility at a new level, developing its own multidisciplinary qualifications as a pioneering model for a theory and practice geared to the future. Indeed, it may in the process itself be becoming the central agency reconciling diverse forms of social activity and (this is ultimately very much within the tradition of German design, albeit at a different level of intensity) taking a productive stand on urgent social problems.

Certainly, this development is not free of contradictions and has not been completely smooth in West Germany either. And of course the future will still contain niches of simple modes of production and draftsmanship in which design will have a role to play. Indeed, it may be that the present day and age is placing too much responsibility on the shoulders of design, maneuvering it into a highly ambivalent key position. Yet a mixture of rationalism and empirical experience is today forcing politicians, economists, and everyone else to take design seriously as a source of social innovation, and they are encouraging design to take on this realistic role and to give it real substance. This may mean, incidentally, that culture is reappearing as civilization and in this form becoming universally applicable. After all, the task is still to organize all areas of society in an intelligent, non-hierarchical, in other words, humane manner. For besides the often stimulating visual effect, the fact that the true quality of design does not strike the eye often provides the occasion and the reason for concerning oneself intellectually with design . . . and perhaps with German design in particular.

Brigitte Wolf **Design in Daily Life**

In everyday life, human beings need and use a wide variety of objects. And these objects, their useful properties, and the way we use them all in turn affect our everyday lives. In this context, the desire for a particular product is usually connected with the notion of a certain lifestyle and a certain quality of life. In the course of time, however, changes occur in the significance of objects, the role they play in our lives, their appearance, the way they are produced, distributed, and used. Everyday culture – that is, the material environment in which we live – would appear to be shaped by the complicated interplay of various factors: not only by what is technologically feasible and what is actually used in daily life, but also by external factors such as aesthetic preferences, changing lifestyles, and not least problems of energy resources and the environment. We can gain insights into the history of the Federal Republic of Germany by considering the products and designs typical of particular periods.

The Fifties
The social situation in the early years of the Federal Republic can be summed up in a single word: shortage. People's lives were ruled by material hardship, fundamental supply problems, and the need to carry out the most urgent tasks connected with rebuilding a country that lay in ruins. There was a shortage of everything – in housing, household goods and furniture, clothing, articles of personal hygiene, means of transportation, and production plants. In other words, demand was enormous, while supply was extremely meager. It goes without saying that under such conditions people regarded the appearance of objects – i.e. their design – let alone the call for something like "good form" (this term was coined by Max Bill in 1948) as irrelevant. Instead, efforts were dedicated above all to securing the bare necessities and to restoring something like normal everyday life and industrial production. All sectors of industry saw rapid development, particularly in the plastics industry, a hitherto relatively unknown sector where new materials (duroplastic and thermoplastic) made possible new forms and manufacturing processes. Manufacturers who knew how to exploit these technical developments found a ready market for their products.

The kidney-shaped table is a good example of a successful product whose design took account of both the actual habits and conditions of people's lives and the technological potential of the day. Its shape was inspired by contemporary artistic currents (as represented, for example, by Jean Arp and Henry Moore). Such new forms could be manufactured without difficulty from the new materials, including such forms as drew their inspiration from art. Moreover, they corresponded to the "new" feeling for life people experience during a period of economic upsurge. The kidney-shaped table was light, portable, and affordable. It was ideally suited to cramped housing conditions, and could be used for a number of different purposes. In this case, supply and demand complemented each other perfectly, and the kidney-shaped table became the symbol of the decade. Yet it was not associated with "good form," nor was it linked with the name of a particular designer; rather, it has become the epitome of "anonymous" design.

Inexpensive, mass-produced articles represent one side of the world of merchandise during the fifties. At the same time, designers taking up the Bauhaus tradition developed outstanding products which corresponded to what was – and still is – considered to be "good form." Wagenfeld, Löffelhardt, Eiermann – to name but a few – were responsible for pioneering achievements in the field of design, accomplishments which were probably possible in such concentrated form only in that decade, for it was then that the Bauhaus ideas, suppressed for so long under fascism, were finally given free rein again. Even in the case of mass-produced goods, the freedom of scope offered within the limits set by producer and consumer interests was greater than it has ever been since.

Designers were not forced to subordinate their work to marketing and sales policy, statutory safety regulations and norms did not yet play a significant rule, and new products faced little competition. During this period, designers focussed their attention on furniture and household appliances, paying scant regard to capital goods and technical products. Using materials both new (plastics) and traditional (wood, metal, textiles, etc.), alone or in combination, they developed product designs that were functional and practical, and which are nowadays regarded as "design classics."

At the same time, the German government and state agencies ambitiously endeavored to give the population an aesthetic education and to win them over to the idea of "good form." Aesthetic education began at school level with the Werkbund kits, and was carried on at adult level with numerous facilities offering advice on homemaking. These attempts at education did not, however, result in the commercial success of "good form"; kidney-shaped tables and inexpensive household goods, often made from plastic, continued to be the big sellers. By the end of the decade, it was possible to think of this state-inspired attempt at popular education in aesthetics as having failed. The people were much more concerned with forgetting the shortages and hardships caused by World War II, and with banishing the memories of enforced "functionalism" (such as clothing made out of uniforms, kitchen equipment made out of the instruments of war, and toys made out of cartridge-cases). It was now time to bring a little color into the domestic life it had been so hard to re-establish. The ensuing "German economic miracle" found emotional expression among other things in the fact that, once the major necessities of life had been provided for, people began to surround themselves with "decorations" which did not as such have to be functional (pretzel stands, vases, bowls, collections of ornamental cups, etc.). By the end of the fifties, most families had their own apartment and a basic stock of furniture and household goods. As a consequence, consumer interests began to change.

The Sixties

Electrical appliances, particularly for the home, were the big sellers of the sixties. Washing-machines, spin dryers, electric ranges and vacuum cleaners became available to simplify and ease housework, and there were also machines for personal hygiene, such as electric hair-dryers and shavers. Household electrical goods were becoming less and less of a luxury. In the course of the decade, the spectrum of electrical "home helps" broadened to include almost a hundred different appliances, ranging from washing-machines, coffee-makers and vacuum cleaners to shoe-polishers and air-humidifiers. And more and more households possessed TV sets, radio-phonographs, and other products of the budding entertainment industry.

The success and rapid spread of the electrical appliances can above all be attributed to the fact that they made routine housework – such as cooking, laundering, dishwashing, and cleaning – easier and thus led to a reduction in the necessary physical labor input. The automation of housework was lauded as the result of a form of technological progress which people expected would relieve them of a great part of their work-load. Initially, however, they did not know how to use these machines

and had to learn to do so – after all, technical changes of this magnitude generally lead to changes in structures of social behavior. Thus, the weekly or monthly "washday" became superfluous, with laundering work now tending to be spread evenly over the whole week. The same occurred in the case of "cleaning days": whereas the house or apartment used to be cleaned from top to bottom in one day – timed to coincide with religious festivals such as Easter or Christmas – such activities were now also spread over the whole year. The extent and intensity of the cleaning activities, then as now, depended on the individual requirements of the particular family.

Behavior patterns also altered in the leisure sphere. The increasing availability of television shaped people's communicative behavior, and this was clearly reflected in the structure of the living-room. The seating, originally arranged in a circle, was now oriented toward the TV set, taking the form of an "L" or a "U." The entertainment offered by television seemed to have become more important to many people than communication between the members of the family.

Initially, the electrical goods market was dominated by a small number of manufacturers, and there were obvious differences between the products each offered. However, this state of affairs did not last long, and a multitude of similar articles was soon available in each of the various product categories. Furthermore, the various manufacturers reached comparable levels of technological development. It became rare for a company to secure a market advantage by introducing new technology, and competing manufacturers were fast to catch up on an improved sales performance that had arisen from a higher level of technical sophistication.

A new situation had arisen in the market-place: it was no longer true that everything on offer was actually purchased. Supply had expanded, in terms of both volume and variety, while demand had become more critical and discerning. Manufacturers suddenly found themselves confronted with the danger of not being able to sell goods they had produced, which prompted them to begin investigating consumer behavior (through market research) in order to plan the manufacture and sale of new products accordingly. Target-groups of purchasers were differentiated as calculable units of demand, and the population thus divided up according to their income and education levels. Goods were henceforth supplied in line with forecast purchasing behavior and adapted to meet the needs of the various target groups of consumers. There was a continual increase in the relative importance of well-thought-out product strategies and the contribution of design to the sales success of a product.

Many people were overwhelmed when faced with the problem of choosing the "right" model out of the wealth of technical appliances now on offer. For the layperson with no previous technical knowledge it was difficult to assess whether the price bore an appropriate relation to the product's practical value. Thus, many purchase decisions were determined by what one could afford. If, on the other hand, one did not need to worry about the price, one simply bought what one liked the look of.

In this context, initiatives were set up among the population to safeguard the rights of the so-called "consumers." In the long term, these organizations have been instrumental in creating statutory provisions and norms aimed at ensuring that the basic interests of buyers and users are upheld. The year 1965 saw the launch of the Stiftung Warentest consumer foundation, which began carrying out comparative tests on similar products. (For example, all washing-machines on the German market were assessed according to criteria set out in a test program.) With a view to providing an independent guide prior to buying, the findings were published in *Test* magazine and disseminated by the regional consumer advisory bureaux. Initially, people did not pay much heed to such information, but the level of acceptance enjoyed by this institution has meanwhile grown steadily, as has its influence on purchasing decisions.

The most important criteria for evaluating and purchasing products were whether they were suited for the uses to which they were to be put and were safe, durable, and easy to handle. By extension the same criteria came to bear on the design process. Designers liked to see themselves as the "consumer's advocate," responsible for designing technical household appliances in such a way that they were easy to handle and operate, and fully functional as required in everyday life. By the end of the sixties, people had developed a critical attitude toward purchasing; company profits – this was for the moment especially true of the household appliance sector – as a consequence became more and more dependent on the so-called "price-performance ratio" of the products they offered.

The Seventies

High productivity on the part of manufacturers and the higher income levels of consumers had resulted in almost all West German households being well-equipped with electrical appliances by the seventies. Although these mechanical aids eased the burden of housework in many respects, there was one thing they were not able to achieve, namely an appreciable reduction in the amount of time taken up by housework. Any time-saving advantages were counterbalanced by the time needed to set up and clean the equipment and by storage problems. The kitchen machine was a case in point: setting it up, switching over from one of its various functions to another, and the complicated and time-consuming cleaning procedure were all factors which resulted in the machine being used only sporadically. In the long term, manufacturers drew conclusions from such empirical user-behavior and developed the electric hand-mixer as an alternative. This largely eliminated the disadvantages

of the kitchen machine while retaining the advantages (electrical stirring, kneading, etc.).

There were also misconceptions over user-behavior in the case of coffee machines. These were developed with a view to enhancing the coffee or breakfast table, serving up fresh hot coffee within convenient reach. However, in real life consumers left their coffee machines standing in the kitchen, a long way from the dining-table, for they were simply too noisy. This canceled out the advantage of convenient hot coffee that the machines were supposed to offer: either the coffee went cold or one continually had to go to the kitchen to fetch it. It therefore became customary to pour the coffee into a thermos flask, which after many years resulted in coffee machines being equipped with insulated jugs.

Although it might seem surprising, washing-machines did not significantly reduce the time spent laundering clothes. Not only had a rise in standards of personal hygiene and the concomitant change in personal cleanliness increased the volume of laundry, the synthetic materials and mixed fabrics favored by the textile industry in the seventies also necessitated a daily change of clothes. Thus, although the now fully automated washing-machine did away with the drudgery of washday, the total amount of time spent on laundering remained almost constant.

Only very gradually did this kind of everyday experience lead to improvements to household appliances being made, for the machines continued all the same to sell well. And to a great extent sales success hinged on product design. It was predominantly men who – especially around Christmastime – purchased electrical appliances, yet they were seldom actually the users of what they had bought. Then as now they relieved themselves of the duty of helping with household chores by making their wives presents of electrical household helps.

Manufacturers were no longer primarily concerned with improving the technical performance and functions of electrical goods, but rather with ensuring that they could be integrated into and applied in the user's everyday life and home environment. It had to be possible for the machines to be "built into" or at least "suited to" their actual operational sphere. Individual machines were no longer in demand, but rather "systems" of appliances which were carefully designed to match each other, in both technical and aesthetic terms: office systems, modular consumer electronic systems, and kitchen systems. In the household, this meant that the task for designers was now to create not so much individual objects as complex kitchen environments that were flexible enough to be adapted to different architectural contexts. The fact that the kitchen was now classified as a place of work meant that designers began to attribute increasing importance to ergonomics. Different work areas were specified, appliances were conveniently installed within easy reach where they were needed – thus reducing distances and set-up times – and operating conditions were optimized. Taking their cue from the numerous studies on "household economy" published in those years, designers attempted to reduce the time spent in kitchen work by streamlining the kitchen in line with the same methods as those used in industry to design workplaces such that a worker can achieve maximum output in a minimum time. Women – who were now pressing more and more strongly for emancipation – were persuaded to believe that they would gain more time for other activities. The kitchen systems were given a visual appearance to match the individual preferences of the consumers, and various "looks" became fashionable, ranging from farm-style to high class. Yet these kitchen workplaces had one big disadvantage, namely their price; only people in high income brackets could afford them.

At the same time there was a growth in the belief that there must be objective criteria by which the qualities of a product could be judged. For in the face of the large differences in price and quality, many consumers felt uncertain of the choice they should make and increasingly began to seek advice in the form of the information and recommendations provided by the Stiftung Warentest. This had now become very popular and was having an increasingly powerful impact on consumer behavior. In the consumer goods sector, a favorable test result was an absolute prerequisite for a sales success. Products which came out of the tests badly were already rejected at the retailer stage and thus had little chance of even finding their way into the shops. As a consequence, new products had to be designed to get the best possible marks in the tests.

The volume and diversity of products on offer continued to expand steadily, and design was predominantly influenced by marketing considerations. Many designers found the scope left them for autonomous decisions and creativity steadily shrinking. In order to minimize sales risks, manufacturers generally oriented themselves toward the most successful product within a particular group of products. Designers were often confronted with pre-established production costs, technical specifications, indeed even shape, color, and decor. For all that, products nevertheless often failed to come up to the users' expectations, and thus did not sell. The manufacturers simply had to cope with "flops" of this sort.

Last but not least, the seventies saw people finally beginning to sense that industrial growth might in fact have its limits. Citizens' action groups were set up to campaign on environmental issues, and their work was instrumental in enhancing awareness and understanding of environmental and energy problems. As a result, changes in behavioral patterns began to occur. When buying new household goods, dishwashers and washing-machines for example, people now took greater account of water and detergent consumption. Conservation and pollution were now key issues, and manufacturers found that many customers were prepared to pay more for an appliance that met certain environmental standards.

The Eighties

The past decade was characterized by the microchip. Electronic data-processing was of course no longer a novelty, but the microchip boosted the efficiency and speed of computers tremendously; the machines that performed these complex calculations became smaller and smaller. By the end of the eighties, a personal computer and/or computer games were to be found in many households.

It is certainly an over-generalization to say that in the eighties it was precisely computers that achieved the optimal combination of user interests and technological possibilities. However, there can be no doubt that people in the eighties were confronted with the need to process and correlate more and more information at an ever-increasing speed. Electronic data-processing would seem to meet this need in an optimal way, and there can be no doubt that this form of information-processing does, in general, have advantages. However, the very speed at which this development is taking place threatens to bring about a considerable disregard for the real interests of the user. In this area, technological progress has ripped itself free of social constraints and now follows laws of its own. The breakneck speed at which the first, second, third, fourth, fifth, etc., generations of computers have been developed has left no room for collecting and evaluating user feedback and drawing consequences therefrom for future developments. Technological aspects have clearly gained the upper hand in product development, and user-oriented criteria have been relegated to the background. At the same time, this technology has imposed completely new demands on the psychological, social, intellectual, and emotional capacities of the users, and this has hitherto been far too seldom the subject of scientific investigation. Indeed, the relationship between users and electronic data-processing machines cannot be adequately explained in terms of the conventional criteria used to date – this is just one of the problems of the computer age.

Moreover, the sheer multiplicity of user interests has complicated the task of defining them, as is shown, for example, in the case of the banking sector. Here, existing computer systems were augmented in the eighties by publicly accessible terminals such as ATMs and statement-printers. This involves two different kinds of user: the bank employee and the customer. For the former, the automation of routine bank transactions is undoubtedly a relief – and furthermore, possible errors in calculations or booking have largely been eliminated. There is no doubt that the machines are also of advantage to the other users, the bank's customers: they are, for example, available outside banking hours, with a check card providing access to tills and thus cash twenty-four hours a day, anywhere in the country. And ergonomic considerations have been taken into account in designing the arrangement, form, and readability of the operating elements. Despite all this, users are often dissatisfied. It takes a relatively long time for the statement-printer to print out the documents; furthermore, these machines are highly prone to malfunctioning, and the customer can thus often not obtain the desired information. The advantages of the ATMs are nullified when they are "out of order," in the process of being restocked, or empty outside banking hours, or when they issue $ 500 in ten-dollar bills, or refuse to issue any money at all because the account is overdrawn. It had, by contrast, been possible to deal with customer requirements individually and quickly in the course of a personal talk with a member of the bank's staff.

The user-friendly design of highly complex computer systems in the service industry and in manufacturing – specifically taking account of the multilevel user structures – will therefore be an important task facing design in the nineties. Yet this entails a dilemma, a dilemma that could also provide a great opportunity, for designers can scarcely rely on ergonomics and market research any more – their traditional sources of scientific reference nor can they draw on some intrinsic logic of form. The advantage of this is that design will perhaps be able to develop further by finding a new basis for itself. The development of technology has simply outpaced those scientific disciplines to which it used to refer. This means that form often no longer follows on from function but is merely a question of habit. In the field of computers in particular, product forms and sizes are retained even though technological advances mean that the products could take on a completely different shape – above all, they could be smaller, more compact, easier to comprehend at a glance, and thus more user-friendly.

Today it would appear that the physiological optimization of the relationship between human beings and machines has not come up to expectations, as the example of the telling-machines demonstrates. A radical expansion of ergonomics is therefore urgently called for. It would seem that a "science of the user," a theoretical basis for design which conceives of human beings as social, thinking, and feeling individuals, is essential for the future, specifically in the case of computers but also with regard to future product design in general. And market research will become obsolete if it does not strive to create and deploy a "holistic" concept of human beings.

Work at present underway in the "experimental design workshops" of some leading German corporations suggests that there is an awareness of these problems. "Prototyping" is already being done by interdisciplinary teams, and since the limitations of individual need-fulfillment are becoming apparent in many areas, the aim must be to develop "concepts" in which the interests of the individual and those of society as a whole are rendered compatible with each other. The task facing design in the future will therefore be not so much the creation of objects and products as the planning of complex "situations."

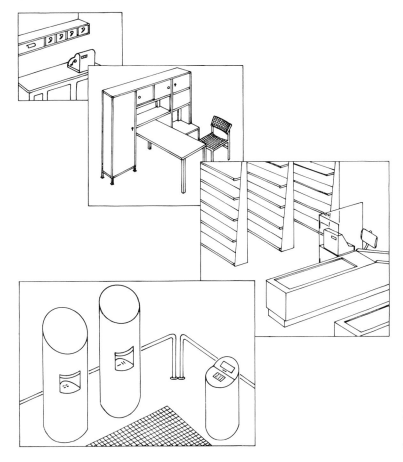

2 *untitled*
1990
Julia Lang

3 *View of the Hochschule für Gestaltung (HfG) Ulm, from the southwest*
1955
Max Bill
Photo: Wolfgang Siol

Gwendolyn Ristant **Ulm**

The longer it is since the Hochschule für Gestaltung (Ulm school) closed its doors, the greater the mythology surrounding it. The influence of the HfG in Ulm has far outlasted its physical existence and has extended beyond national boundaries, for the Ulm school engendered a concept of design not only for individual objects of daily use, but for everyday life, mass production, mass communication, and visual images in general. Interestingly enough, it was not originally conceived as a school of design, but rather as a college of democratic citizenship; and the HfG as it finally emerged continued to be clearly antifascist in thrust and to promulgate a critical stance on political and social affairs.

The roots of this development are to be found in the prehistory and the early days of the school, which were closely connected with resistance to National Socialism and the struggle for a democratic society. Hans and Sophie Scholl, members of the "White Rose" antifascist resistance group, had been executed by the Nazis in February 1943 for alleged high treason. Directly after the war Inge Scholl, their sister, began to campaign for an adult education center as disseminator of democratic ideas in Ulm, a vision that became reality in 1946. The insights she gained through working for the adult education center and the first contacts with émigrés, democratically minded artists, writers and scientists (including Martin Buber, Carl Zuckmayer, Hans Werner Richter, Walter Jens, Werner Heisenberg, Otl

Aicher), and former Bauhaus designers (Max Bill, Helene Nonné-Schmidt) prompted Inge Scholl to set up a foundation in memory of her brother and sister, the object of which was the establishment of a free university.

With the support of her friends Otl Aicher, Max Bill, and Hans Werner Richter, Inge Scholl succeeded, after much effort and numerous political controversies, in convincing General McCloy, the then American High Commissioner, of her idea. McCloy promised her one million Deutschmarks on condition that she raised an equal amount; this she managed to do, in a ravaged and economically crippled Germany. Thus, in 1952, the Hochschule für Gestaltung was finally approved; construction began in 1953 under the direction of Swiss artist and architect Max Bill. The official opening ceremony, at which Walter Gropius gave the inaugural address, took place in 1955.

A school had been created that was unique with respect to the cultural, educational, and design policies pursued. A small group of lecturers and students committed themselves to creating a social, well-designed environment, treating utility objects with as much dedication as was paid to theoretical and empirical analyses of urbanization, technology, industry, and people's life and work contexts. Rather than indulge in styling and the creation of modish designs with an abundance of curves, they investigated the social dimension and its application to the way

4 *Hochschule für Gestaltung, interior view*
c. 1955
Photo: Ernst Scheidegger

5 *Students in the cafeteria. The furniture and crockery are HfG designs, the stool was designed by Max Bill as a seat and carrier.*
Photo: Heiner Jacob

6 *One of the split-level studio flats for final-year students and visiting professors*
Photo: Heiner Jacob

7 *A class held on the terrace outside the cafeteria*

8 *Metal workshop, with Cornelius Clittenhout (workshop supervisor) and Elke Koch-Weser 1955–56*

9 *In the classroom with Tomás Maldonado*

10 *Carnival time at HfG 1958 Photo: Wolfgang Siol*

objects are used, developing systems with as high a degree of transparency as possible. With respect to teaching, an interdisciplinary approach was adopted, the main aim being to achieve a comprehensive unity of theory and practice. Students were not expected to have specific formal qualifications, but rather to have undergone practical training and to possess an understanding of cultural and social complexes. The HfG comprised four departments: Product Design, Visual Communication, Information, and Industrial Construction; in 1961, an Institute for Film Design was attached to the school. The course of studies lasted four years, of which the first year was particularly important because all students had to pass the foundation course before they could be admitted to one of the departments. The syllabus focussed on general design principles, on theoretical and scientific knowledge, and on learning how to draft plans, construct models, and present work. Theory and practice were intended to be evenly balanced, and the aim in both was to develop a sense of social and cultural responsibility. The international character of faculty and student body was an important element of the college's constitution, this being a conscious measure to counter the disastrous nationalism of recent German history. Up to half of the students came from abroad, and the lecturers, for example, from Switzerland (Bill), Argentina (Maldonado), Britain (Fröshaug), France/USA (Moles), Austria (Zeischegg, Lindinger), Switzerland/France (Schnaidt); Gugelot had been born in Indonesia, Bonsiepe lived in Latin America. Of course, there were also German teachers, such as the sculptor and graphic artist Aicher, the film-makers Kluge and Reitz, and the artist and typographer Vordemberge-Gildewart.

The school's extraordinary qualitative significance was based on a total 20 permanent lecturers and 200 visiting professors; and the impact the HfG had on the world of design is

out of all proportion to the number of students who passed through it — only 215 actually graduated, from a total of 640 enrolments.

Although Ulm appears in retrospect to display such homogeneity and unity and to be so representative of a distinctive style, there were many internal controversies over conceptual and educational matters. These led to fierce confrontations and to factions being formed among the staff. In all, it is possible to distinguish six different phases. The era of Scholl, Aicher, Bill, and Zeischegg lasted from 1947 to 1953, years during which the basic concept of the school and its institutionalized structures were hammered out, and finance problems figured largely. The period between 1953 and 1956 saw the building and consolidation of the college under the aegis of Max Bill, the first president, who viewed the HfG as a clear continuation of the Bauhaus tradition and therefore predominantly appointed former Bauhaus figures (Albers, Itten, Nonné-Schmidt, Peterhans). The years 1956 to 1958 saw the beginnings of an open conflict between the older Bauhaus followers and the young lecturers who called for a nonderivative course of studies oriented toward scientific knowledge and theory. (Bill left the college in 1957 in protest at the "Ulm Model" which was adopted on Maldonado's initiative and involved collective administration in the form of a presidential committee.) The 1958–1962 phase saw the spread of scientistic-positivistic notions of a strictly mathematical methodology and form of analysis, purporting to value-free judgments; manifestoes and teaching based on cultural and social design were replaced by working hypotheses, ergonomic investigations, and operational research. From 1962 onward, Aicher, Gugelot, Zeischegg, and Maldonado rebelled against this dogmatism, and — pressure also being brought to bear by the State Government of Baden-Württemberg — the school's constitution was amended. The one-man presidency (held by Aicher, then from 1964 by Maldonado, and finally by Herbert Ohl) was re-introduced, and the students now had only a 33 % rather than 50 % representation on the college committees. The first rudiments of a design theory were sketched, and the career profile became more directly related to industry. By 1967, it was becoming increasingly clear that financial disaster was imminent: the Geschwister Scholl Foundation was heavily in debt, lecturers had to be dismissed and courses cut. As a result of intensified political controversies within the Federal and State Governments, public subsidies were withdrawn and the State Government demanded that the HfG be annexed to the Ulm Engineering College and comply with the State Law governing higher education. Lecturers and students were divided over the best strategy for resistance. In October 1968, the lecturers refused to hold classes because of the untenable financial and staffing situation, and in November the Baden-Württemberg State Parliament, in which the Conservatives held the majority, ordered that the HfG be closed.

In December 1968, State Prime Minister Hans Filbinger, who – as was later revealed – had shared responsibility as judge during the Nazi period for death sentences in wartime courts-martial – justified the closure of the HfG with the following words: "We want to create something new, and that requires the liquidation of the old." What he meant by "the old" was the experiment of an alternative, free, interdisciplinary college of design. It was possible to "liquidate" an institution, but the concept of an innovative and cultural form of design lives on.

11 *Experimental presentation in the laboratory for perception studies under the guidance of Meruyu W. Perrine 1960*
Photo: Wolfgang Siol

12 *Members of the Gugelot development group 1959*
Photo: Wolfgang Siol

13 *HfG faculty meeting 1958*

14 *Variations on punched holes.*
The circles have a diameter of 3 mm, and the distance between them is variable.
1965—66
Axel Lintener (class of Gui Bonsiepe)

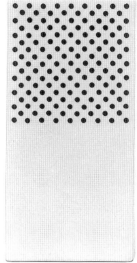  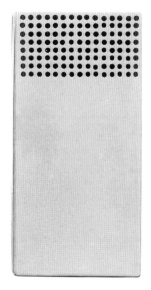

15 *Variations on punched holes.*
Mixed grids with variable distances between the elements and different-sized elements; square outline shape
1965—66
Christian Franz (class of Gui Bonsiepe)

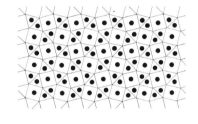 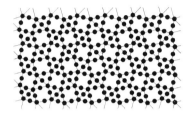 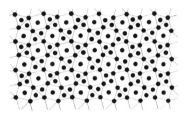

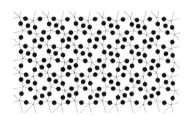  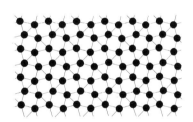

16 *Non-orientable surface*
1965—66
Christian Franz

17 *Non-orientable surface*
1965—66
Dirk Schmauser ▷

18 *Non-orientable surface.*
3 cuts. Face-cut and seams are along a square grid
1965—66
Hans Ulrich Schack ▷▷
(class of Gui Bonsiepe)
Photos: Roland Fürst

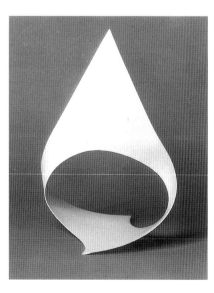 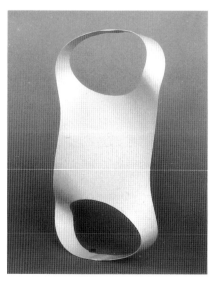 

19 *Paper-tissue holders (stacked)*
1956
Basic training course
Photo: Wolfgang Siol

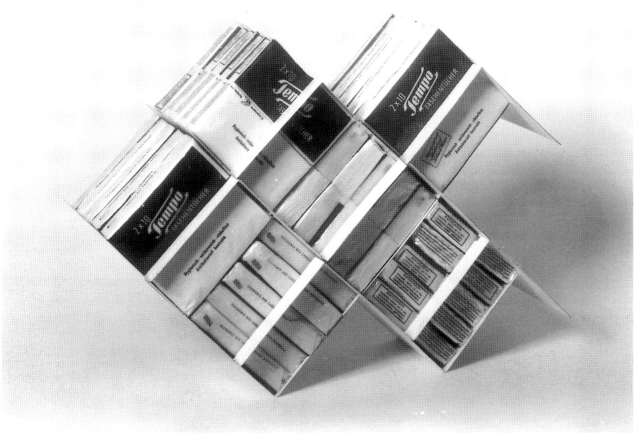

20 *Paper-tissue holders (filled)*
1956
Basic training course
Photo: Wolfgang Siol

21 *Non-orientable surface*
1958–59
Ulrich Burandt (class of Tomás
Maldonado)

22 *Stackable ashtrays*
1966–67
Walter Zeischegg
Helit, Kierspe (Presswerk
Westfalen Friedrich Hefendehl
GmbH & Co. KG)

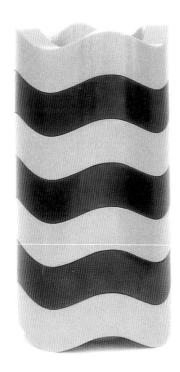

23 *Three-dimensional formal*
exercises using a 3 D lattice of
isometric elements
1965–66
Georg Hilsmann (class of Gui
Bonsiepe)
Photo: Roland Fürst

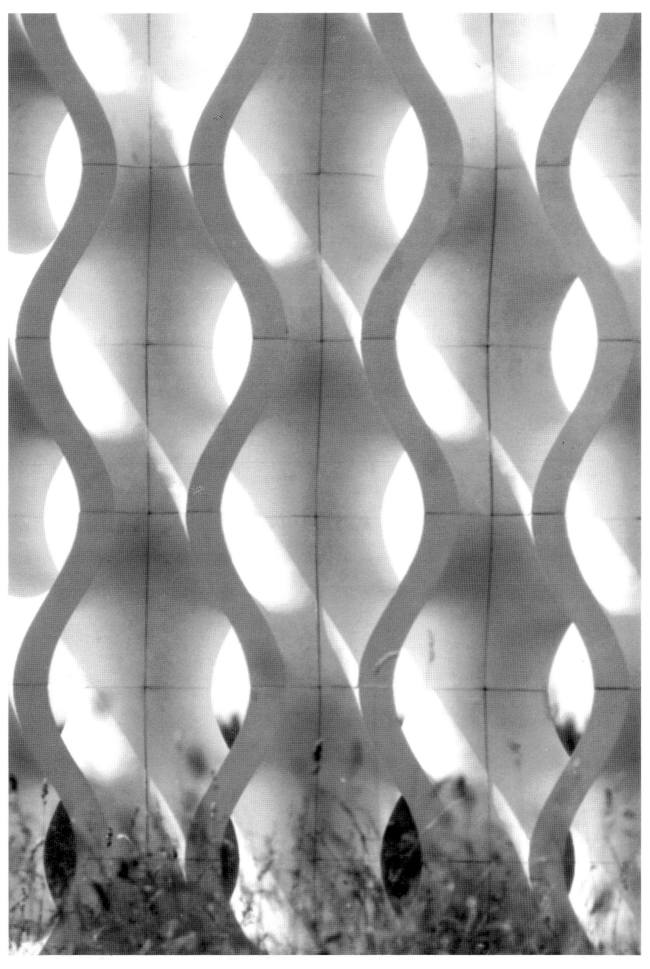

24 *Trelliswork wall*
Identical concave elements are
used to create a trellislike sur-
face.
1964–65
Walter Zeischegg
Photo: Walter Zeischegg

25 *Street lighting*
1965–66
Peter Hofmeister, Thomas Mentzel, Werner Zemp (class of Walter Zeischegg)
Photo: Roland Fürst

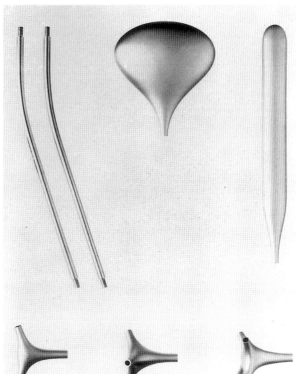

26 *Street lighting (components)*
1965–66
Peter Hofmeister, Thomas Mentzel, Werner Zemp (class of Walter Zeischegg)

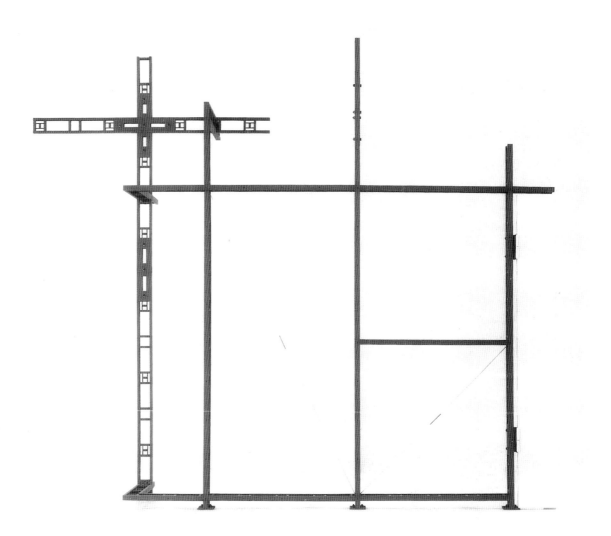

27 *Scaffolding of folded sheet metal*
1956–57
Department of Architecture and Town Planning (class of Konrad Wachsmann)
Photo: Wolfgang Siol

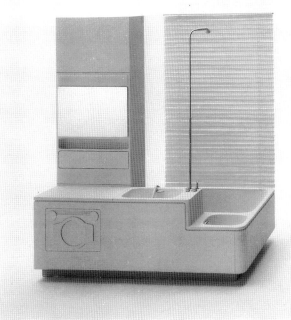

28, 29, 30 *Sanitary unit,
modular system
1963–64
Building Department and Institute for Industrialized Construction (class of Herbert Ohl)
Photos: Roland Fürst*

31 *Bathroom unit.
The telescoping shower is at
full extension, the blind lowered to catch splashing water.
1961–62
Walter Kiehlneker
Department of Product Design
(class of Walter Zeischegg)
Photo: Wolfgang Siol*

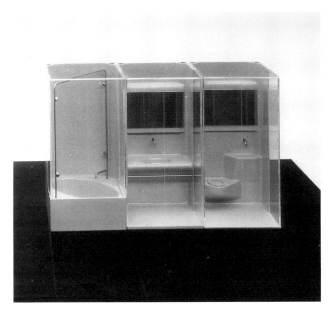

32 *Student dormitory built
using cellular rooms, assembly
of the room cells
1962–63 (1957–63)
Institute for Industrialized
Construction (Director: Herbert Ohl)
Photo: Wolfgang Siol*

33 M125 *furniture system*
1957 (developed from 1950)
Hans Gugelot
Wilhelm Bofinger, Ilsfeld
Photo: Christian Staub

34 M125 *furniture system*
(without doors)
1957 (developed from 1950)
Hans Gugelot
Wilhelm Bofinger, Ilsfeld
Photo: Christian Staub

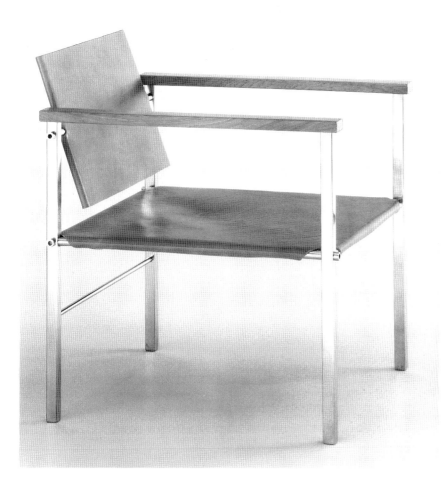

35 SBM680 *steel tube arm-*
chair, collapsable
1958
Ernst Moeckl, Karl Heinz Berg-
miller
Wilde & Spieth GmbH & Co.,
Esslingen
Photo: Christian Staub

36 *Table frame, joints*
1958
Ernst Moeckl, Karl Heinz Berg-
miller
Wilde & Spieth GmbH & Co.,
Esslingen
Photo: Christian Staub

37 *Table, collapsable*
1958
Ernst Moeckl, Karl Heinz Berg-
miller
Wilde & Spieth GmbH & Co.,
Esslingen
Photo: Christian Staub

38 PK-G combined radio and
phonograph
1954–55
Hans Gugelot
Max Braun, Frankfurt (now:
Braun AG, Kronberg)

39 FS-G *television-set*
1954–55
Hans Gugelot
Max Braun, Frankfurt (now:
Braun AG, Kronberg)

40 G12 *turntable*
1954–55
Hans Gugelot
Max Braun, Frankfurt (now:
Braun AG, Kronberg) ▷

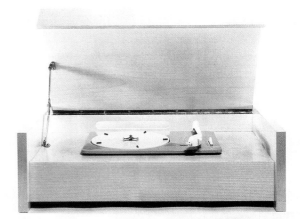

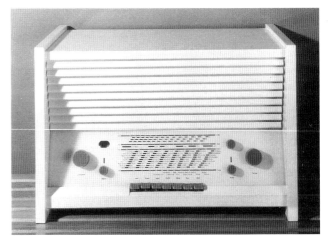

41 G11 Super *radio*
1954–55
Hans Gugelot
Max Braun, Frankfurt (now:
Braun AG, Kronberg)

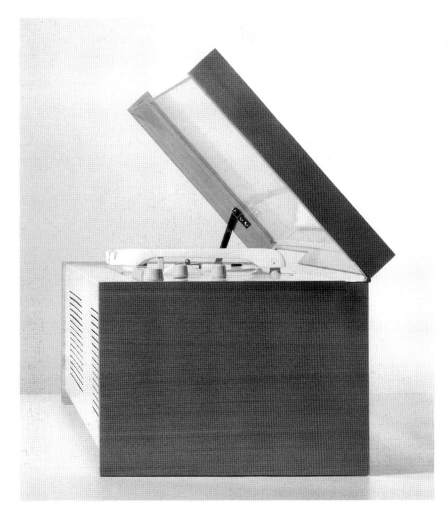

42 SK4 *combined radio and*
phonograph
1956
Hans Gugelot, Dieter Rams
Max Braun, Frankfurt (now:
Braun AG, Kronberg)

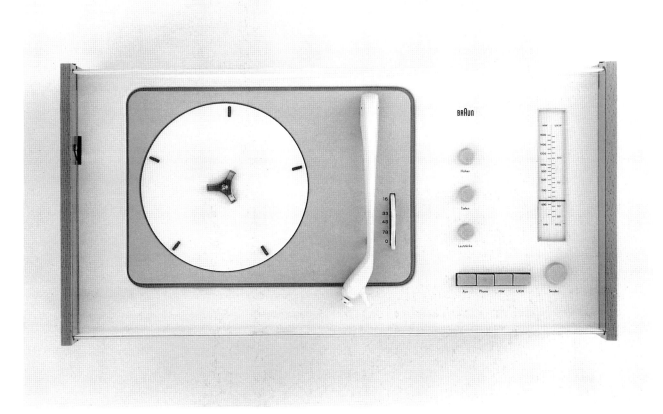

43 SK4 *combined radio and*
phonograph
1956
Hans Gugelot, Dieter Rams
Max Braun, Frankfurt (now:
Braun AG, Kronberg)
Photo: Wolfgang Siol

44 Helit 6204 *filecard-trolley*
1966–67
Walter Zeischegg, Dieter
Raffler
Helit, Kierspe (Presswerk
Westfalen Friedrich Hefendehl
GmbH & Co. KG)
Photo: Wolfgang Siol

45 *Helit card files*
1966–67
Walter Zeischegg, Dieter
Raffler
Helit, Kierspe (Presswerk
Westfalen Friedrich Hefendehl
GmbH & Co. KG)
Photo: Wolfgang Siol

46 Unidata *universal storage-system for all forms of storage-media*
1963—64
Ulm Development Group 6 (Tomás Maldonado, Rudolf Scharfenberg, Gui Bonsiepe)
Alex Lindner GmbH, Nürtingen
Photo: Wolfgang Siol

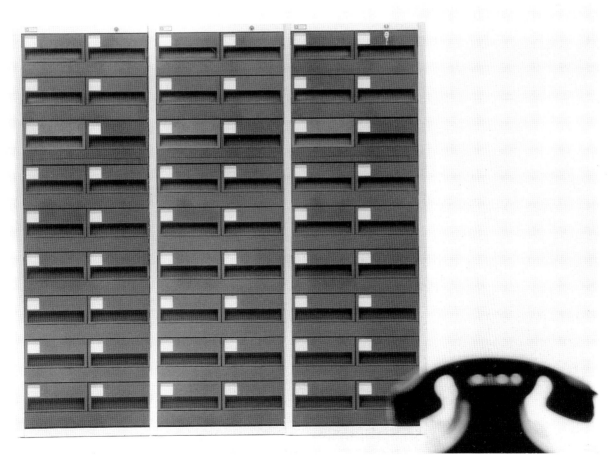

47 Unidata *universal storage-system*
LKS92 *punchcard-cupboard*
1963—64
Ulm Development Group 6 (Tomás Maldonado, Rudolf Scharfenberg, Gui Bonsiepe)
Alex Lindner GmbH, Nürtingen
Photo: Wolfgang Siol

48, 49, 50 TC100 *compact crockery*
1958–59
Hans Roericht (master's degree project)
Department of Product Design
Porzellanfabrik Waldershof, Oberpfalz (now available under the brandname Thomas, produced by Rosenthal AG, Selb)
Photos: Wolfgang Siol

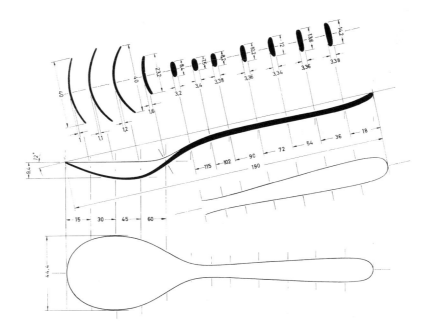

51 *Cutlery (technical drawing)*
1957–58
Ernst Moeckl (master's degree project)
Department of Product Design
Alpaccawerke, Neu-Ulm
Photo: Christian Staub

52 Piccolo *cutlery set*
Before 1960
Hans Gugelot, Rido Busse
Müller & Schmidt Pfeilring-
werke GmbH & Co. KG and
Grasoli Werk GmbH & Co. KG,
Gebr. Grah (now Carl
Mertens, CMS Grasoli
GmbH & Co.)
Photo: Wolfgang Siol

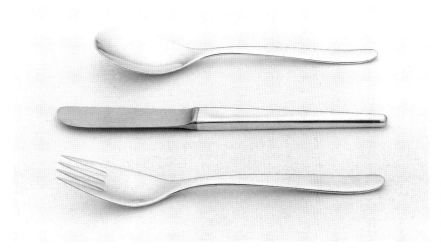

53 *Cutlery*
1957–58
Ernst Moeckl (master's degree project)
Department of Product Design
Alpaccawerke, Neu-Ulm
Photo: Christian Staub

54 RKD114 *electronic measuring-instrument*
1962–63
Ulm Development Group 6
(Tomás Maldonado, Rudolf Scharfenberg, Gui Bonsiepe)
Josef Neuberger, Munich
(now Neuberger Mess-instrumente GmbH)

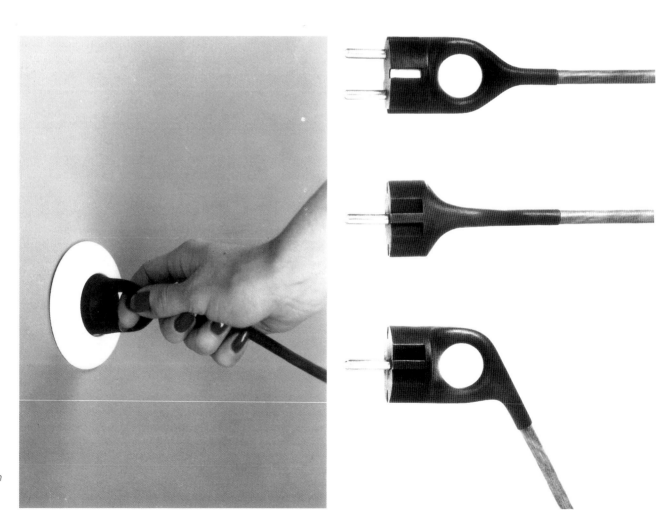

55, 56 *Soft PVC plug for appliances*
1958–59
Aribert Vahlenbreder
Department of Product Design
(class of Walter Zeischegg)
Photo: Wolfgang Siol

57 GRV553 *radial drill*
1963–64
Hans Gugelot, gugelot design
gmbh
Girards Werkzeugmaschinen
GmbH, Hagen

58 *Oscilloscope*
1959
Hans von Klier (master's
degree project)
Department of Product Design
Telefunken, Ulm
Photo: Wolfgang Siol

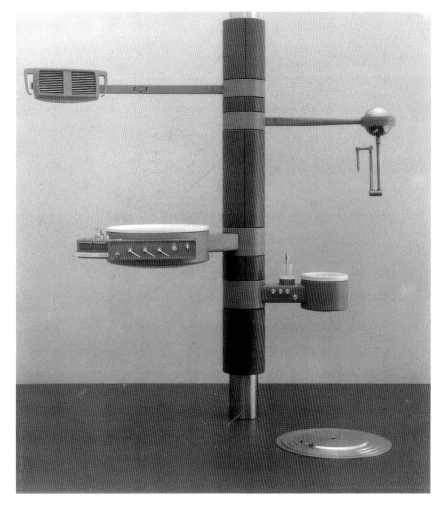

59 *Dentist's workplace unit*
1961–62
Peter Emmer, Peter Beck,
Reinhold Deckelmann, Dieter
Reich
Department of Product Design
(class of Walter Zeischegg)

60 *Kitchen clock with timer*
1956–57
Max Bill, Ernst Moeckl
Gebr. Junghans AG,
Schramberg (now Junghans
Uhren GmbH)
Photo: Wolfgang Siol

61 *Letter-scales*
1963–64
Werner Zemp
Department of Product Design
(class of Tomás Maldonado)
Photo: Roland Fürst

62 *Teaching-machine*
1964–65
Kai Ehlert, Hans-Jürgen
Lannoch, Sudhakar Nadkarni,
Peter Kövari
Department of Product Design
(class of Tomás Maldonado)
Photo: Roland Fürst

63 Pfaff 80 _sewing-machine_
_1958–59_
Hans Gugelot, Herbert Lin-
dinger, Helmut Müller-Kühn
Pfaff AG, Kaiserslautern (now:
Pfaff-Industriemaschinen
GmbH)

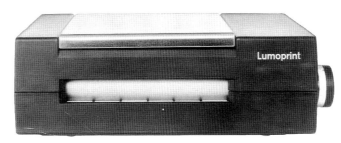

64 Lumoprint L250 _office_
copier
_1962_
Hans Gugelot, Hans Sukopp
LUMOPRINT Zindler KG, Ham-
burg

65 Carousel S _slide-projector_
_1963_
Hans Gugelot, gugelot design
gmbh
Kodak AG, Stuttgart

66 _Iron_
_1958–59_
Reinhold Weiss (master's
degree project)
Department of Product Design
Photo: Wolfgang Siol

67, 68 *Rotary tedder*
1965–66
Eberhard Wahl (master's degree project)
Department of Product Design
Photo: Stritzinger

69 Autonova "fam"
1964–65
Michael Conrad (HfG), Pio Manzoni (HfG), Fritz B. Busch

70 Autonova "fam" *(road view)*
1964–65
Michael Conrad (HfG), Pio Manzoni (HfG), Fritz B. Busch

◁ **71** *Train for Hamburg sub-
way-system*
1964
*Hans Gugelot, Herbert Lin-
dinger, Helmut Müller-Kühn
(color consultants: Otl Aicher,
Peter Croy)
Linke-Hofmann-Busch GmbH,
Salzgitter; Kiepe, Düsseldorf
Photo: Kai Ehlert*

72 *Train for Hamburg sub-
way-system, Hamburger
Hochbahn AG (study of a
model)*
1960–61
*Hans Gugelot, Herbert Lin-
dinger, Helmut Müller-Kühn
(color consultants: Otl Aicher,
Peter Croy)*

73 *Train for Hamburg sub-
way-system*
1960–61
*Hans Gugelot, Herbert Linding-
er, Helmut Müller-Kühn (color
consultants: Otl Aicher, Peter
Croy)
Photo: Wolfgang Siol*

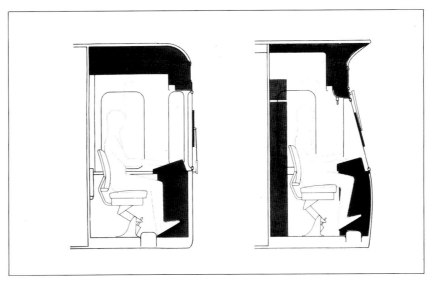

74 *Train for Hamburg sub-
way-system, driver's cabin
(draft)*
1960–61
*Hans Gugelot, Herbert Lin-
dinger, Helmut Müller-Kühn
Photo: Wolfgang Siol*

75 Corporate image for Lufthansa's Boeing fleet with
color, typeface, and logo as
distinguishing features
1961–62 (until 1964–65)
Ulm Development Group 5
(Otl Aicher, Tomás Gonda,
Fritz Querengässer, Hans
Roericht)
Department of Visual Com-
munications

76 In-flight crockery
Deutsche Lufthansa AG
1961–62 (until 1964–65)
Ulm Development Group 5
(Otl Aicher, Tomás Gonda,
Fritz Querengässer, Hans
Roericht)
Department of Visual Com-
munications
J. Buchsteiner, Gingen; KAHA
Kunststoffwerk K. Hädrich
GmbH & Co. KG, Giessen
Photo: Roland Fürst   ▷

77 Lufthansa in-flight crockery
1961–62 (until 1964–65)
Ulm Development Group 5
(Otl Aicher, Tomás Gonda,
Fritz Querengässer, Hans
Roericht)
Department of Visual Com-
munications
J. Buchsteiner, Gingen; KAHA
Kunststoffwerk K. Hädrich
GmbH & Co. KG, Giessen;
U. Buchholtz GmbH & Co. KG,
Berlin
Photo: Roland Fürst

78 Prototype rail station
system (1st prize in the
competition held by the City
of Ludwigshafen and BASF)
1967–68
Karl Gröbli, Jean-Claude Ludi,
Rudolf Schaerer, Michael
Weiss
Departments of Product De-
sign, Construction, and Visual
Communications (classes of
Herbert Lindinger and Claude
Schnaidt)
Carboplast GmbH, Marl

79, 80 *Advertising-series for
the Hermann Miller Collection
1961–62
Photograph by Wolfgang Siol,
design by Otl Aicher and
Tomás Gonda
Department of Visual Com-
munications
Contura SA, Birsfelden,
Switzerland
Photo: Wolfgang Siol*

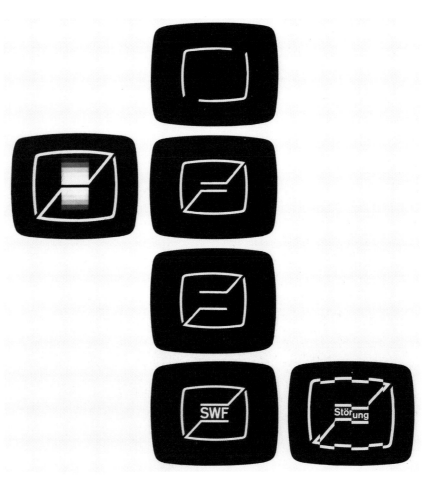

81 *Television-screen logo for
Südwestfunk Broadcasting
Corp., Baden-Baden:
variations of the sign
1966–67
Herbert W. Kapitzki
Department of Visual Com-
munications*

82 *Cloakroom hook*
1957–58
Photo: Wolfgang Siol

83 *Hook and hat*
1957–58
Photo: Wolfgang Siol

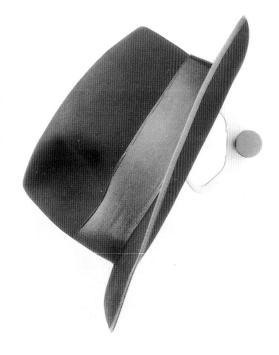

84 *Television-screen sign for*
disruptions in transmission
1965–66
Michael Klar
Department of Visual Com-
munications
(class of Herbert W. Kapitzki)

Gwendolyn Ristant Other Manifestations of the Fifties

Memories are often deceptive. In retrospect, it appears as though outside the Ulm sphere of influence German design of the fifties and early sixties produced nothing but asymmetrical, rounded, brightly colored surfaces and objects – as though curving, oblique, compressed, or bulbous forms dominated the world of interiors and artefacts. The kidney-shaped table is the incarnation of all these associations. On closer examination, however, this memory proves to be false. For this period of intensive reconstruction and emergent prosperity, indeed of new affluence for many, was in fact characterized by a remarkable heterogeneity.

Once the bulk of the rubble had been cleared and the crippled economy had slowly begun to reorganize itself, an urgent quantitative and qualitative need for design arose, and not only in the private domain of household and consumer goods: for the capital goods – tools, machines, means of transportation – were also urgently required. The young republic was surging ahead, the old materials, functions, and infrastructures were no longer adequate. Scarcely had the severest hardship been overcome than the nation began to discuss taste, perfection of form, beautification of life, and new or more elegant styles of homemaking. Space-saving, folding, and adaptable furniture was designed for the typical small-family apartment. The famous SE 18 folding chair, dating from 1952, which is still manufactured today, and Egon

Eiermann's 1949 sprung swivel chair are well-known examples of a form of modernity that avoided all elaborate styling and ornamental curves. The same could be said of the wall and ceiling lighting created by Braun-Feldweg or Wagenfeld, of Schneider-Essleben's functional office systems, and of the glasses, glass objects, and porcelain tableware designed by Löffelhardt, Engler, or Wagenfeld. These were undoubtedly the dominant personalities of the age in the field of consumer goods design, alongside the designers from the HfG in Ulm and Dieter Rams, a kindred spirit of theirs, who together with Hans Gugelot from Ulm created the typical look of Braun products and thus contributed to that company's breakthrough in the market.

The new way of life was supposed to be practical, functional, and modern. Surfaces sparkled hygienically with their new coatings, the Formica kitchen became a dream in white for the new housewife – or the working wife, who was soon to become a force to be reckoned with. Plastic and the newly developed chrome-plated steel both became respectable materials. Unbreakable plastic beakers, bowls, and salad servers testify just as strongly to this new euphoria of practicality as does the soft PVC sheeting which was used to cover walls and furniture, for curtains or table-cloths. Those who could afford it and who wished to display their daring-yet-discreet taste also bought themselves a simple, functional gray-and-white radio or even an audio combination from

85 Trans-Europa-Express TEE
German Federal Railways
VT11.5 (601) *diesel multiple unit*
1957
German Federal Railways Central Office, Munich; Maschinenfabrik Augsburg-Nürnberg (MAN), rail vehicle factory; Linke-Hofmann-Busch (LHB); Wegmann & Co. BBC Brown Boveri AG; MTU; Maibach; MAN; Daimler-Benz AG
Photo: Först

86 *German Federal Railways ET30 (430) three-car over-head-contact electric train for local and rapid-transit traffic 1956 Produced by all the major German railcar manufacturers; AEG Aktiengesellschaft, BBC Brown Boveri AG, Siemens-Schuckert Werke*

87 *Omnibus*
c. 1965
Designed by the manufac-
turers
Klöckner-Humboldt-Deutz
AG, Ulm (now Klöckner-
Humboldt-Deutz AG,
Cologne)

Expediency and luxury, streamlin-ing and functionality, handy objects for everyday use and off-beat bric-à-brac, noble materials and new syn-thetics: these were the parallel and competing developments of the day. Products design claimed to be pro-viding socially oriented, functional forms, while at the same time en-couraging the spectacular, the un-conventional, and the colorful.

Simultaneously, industrial design was also progressing in the technol-ogy sector, with new types of optical equipment, transport vehicles, con-veyor-belts, control consoles, lathes, injection molding apparatus, etc. All these industrial machines were characterized by remarkably clean, far-sighted, and innovative forms and functions that were developed in cooperation with technical drafts-men and engineers.

88 BMW Isetta Export
c. 1956
Designed by the manufac-
turers
BMW AG Bayerische
Motorenwerke Aktien-
gesellschaft, Munich

Braun to replace the old wooden, gold-trimmed radiogram monstro-sity. But now that, economically speaking, things were starting to look up again, the Germans did not just want to sit at home – they wanted mobility outside the house. People started to develop a taste for travel. Those who had already achieved a certain degree of afflu-ence acquired the vehicle that matched their wallet: a Lloyd runa-bout, a BMW Isetta 150, or a Mer-cedes 300 SL. Traveling by public transport could also be a pleasant experience, and those who had the money went dashing up and down the country on the German Federal Railway's new Trans-European Ex-press.

Thus the period in question saw much that did not come out of Ulm: not just the kidney-shaped table but a whole variety of products and sys-tems paved the way for what was later to be called "good form"; some of these are still being pro-duced today, and they do not seem to have aged at all. These were the experiments of a society in the pro-cess of reconstruction, which was seeking to rediscover good taste and design but was still unsure of itself.

89 *Dethleffs* Globetrotter
c. 1958
Designed by the manufac-
turers
Dethleffs Wohnwagenwerk,
Isny

90 BMW 501 *limousine*
1951–52 six-cylinder model
1955 eight-cylinder model
Designed by the manufac-
turers
BMW AG Bayerische
Motorenwerke
Aktiengesellschaft, Munich

91 Mercedes-Benz 300 SL
Roadster
1956–57
Designed by the manufac-
turers
Daimler-Benz AG, Stuttgart

92 *Steering-wheel*
1958
Metal and plastic
Interform Wolfsburg
Volkswagen AG, Wolfsburg
Photo: Interform Wolfsburg

93 ◁ VW-Microbus *special
model*
c. 1962
*Designed by the manufac-
turers*
Volkswagen AG, Wolfsburg

94 *Circular billboard in Frankfurt*
c. 1960
*Deutsche Städtereklame,
Frankfurt*

95 VW Karman Ghia 1200
Coupé
c. 1960
Ghia S.p.A., Turin
Volkswagen AG, Wolfsburg

96 6-122 *pressure-gage*
1952
*Designed by the manufac-
turers*
*Elektron & Co. GmbH, Stutt-
gart*

97 *Kitchen unit with all-purpose cupboards for kitchen appliances*
1957-58
Designed by the manufacturers
Poggenpohl KG Möbelwerke, Herford (now: Poggenpohl Möbelwerke GmbH & Co.)
Photo: W. Bartel

98 WKS4 *kitchen unit*
c. 1957
Sep Ruf
WK Sozialwerk-Möbel, Stuttgart (now: WK Wohnen Einrichtungs GmbH, Leinfelden)

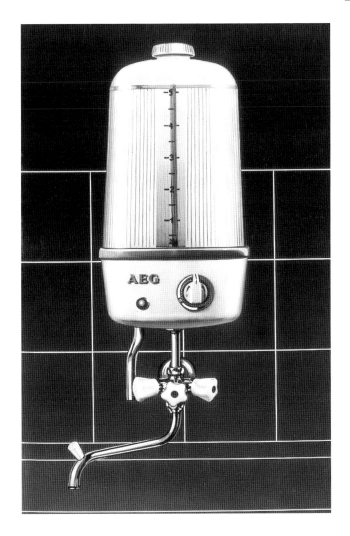

99 Thermofix *boiler*
1960–62
Metal and glass
Designed by the manufacturers
AEG Allgemeine Elektricitäts-Gesellschaft, Berlin (now: AEG Aktiengesellschaft Hausgeräte, Nuremberg)

100 DHS *dual-tank waterheater*
1957
Offelsmeyer
Stiebel-Eltron, Holzminden (now: Stiebel-Eltron GmbH & Co. KG)

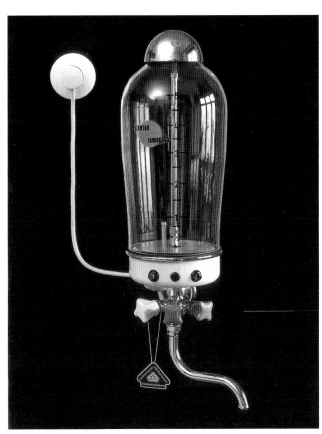

101 *Electric samovar*
1956–58
Designed by the manufacturers (K. Theiss, E. Henke Jr.)
Fabrik für Elektrotechnischen Bedarf GmbH Theiss & Henke, Kaan-Marienborn
Photo: Hans Wolpert

102 Sintrax coffee-percolator
c. 1962
Fireproof Jena glass
Bruno Mauder
Jenaer Glaswerk Schott &
Gen., Mainz (now: Schott
Glaswerke)
Photo: Willi Moegle

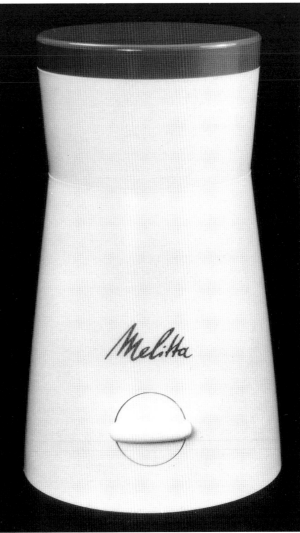

103 *Bosch mixer*
1957
Bernhard Jablonski
Robert Bosch GmbH, Stuttgart

104 *Melitta coffee-grinder*
with integrated timer
1960
Plastic body
Liselotte Kantner
Melitta-Werke Bentz & Sohn,
Minden (now: Melitta-Werke)

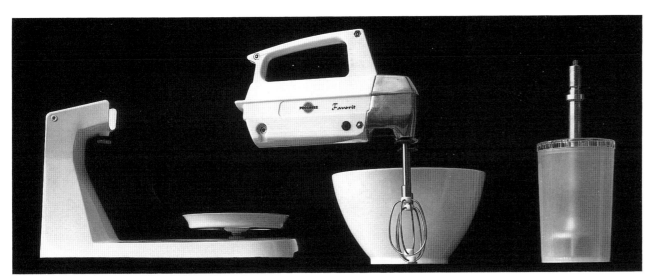

105 *KHG* Favorit *handheld*
mixer
c. 1960
Diecast aluminum and plastic
Erich Slany
Progress Verkauf GmbH, a
division of Mautz & Pfeiffer,
Stuttgart (now: Progress Elek-
trogeräte GmbH, Nürtingen)

106 OGL3 *gas-fired space-heater*
1953–55
Designed by the manufacturers
Junkers & Co. GmbH, Wernau
Photo: Barth

107 Voss Germane 7110 *convector heater*
1955–56
Metal
Wilhelm Wagenfeld
Vosswerke AG, Sarstedt

108 Oranier "Neue Form"
all-purpose nozzle burner
1958–59
Cast iron
W. Ebert
Frank'sche Eisenwerke AG,
Adolfshütte

109 *Electric heater*
1958
Sheet metal
Designed by the manufacturers (Peter Sieber)
AEG Allgemeine-Elektricitäts-Gesellschaft, Frankfurt (now: AEG Aktiengesellschaft)

110 *Small fan-heater*
1959
Duroplastic
Designed by the manufacturers
AEG Allgemeine-Elektricitäts-Gesellschaft, Frankfurt (now: AEG Aktiengesellschaft)

111 GK155W *wall-mounted refrigerator*
1960
Thermoplastic
Bernhard Jablonski
Robert Bosch GmbH, Stuttgart

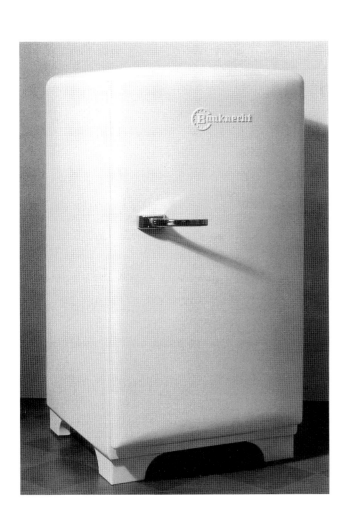

112 *Refrigerator*
c. 1956
Sheet steel and plastic
Designed by the manufacturers
G. Bauknecht GmbH, Stuttgart (now: Bauknecht Hausgeräte GmbH)
Photo: Willi Moegle

113 *Compressor refrigerator*
1960
Sheet steel, plastic, and metal grid
Designed by the manufacturers
Siemens Elektrogeräte GmbH, Munich

114 *Coffeepot (1st prize,*
Silver Coffeepot Competition)
1958–59
Silver, ebony
Alfred Danner
E. Walter Werkstätten
P. Bruckmann & Söhne,
Heilbronn
Photo: Tiede

115 *Coffeepot (2nd prize,*
Silver Coffeepot Competition)
1958–59
Silver, palisander wood
Helmut Warneke
Gebrüder Deyhle, Schwäbisch
Gmünd (now: Gebrüder
Deyhle GmbH & Co.)
Photo: Menzel

116 *Pots*
(3rd prize, Silver Coffeepot
Competition)
1958–59
Silver, ebony
Karl Dittert
E. Walter Werkstätten
P. Bruckmann & Söhne,
Heilbronn

117 3774 *eggcup*
1953–54
Cromargan
Wilhelm Wagenfeld
WMF Württembergische
Metallwarenfabrik AG, Geis-
lingen
Photo: K. Schumacher

118 511 *table-service*
1957
Porcelain
Heinrich Löffelhardt
Porzellanfabrik Schönwald,
Schönwald
Photo: Willi Moegle

119 Krokus *tea-set*
1955–56
Porcelain
Hubert Griemert
Staatliche Porzellanmanufak-
tur Berlin, Berlin (now: KPM)
Photo: Baumann ▷

120 Stockholm *coffee-service*
(form 7, *with 0707 cobalt blue*
decoration)
1961
Stoneware
Liselotte Kantner
Melitta Werke Benz & Sohn,
Minden (now: Melitta-Werke)

121 Grazie coffee-set
1956
Porcelain
Karl Leutner
Porzellanfabrik Heinrich & Co.,
Selb (now: Heinrich Porzellan
GmbH)
Photo: Willi Moegle

122 2075 coffee-set
1961–62
Porcelain
Heinrich Löffelhardt
Porzellanfabrik Arzberg,
Arzberg
Photo: Willi Moegle

123 *Teapot*
1957
Porcelain
Trude Petri-Raben
Staatliche Porzellanmanufak-
tur Berlin, Berlin (now: KPM)
Photo: Baumann

124 Atlanta 4200 *cutlery-set*
1954–55
Cromargan or silver
Wilhelm Wagenfeld
WMF Württembergische
Metallwarenfabrik AG, Geis-
lingen

125 Pott 83/783 *cutlery-set*
1950–51 (reworked Gretsch
design of 1942)
Silver or Argentan
Hermann Gretsch, Wilhelm
Wagenfeld
C. Hugo Pott, Solingen (now:
C. Hugo Pott GmbH & Co. KG)

126 *Cutlery-set (model) (1st*
prize, WMF Cutlery Competi-
tion)
1959
Fritz Weidler (class of Karl Dit-
tert), State College of Indus-
trial Art, Schwäbisch Gmünd

127 2722 *cutlery-set*
1956
18/8 nickel chromium steel,
stainless steel
Carl Pott
C. Hugo Pott, Solingen (now:
C. Hugo Pott GmbH & Co. KG)
Photo: Willi Moegle

128 3130 *dinner-plates*
1960
Ovenproof glass
Heinrich Löffelhardt
Jenaer Glaswerke Schott &
Gen., Mainz (now: Schott
Glaswerke)
Photo: Willi Moegle

129 WMF Form 3600 *cutlery-*
set
1952–53
Polished Cromargan
Wilhelm Wagenfeld
WMF Württembergische
Metallwarenfabrik AG,
Geislingen

130 3182 *ragout dishes*
1958–59
Ovenproof glass
Heinrich Löffelhardt
Jenaer Glaswerke Schott &
Gen., Mainz (now: Schott
Glaswerke)
Photo: Willi Moegle

131 3109 *casserole, with*
3108 *flat lid*
Photo c. 1960
Ovenproof glass
Heinrich Löffelhardt
Jenaer Glaswerke Schott &
Gen., Mainz (now: Schott
Glaswerke)
Photo: Manfred Boersch

132 *Bowl*
1957
Porcelain
Karl Leutner
Porzellanfabrik Heinrich & Co.,
Selb (now: Heinrich Porzellan
GmbH)
Photo: Willi Moegle

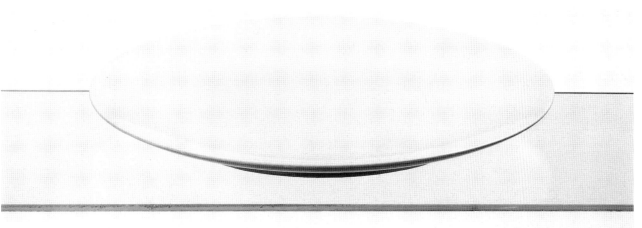

133 *3528 dessert-plate*
1958–59
Acrylonitrile and polystyrene
mixture
Ernst Moeckl
Hünersdorff-Bührer, Ludwigs-
burg (now: Hünersdorff
GmbH)
Photo: Willi Moegle

134 SE42 *chair*
1949
Egon Eiermann
Wilde + Spieth, Esslingen
(Wilde + Spieth GmbH & Co.)
Photo: Werbetechnik

135 Casala 3110/0 *and*
3110/6 *stackable chairs*
1958
Ernst Dettinger
Carl Sasse KG, Lauenau (now:
Casala-Werke Carl Sasse
GmbH & Co. KG)
Photo: Willi Moegle   ▷

136 VB101w *chair*
1952–53
Hans Th. Baumann
Fehlbaum Vitra GmbH, Weil
(now: Vitra GmbH)
Photo: Reiss-Ensinger   ▷▷

137 EL121 *stool*
c. 1953
Eduard Ludwig
Domus KG H. Schoeck,
Schwaikheim
Photo: Willi Moegle

138 SE18 *folding chair*
1952
Egon Eiermann
Wilde + Spieth, Esslingen
(Wilde + Spieth GmbH & Co.)
Photo: Karro Schumacher   ▷

139 SR1 *chair*
Prior to 1962
Bodo Rasch
Wilde + Spieth, Esslingen
(Wilde + Spieth GmbH & Co.)
Photo: Willi Moegle   ▷▷

140 452 *armchair*
1957
Herbert Hirche
Wilkhahn, Espelkamp (now:
Wilkhahn, Bad Münder)
Photo: Bruno Rieth

141 PSE58 *armchair*
1958–59
Paul Schneider-Esleben
H. Kaufeld, Brake (now: Hans
Kaufeld & Co., Bielefeld)
Photo: Charles Wilp   ▷

142 1152K *armchair*
1956
Helmut Magg
Deutsche Werkstätten Ferti-
gungsgesellschaft mbH,
Munich (now: DeWe
Deutsche Werkstätten Ferti-
gungsgesellschaft mbH)
Photo: Erskine   ▷▷

143 Mandarin T80 *table*
1958–59
Teak
Harald Roth
Casa GmbH, Munich
Photo: Willi Moegle

144 WR184 *table*
1960
Walnut, cherry, or teak
Q. Punzmann
Wilhelm Renz KG, Böblingen
Photo: Willi Moegle

◁ **145** 529 *dining-table*
Prior to 1957
Teak or cherry, plastic top
Herbert Hirche
Wilkhahn, Espelkamp (now:
Wilkhahn, Bad Münder)
Photo: Bruno Rieth

146 T57 *tea-table*
c. 1958
Steel tubing, teak, palisander
or dark tropical wood, or plas-
tic
Ernst Kirchhoff
Casa GmbH, Munich
Photo: Willi Moegle

147 62399 *shell-pattern plastic sheeting*
1955
Polyvinyl chloride
Designed by the manufacturers
Acella, Benecke, Hanover

148 Sandra 9675 *fabric*
c. 1957
Peter Herkenrath
Heinrich Habig AG, Herdecke

149 *Furnishing-fabric*
c. 1957
Silk, warp yarn natural silk
Students of Georg Muche,
College of Textile Engineering,
Krefeld
Photo: O. Rathgeber

150 Sita 9720 *fabric*
c. 1957
Emil Schumacher
Heinrich Habig AG, Herdecke

151 Sandra 9670 *fabric*
c. 1957
Rolf Cavael
Heinrich Habig AG, Herdecke

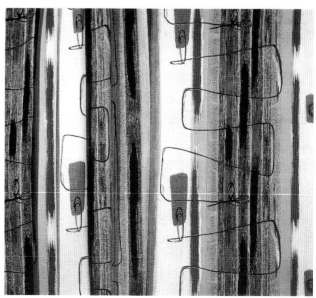

152 Capri *printed fabric*
1958–59
Margret Hildebrand
Stuttgarter Gardinenfabrik
GmbH, Herrenberg
Photo: Michael Wolgensinger

153 17331 *wallpaper*
c. 1960
Kurt Kranz
Marburger Tapetenfabrik
J. B. Schaefer GmbH, Kirch-
hain (now: Marburger
Tapetenfabrik J. B. Schaefer
GmbH & Co. KG)
Photo: Kleinhempel

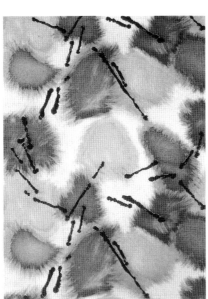

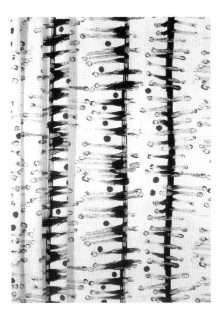

◁◁ **154** Sandra 9673 *fabric*
c. 1957
Alexander Camaro
Heinrich Habig AG, Herdecke

◁ **155** 8655 *fabric*
c. 1957
Hubert Berke
Heinrich Habig AG, Herdecke

156 Sandra 9712 *fabric*
c. 1957
Fritz Winter
Heinrich Habig AG, Herdecke

157 *Office desks*
1953
Steel runner-like legs, steel drawers, Plastipol desk top
George Leowald
Pohlschröder & Co. KG, Dortmund
Photo: Heidersberger

158 Bukama Kornett *stapler*
1957
Steel plate
E. Haubold
Bukama GmbH, Hanover
Photo: Lieb ▷

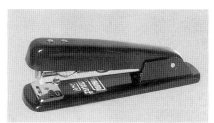

159 Develop DE 36 *electric copying-machine*
1952
Designed by the manufacturers
Develop KG Dr. Eisbein & Co., Stuttgart (now: Develop Dr. Eisbein GmbH & Co., Gerlingen) ▷

160 Badenia "Vier Spezies" *calculator*
1955–56
Diecast light metal
Wilhelm Braun-Feldweg
Math. Bäuerle GmbH, St. Georgen (now: Tobias Bäuerle GmbH & Co. KG)
Photo: Breyer/Lott

161 abc *portable typewriter*
1954–55
Diecast steel and aluminum
Wilhelm Wagenfeld
Kochs Adlernähmaschinen Werke AG, Bielefeld (now: Kochs Adler AG) ▷

162 *Card-punching machine with calculating and print-out features*
c. 1956
Designed by the manufacturers
Kienzle Apparate GmbH, Villingen (now: Mannesmann Kienzle GmbH)

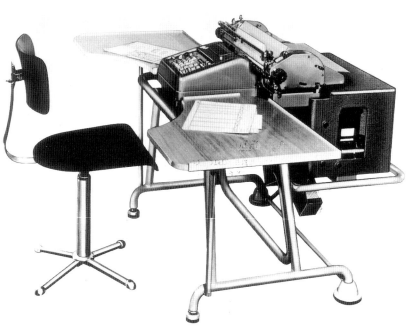

163 Siemens 100 *teletyper*
1958
Designed by the manufacturers
Siemens & Halske AG, Munich (now: Siemens AG) ▷

164 Zeitgewinn *office furniture system*
1960
Steel and walnut
Peter Raacke
VOKO Büromöbelfabriken, Giessen (now: VOKO Franz Vogt & Co. KG)
Photo: Karro Schumacher

◁ **165** Assistent *table-top telephone*
1958–59
D. Blumenau
SEL Standard Elektrik Lorenz AG, Stuttgart
Photo: Günter Senfft

166 VOKO Transparent *filing-system*
1962–63
Sheet and steel tubing
Peter Raacke
VOKO Büromöbelfabriken, Giessen (now: VOKO Franz Vogt & Co. KG)

◁ **167** Assmann Universa *dictaphone*
1957
Metal
Günter Kraatz
Wolfgang Assmann GmbH, Bad Homburg
(now: Assmann Informatik 2000 GmbH)

◁ **168** Alpina *all-purpose calculator*
1960
Designed by the manufacturers
Alpina Büromaschinenvertrieb Grossbovensiepen KG, Kaufbeuren

169 Zeitgewinn *office furniture system*
1960
Steel and walnut
Peter Raacke
VOKO Büromöbelfabriken, Giessen (now: VOKO Franz Vogt & Co. KG)
Photo: Karro Schumacher

◁ **170** EBA-Tarnator allround 200 *shredder*
1961
Adolf Ehinger Jr.
Adolf Ehinger Maschinenfabrik, Balingen

171 Standard WL *microscope*
c. 1957
Designed by the manufac-
turers
Carl Zeiss, Oberkochen

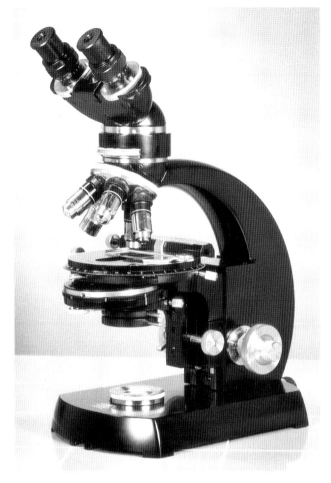

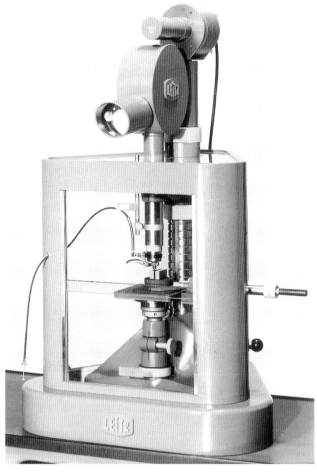

172 Ultra Projectometer
1952
Cast iron, aluminum
Designed by the manufac-
turers
Ernst Leitz GmbH, Wetzlar

173 Ni2 *surveyor's level*
1950
Metal
Designed by the manufac-
turers
Carl Zeiss, Oberkochen

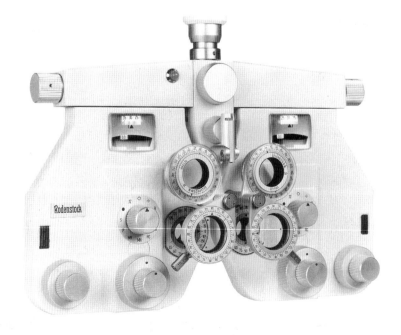

174 Phoropter *refraction-*
apparatus
1961
Metal
Willy Herold
Optische Werke Rodenstock,
Munich
Photo: Anker

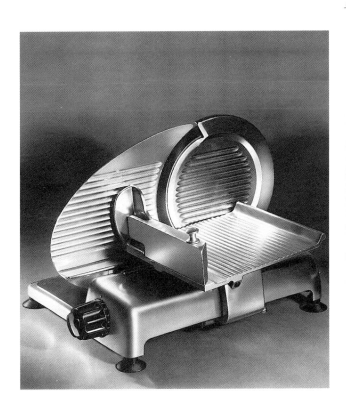

175 VE6 *electric food-slicer*
1959
Designed by the manufac-
turers
Bizerba-Waagen-Verkaufs-
gesellschaft mbH, Balingen
(now: Bizerba Waagen und
Maschinenfabriken)

176 OP3 *fully automatic price-*
calculating scales
1954
Cast aluminum
Designed by the manufac-
turers
Bizerba-Waagen-Verkaufs-
gesellschaft mbH, Balingen
(now: Bizerba Waagen- und
Maschinenfabriken)
Photo: Schmid

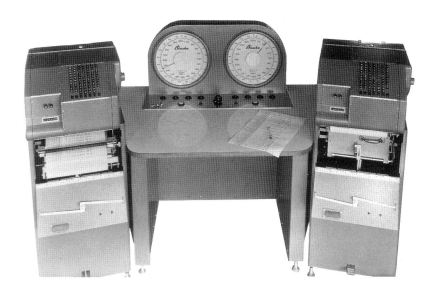

177 *Weighing-desk, with re-*
mote display unit and button-
operated pressure gages for
two weighing-points
Before 1958
Designed by the manufac-
turers
Bizerba-Waagen-Verkaufs-
gesellschaft mbH, Balingen
(now: Bizerba Waagen- und
Maschinenfabriken)

178 *Porcelain for technical purposes*
Prior to 1954
Designed by the manufacturers
Staatliche Porzellanmanufaktur Berlin, Werk Selb (now: KPM)
Photo: Anton Stankowski

179 Model 19 *visual display unit*
1959
Metal, plastic
Designed by the manufacturers
Siemens & Halske AG, Munich (now: Siemens AG)

180 *Display of laboratory glassware, Hanover Fair*
1956
Arnold Bode
Jenaer Glaswerke Schott & Gen., Mainz (now: Schott Glaswerke)
Photo: Heidersberger

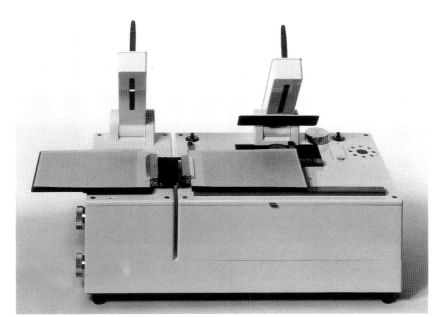

181 *Extinction meter with integral recorder*
c. 1954
Metal
Designed by the manufacturers
Carl Zeiss, Oberkochen
Photo: Friedrich Emich

182 *Control panels at RWE's Thingen power-station in the Black Forest*
1957
Designed by the manufacturers (Peter Sieber)
AEG Allgemeine-Elektricitäts-Gesellschaft, Frankfurt (now: AEG Aktiengesellschaft)
Photo: Krucker

183 *Rotary blower for 3-phase and single-phase alternating current*
c. 1958
Gray cast iron, aluminum
Designed by the manufacturers
Elektror Karl W. Müller, Esslingen
Photo: Blasczyk

184 *STS 43/53/8-STR/12/P steel rod conveyor-belt*
1961
Designed by the manufacturers
Hans Holger Wiese Förderanlagen, Hanover (now: Hans Holger Wiese GmbH & Co. KG, Burgwedel)

185 German standard JEG *motor* ZET
1961
Designed by the manufacturers
Richard Zimmermann KG, Denkendorf

186 *Turbine at Altbach II power-station*
1960–61
Designed by the manufacturers (Peter Sieber)
AEG Allgemeine Elektricitäts-Gesellschaft, Frankfurt (now: AEG Aktiengesellschaft)

187 RV50 *turret lathe*
c. 1951
Cast-iron monocoque construction
Designed by the manufacturers (Walter Möbius)
Gildemeister & Co. AG, Bielefeld (now: Gildemeister Automatische Drehmaschinen GmbH)

188 P1250 *cylindrical toothcutter*
c. 1962
Walter M. Kerting
Pfauter Walzfräsmaschinenfabrik, Ludwigsburg (now: Hermann Pfauter GmbH & Co. Werkzeugmaschinenfabrik)

189 23N/13 *lever-operated upright punching-machine*
c. 1961
Designed by the manufacturers
Muhr & Bender, Attendorn (now: Muhr und Bender Maschinenbau GmbH)
Photo: Jupp Schmies

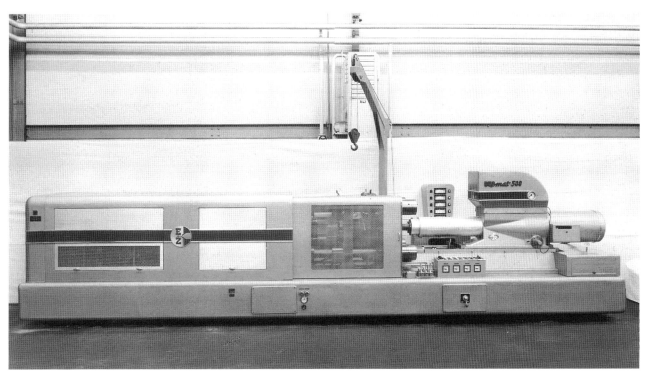

190 DUOmat 500s *injection molding machine with integrated unit for screw injection*
1958
Designed by the manufacturers
Eckert und Ziegler GmbH, Weissenburg
Photo: Max Göllner

191 Bremen *unit column crane*
1956
Klaus Flesche
MAN Maschinenfabrik Augsburg-Nürnberg AG, Nuremberg (now: MAN GmbH, Munich)

192 415 *4.5-ton truck with forward cab*
1956
Klaus Flesche
MAN Maschinenfabrik Augsburg-Nürnberg AG, Nuremberg (now: MAN GmbH, Munich)

193 PHB *traveling bridge crane*
Prior to 1962
Pohlig-Heckel-Bleichert
Vereinigte Maschinenfabriken AG, Rohrbach

194 MD195 *combine harvester*
1955
Designed by the manufacturers
Heinrich Lanz AG, Mannheim

195 V70b *mobile crane*
c. 1950
W. A. Golka
DEMAG AG, Duisburg (now: Mannesmann Demag AG)

196 B504 *all-purpose fully hydraulic bulldozer (equipped with dipper shovel in the crawler-driven version)*
1956
Steel
Designed by the manufacturers
DEMAG Baggerfabrik GmbH, Benrath, Düsseldorf (now: Mannesmann Demag AG, Duisburg)

197 *16-ton hydraulic press*
1960
Metal
Odo Klose
FMA Pokorny, Frankfurt

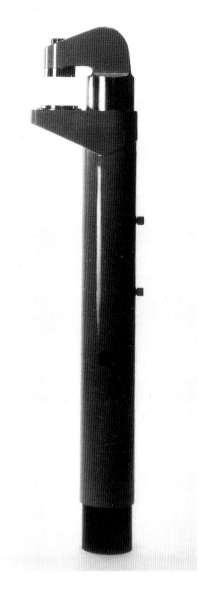

198 *Plug for precision instruments*
Before 1964
Designed by the manufacturers
Rohde & Schwarz, Munich (now: Rohde & Schwarz GmbH & Co. KG)

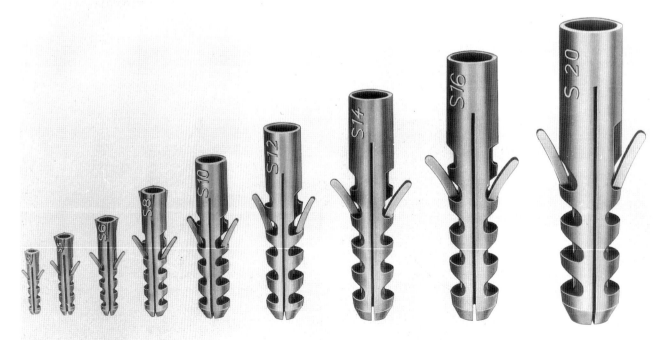

199 Fischer S4 – S20 *hole-plugs*
1958
Thermoplastic
Artur Fischer
Fischer-Werke, A. Fischer, Tumlingen (now: Fischerwerke Artur Fischer GmbH & Co. KG)

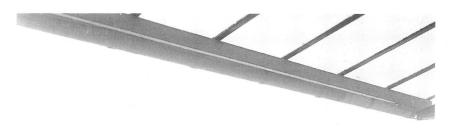

200 K251 *stackable baskets*
Before 1960
Light metal
Designed by the manufacturers
Zarges-Leichtmetallbau KG, Weilheim (now: Zarges Leichtbau GmbH)

201 *Stackable boxes*
Prior to 1960
Light metal
Designed by the manufacturers
Zarges-Leichtmetallbau KG, Weilheim (now: Zarges Leichtbau GmbH)

202 *Stackable table service (draft)*
1960
Mosche Kohen, Ulm

203 Form 1100 *dishes*
1957–58
Porcelain
Heinrich Löffelhardt
Porzellanfabrik Arzberg, Arz-
berg
Photo: Willi Moegle

204 System B1100 *stackable*
crockery
1962
Porcelain
Heinz H. Engler
Porzellanfabrik Weiden Gebr.
Bauscher, Weiden

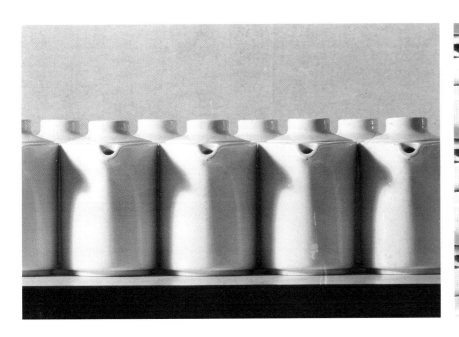

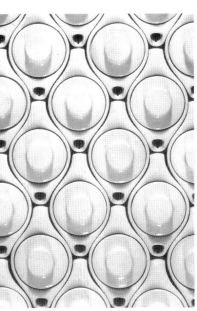

205 Schönwald 498 *hotel crockery*
1961
Heinrich Löffelhardt
Porzellanfabrik Schönwald, Schönwald
Photo: Willi Moegle

206 System B1100 *stackable crockery: jugs*
1961
Porcelain
Heinz H. Engler
Porzellanfabrik Weiden Gebr. Bauscher, Weiden

207 System B1100 *stackable crockery: coffeepots*
1961
Porcelain
Heinz H. Engler
Porzellanfabrik Weiden Gebr. Bauscher, Weiden

208 *Secondary clock (regulator)*
1956
Siemens-Design
Siemens AG, Munich

209 *Advertising column with clock*
Before 1960
Deutsche Städtereklame, Frankfurt

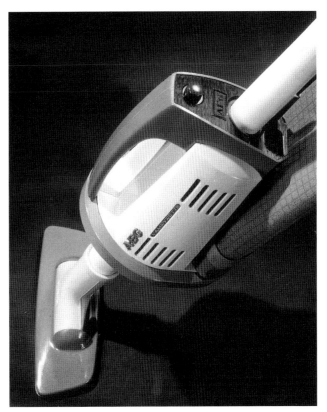

210 Starlet *carpet-sweeper*
1958
Plastic casing
Erich Slany
Leifheit AG, Nassau

211 Vampyrette K *vacuum-cleaner*
1959
Plastic casing
Designed by the manufacturers
AEG Allgemeine Elektricitäts-Gesellschaft, Berlin (now: AEG Aktiengesellschaft Hausgeräte, Nuremberg)

212 P110 *single-disk floor-polisher*
1956
Erich Slany
Progress Verkauf GmbH, a division of Mautz & Pfeiffer, Stuttgart (now: Progress Elektrogeräte GmbH, Nürtingen)
Photo: Richard Schenkirz

213 Super VS 205 *cylinder vacuum-cleaner*
1960
Plastic casing
Siemens-Design
Siemens Elektrogeräte GmbH, Munich

214 Rapid VR 15 *hand vacuum-cleaner*
c. 1960
Plastic casing
Siemens-Design
Siemens Elektrogeräte GmbH, Munich

215 *Automatic heat-con-*
trolled iron
1960
Aluminum, sheet iron, plastic
Graf Goertz
Rowenta Metallwarenfabrik
GmbH, Offenbach (now:
Rowenta-Werke GmbH)
Photo: Stook

216 EBL26S *heat-controlled*
iron
Prior to 1961
Steel base
Designed by the manufac-
turers
Prometheus GmbH, Eschwege
(now: Prometheus GmbH, Sel-
ters-Eisenbach)

217 *Automatik SE iron*
1958
Chrome-plated sheet steel,
aluminum, molded plastic
Siemens-Design
Siemens Elektrogeräte GmbH,
Munich
Photo: Eggle

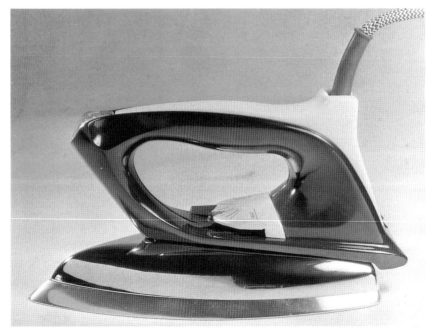

218 *Starch- and water-sprink-*
ler for ironing clothes
1956
Lupolen
Wilhelm Wagenfeld
Joh. Buchsteiner, Gingen

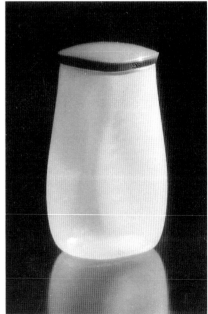

219 HS 32 F *automatic range with wide oven*
1961
Enameled sheet steel
Siemens-Design
Siemens Elektrogeräte GmbH, Munich

220 THB2 *stove*
1956
Enameled sheet steel
Designed by the manufacturers
Siemens-Schuckert Werke AG, Erlangen, Berlin (now: Siemens AG, Munich)

221 Vitavit *pressure-cooker*
1953
Aluminum
Designed by the manufacturers
Rudolf Fissler KG, Idar-Oberstein (now: Fissler GmbH)
Photo: Franz Lazi jr.

222 Schneidboy *vegetable-
slicer*
1954
Polystyrene
*Designed by the manufac-
turers*
*Ritter Werk F. Ritter & Sohn,
Pasing, Munich (now: Ritterwerk GmbH, Gröbenzell)*

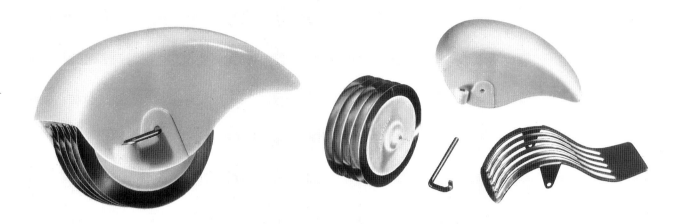

223 M100 *multipurpose
whisk*
1960–61
*Designed by the manufac-
turers (Graf Bernadotte, Acton
Bjorn)*
*ESGE Elektromotoren & Ap-
paratebau GmbH Gschwend
& Springer KG, Neuffen (now:
ESGE electronic GmbH)*

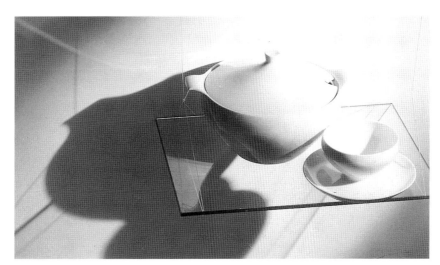

224, 225 411 *table-service*
1953–54
Porcelain
Heinrich Löffelhardt
Porzellanfabrik Schönwald,
Schönwald
Photo: Willi Moegle

226 *Light-switch*
1959
Plastic
Designed by the manufac-
turers
GIRA Elektrotechnische Indus-
trie Gustav Giersiepen KG,
Radevormwald (now: GIRA
Gustav Giersiepen GmbH &
Co. KG)

227 *Light-switches, sockets*
and bell pushes
1956
Molded plastic casing
Designed by the manufac-
turers
Busch-Jaeger Dürener Metall-
werke KG, Lüdenscheid (now:
Busch-Jaeger Elektro GmbH)

228 *Rechargeable flashlights*
c. 1955
Plastic casing
Designed by the manufac-
turers (Peter Sieber)
AEG Allgemeine Elektricitäts-
Gesellschaft Zählerfabriken,
Hamelin (now: AEG Aktien-
gesellschaft, Serienprodukte,
Zähler und Elfa)

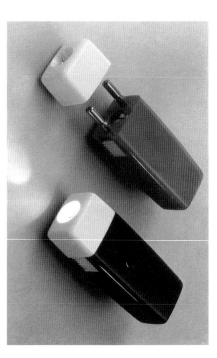

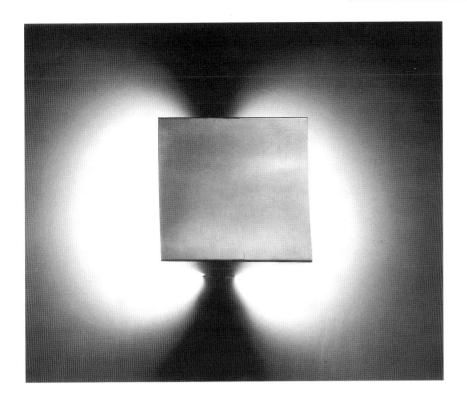

229 Britz *wall-lamp*
1962
Metal shade, adjustable
Wilhelm Braun-Feldweg
DORIA-Werk, Fürth

230 Britz *wall-lamp*
1962
Metal shade, adjustable
Wilhelm Braun-Feldweg
DORIA-Werk, Fürth

231 *Wall-lamp*
c. 1955
Plastic
Hoffmann-Lederer
Hecht, Darmstadt
Photo: O. Rathgeber

232 6026/5021 *wall-lamp for corners*
1955
Porcelain and glass
Wilhelm Wagenfeld
Lindner Licht GmbH, Bamberg

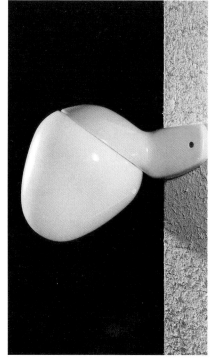

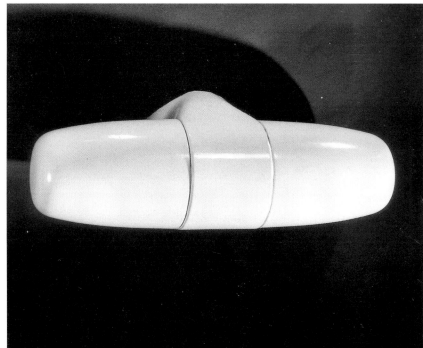

233 6078/5077 *wall-lamp*
1958
Porcelain and glass
Wilhelm Wagenfeld
Lindner Licht GmbH, Bamberg

234 6030/5030 *outside wall-lamp*
1954
Porcelain and glass
Wilhelm Wagenfeld
Lindner Licht GmbH, Bamberg

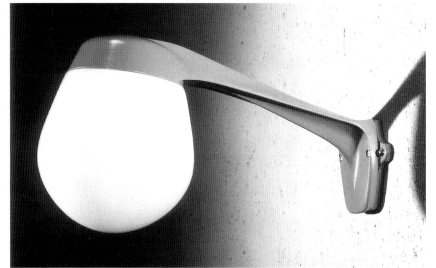

235 Combal 6321.1 *wall-lamp*
1957
Light metal and glass
Wilhelm Wagenfeld
Lindner Licht GmbH, Bamberg

236 6320/5000 *outside wall-lamp*
1958
Light metal and glass
Wilhelm Wagenfeld
Lindner Licht GmbH, Bamberg

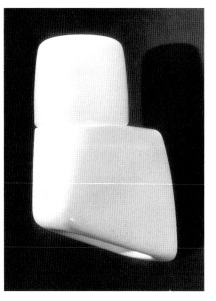

237 6421.1 *wall-lamp*
1959
Wilhelm Wagenfeld
Lindner Licht GmbH, Bamberg
Photo: Hörlein

238 ELROYAL 6401 *dome lamp*
1959
Wilhelm Wagenfeld
Lindner Licht GmbH, Bamberg

239 billo 72691 *anglepoise desk-lamp*
1958
Designed by the manufacturers
Leuchtenfabrik Egon Hillebrand, Neheim-Hüsten (now: Hillebrand GmbH & Co., Egon Hillebrand Leuchten, Arnsberg)

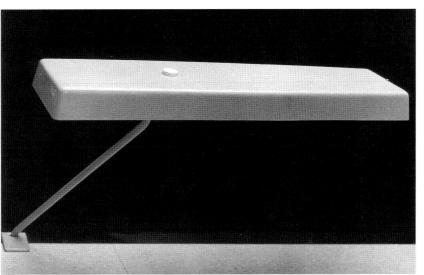

240 *Desk-lamp*
1958–59
Designed by the manufacturers (Klaus Seeliger)
AEG Allgemeine Elektricitäts-Gesellschaft Zählerfabrik, Hamelin (now: AEG Aktiengesellschaft Lichttechnik, Springe)

241, 242 *Red lighting and ultraviolet lamp*
1962
Plastic and sheet steel
Hans Greiser
Meyer & Söhne, Ihmert

243 Leica M3 *camera*
1954
Injection-molded aluminum,
brass, and precious metals
Designed by the manufac-
turers
Ernst Leitz GmbH, Wetzlar
(now: Leica GmbH, Solms)

244 Sixtino *hand-held*
exposure-meter
1960
Metal and plastic
Designed by the manufac-
turers
P. Gossen & Co. GmbH, Er-
langen (now: Gossen GmbH)

245 Cornet R *electronic flash-*
gun
1960
Bernhard Jablonski
Deutsche Elektronik GmbH,
Wilmersdorf, Berlin

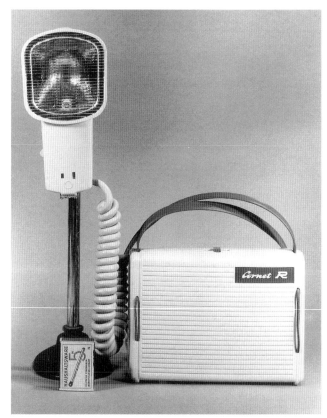

246 Uher 4000 Report S
*portable all-transistorized
tape-recorder
1961–62
Metal and plastic*
Albert Liebe
*Uher-Werke Munich GmbH,
Bad Homburg*

247 Prado 250 *miniature
film-projector
c. 1951
Sheet steel and cast iron
Designed by the manufac-
turers*
*Ernst Leitz GmbH, Wetzlar
(now: Leica GmbH, Solms)*

248 Solo-Boy *miniature radio
Before 1961
Designed by the manufac-
turers*
Grundig AG, Fürth

249 *Prototype radio-housing*
c. 1953
Walter Schwagenscheidt, Tassilo Sittmann, Helmut Dornauf
(Kronberger Werkstatt für Gestaltung)
Photo: Ruth Gerhardt

250 *Prototype radio-housing*
c. 1957
Walter Schwagenscheidt
(Kronberger Werkstatt für Gestaltung)
Photo: Ruth Gerhardt

251 *Prototype radio-housing*
c. 1957
Walter Schwagenscheidt
(Kronberger Werkstatt für Gestaltung)
Photo: Ruth Gerhardt

252 Soloform 5008 *bowl-shaped sofa*
1954
Steel tub and cushioning-material
Hans Hartl
Polstermöbelfabrik Eugen Schmidt GmbH, Darmstadt

253 E19 *bench and* E16 *arm-chair*
1956–57
Wickerwork
Egon Eiermann
Heinrich Murman, Johannisthal-Kronach

254 5825 *sofa*
Prior to 1958
Rudolf Frank
Lukas Schnaidt, Steinheim (now: Lukas Schnaidt GmbH & Co. KG)
Photo: Willi Moegle

255 Marina *dishes*
1954–55
Wilhelm Braun-Feldweg
Kristallglaswerk Hirschberg
der Steinkohlenbergwerke
Mathias Stinnes AG, Essen
(now: Kristallglaswerk
Hirschberg, Allendorf, Mar-
burg)

256 2005 *liqueur-set*
1955
Heinrich Löffelhardt
Vereinigte Farbenglaswerke
AG, Zwiesel (now: Schott-
Zwiesel Glaswerke AG)
Photo: Willi Moegle

257 15009 and 15010
cocktail-set
1959
Crystal
Wilhelm Braun-Feldweg
Peill & Putzler Glashütten-
werke GmbH, Düren   ▷

258 *Liqueur-glasses*
Prior to 1962
Wilhelm Wagenfeld
Vereinigte Lausitzer Glas-
werke, Weisswasser
Photo: Dore Bartcky   ▷

259 *Brandy-glass*
1951–52
Wilhelm Wagenfeld
WMF Württembergische
Metallwarenfabrik AG, Geis-
lingen
Photo: Schumacher

260 Parabol *ashtray*
1953
Porcelain with black glazing
Trude Petri-Raben
Staatliche Porzellanmanufak-
tur Berlin, Werk Selb (now:
KPM)
Photo: Willi Moegle

261 Form WL *candleshade*
1957
Egon Eiermann
Richard Süssmuth Glashütte,
Immenhausen (now: Süss-
muth Glashütte GmbH)
Photo: Elisabeth Klein

262 *1363003 cocktail-shaker*
1959
Silver-plated with Argentan
Wilhelm Wagenfeld
WMF Württembergische
Metallwarenfabrik AG,
Geislingen

263 *Sugar-tongs*
1956
Plated with Cromargan or
Argentan
Wilhelm Wagenfeld
WMF Württembergische
Metallwarenfabrik AG,
Geislingen

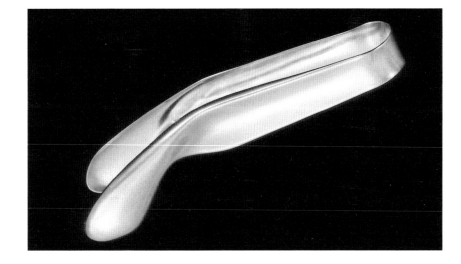

264 Form Jacqueline *coffee-set*
c. 1963
Porcelain
Designed by the manufacturers
C. M. Hutschenreuther Arzberg Porzellan AG, Hohenberg (now: Porzellanfabriken Hutschenreuther, Selb)

265 *From the* Werkbund
boxed set: "The set table"
1955
Deutscher Werkbund, Berlin

266 *From the* Werkbund
boxed set
"A table for work purposes":
1955
*Workplace for the housewife
Chair, table, kitchen appli-
ances
Deutscher Werkbund, Berlin*

267 Werkbund boxed set
"A table for work purposes"
(open)
1955
*Apparatus for the parents,
meaningful toys for small children, books, paint-box, etc.,
for older children. In the dou-
ble bottom there is a black
Formica-topped worktable
and a black stool.
Deutscher Werkbund, Berlin*

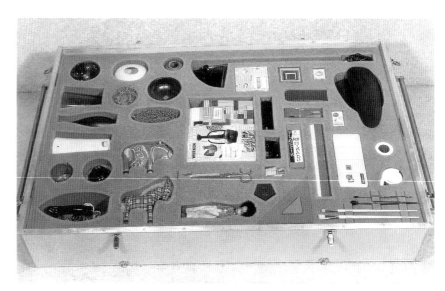

Gwendolyn Ristant **Good Form**

The sixties in West Germany were characterized by a consolidation process that made the economic and social misery of the immediate post-war years seem little more than a bad dream. Unemployment seemed to have been banished for good – indeed, in the period of the dawning "economic miracle" foreign workers were recruited because the German workforce was not large enough.

Product design had also undergone a process of consolidation; the "polystyle" phase was over, where old Bauhaus virtues and new experiments in form, the ephemeral and the lasting, the unconventional and the respectable, had rubbed shoulders. It was no longer just taste that was called for, but "good form" as well. This was not to be left to subjective judgment, and the hunt for criteria for objectively good design was on. The stores were full of merchandise, and the consumer was beginning to lose his bearings in the product jungle. Design – in Germany the English word was not yet current, "shaping" (Gestaltung) or "forming" (Formgebung) still being preferred – had allied itself more closely to industry's requirements, and mass production was now the magic word. Albeit from different standpoints, designers and industry both agreed that criteria for evaluating product design needed to be developed. Manufacturers realized that good, practical, and elegant design would sell more goods than the hitherto rather haphazard approach. The industrial designers, for their part, were working with renewed in-spiration on their dream of establishing aesthetic, functional, and technical categories for defining good design.

The sixties were characterized by three interconnected developments: products and their design became increasingly influenced by *technology*, design could be put on an *objective* footing through universally accepted criteria, and a tendency towards *didactism* emerged. The motives for propagating and promoting well-planned, utilizable industrial design were of course not exclusively of a social and cultural nature – economic interests were also at stake. The national representative body of German design, the Rat für Formgebung (German Design Council), had been founded relatively early, in 1953, but the full significance of its remarkably far-sighted statement of policy was not realized until the following decade; the goal of the Council was "to promote all efforts deemed appropriate to achieve optimal design for German products, both in the consumer's interest and in order to make more competitive the products of German industry and craftsmanship." An awareness of the social and economic relevance of design led in subsequent years to widely varying forms of design promotion, above all by the state. Colleges of design were expanded and new ones were founded, and regional design centers were set up to complement the Rat für Formgebung: in 1962, the Design Center in Stuttgart was opened, followed in 1969 by the

268 LB-System *shop display*
c. 1961
Wood, metal, plastic
Heinz Hochberger
Huwil-Werke GmbH, Ruppich-terroth, Cologne

269 *Automatic letter-sorter*
1965
Designed by the manufac-turers
Siemens & Halske AG, Munich
(now: Siemens AG)

270 1220 endless seating-system
1968
Polyester
Friso Kramer
Wilkhahn, Eimbeckhausen
(now: Wilkhahn, Bad Münder)
Photo: Roland Fürst

271 V 320 *diesel locomotive*
("Gute Form" exhibition,
London 1965)
1961–62
Developed jointly by the Ger-
man Federal Railways Central
Office, the Henschel works,
and MAN (Klaus Flesche)
Henschel-Werke GmbH,
Kassel

272 *Restaurant with vending*
automats
Before 1967
Designed by the manufac-
turers
DWM-Automatenbau GmbH,
Berlin

273 Amphicar 770 *amphib-*
ious vehicle
1961
Designed by the manufac-
turers (Hans Trippel)
Deutsche Waggon- und Ma-
schinenfabriken GmbH, Berlin

International Design Center in West Berlin. In addition, consumer associations appeared on the scene, lobbying for good product design and co-sponsoring design competitions and awards promoted by state design institutions and/or private companies. The belief that it was possible to find universally valid objective criteria for judging the design of industrial goods (function, aesthetic impression, ease of operation, durability, safety, appropriacy of materials, innovation, etc.) soon developed into a design code, indeed a veritable canon. The products which were deemed by the numerous juries to be worthy of an award had to prove their worth in terms of these criteria. As a consequence, it soon became possible to discern a typically German product design, a "German style" – although the designers rejected this notion. Modest in appearance, functional in use, matter-of-fact, with neat right-angles, in white, gray or black, without ornamentation, with no more than precise, technically necessary details: such was the look of those mass products which conformed to the ideal of good design. And it was only logical that most of the award-winning products should come from the technology-oriented sphere: domestic appliances, machines, cameras, radios, audio equipment, televisions. Articles of office and household furniture also lost their individuality, for it was furniture systems and unit furniture that were adjudged to constitute good design.

The epitome of the idea of an objectifiable "good form" (this was the title given to the most important German design competition, a nationwide award organized by the German Design Council from 1969 onwards) was the Braun Corporation, whose products received awards with above-average frequency. This was the company that as early as 1955 had been part of the exclusive avant-garde in terms of its product design. The design program, which had begun with radio and audio combinations designed by

274 *Bus-stop (model)*
1966
G. Joseph (class of Herbert Oestreich, Commercial Arts College, Kassel)
(In the background: a model automobile for town use, 1965, U. Schneider)

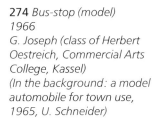

275 *Information panel for bus-stop (submitted to the competition held by the German Design Council, Darmstadt, the City of Ludwigshafen, and BASF AG, 1968)*
1967–68
Steel
Odo Klose, F. Niggemann, U. Reif
Wilhelm Quante, Wuppertal

the HfG lecturer Hans Gugelot, was consistently pursued by Dieter Rams – who is today still head of Braun's design department – and extended to include other product areas. Objects such as the T 1000 multi-band radio (1962), the Sixtant electric shaver (1962), the KM 2 kitchen appliance (1964), or the TFG 1 table lighter (1966) are now legendary and have long since become sought-after cult objects and collectors' items for a large fan club.

Yet this is precisely what the advocates of objective criteria for high-quality design wanted to avoid: good form was intended to be timeless and down-to-earth. For it was in the sixties that West Germany regained confidence in its design and its taste for the first time since the end of the war.

276 *Bus-stop (model) (submitted to the competition held by the German Design Council, Darmstadt, the City of Ludwigshafen, and BASF AG, 1968)*
1967–68
Steel, sheet metal, plastic, glass
Hubert Zimmermann, Dieter Oestreich

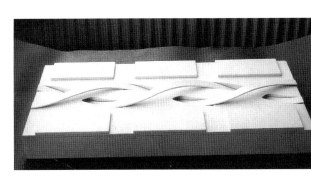

277 *Porsche 911 sportscar ("Gute Form" exhibition, London 1965)*
1964
Sheet steel, box frame
Designed by the manufacturers
Ferdinand Porsche KG, Stuttgart (now: Porsche AG)
Photo: Grünke

278 *"Psychodynamic street" (model) (1st prize at the "Tomorrow's Street" competition held by the Passavantwerke, Michelbacherhütte, in conjunction with the German Design Council, Darmstadt)*
1968
H. Goepfert, J. P. Hölzinger

279 Wegavision 3000L *television-set (white)*
c. 1964
Designed by the manufacturers
WEGA-Radio GmbH, Fellbach
(now: Sony-WEGA-Production GmbH, Selb)

280 Wegavision 3000L *television-set (black)*
c. 1964
Designed by the manufacturers
WEGA-Radio GmbH, Fellbach
(now: Sony-WEGA-Production GmbH, Selb)

281, 282 WEGA 142 *radio receiver (German Federal "Gute Form" Prize, 1969)*
1967–68
H. Völker
WEGA-Radio GmbH, Fellbach
(now: Sony-WEGA-Production GmbH, Selb)
Photos: Willi Moegle

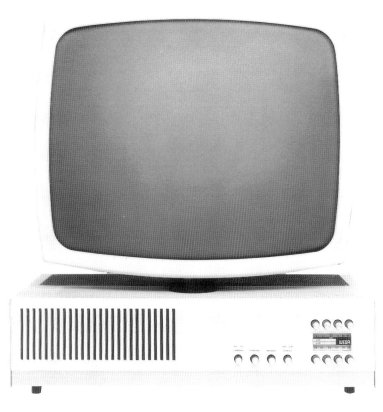

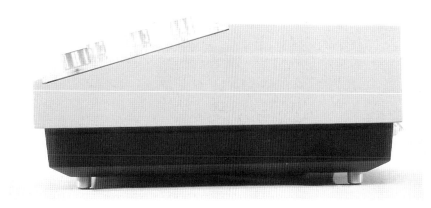

283 L55 hi-fi *loudspeakers*
1969
Designed by the manufac-
turers
AEG-Telefunken,
Braunschweig (now: AEG
Aktiengesellschaft, Frankfurt)

284 REVOX A77 *tape-*
recorder
1967
Wood, plastic, metal
Designed by the manufac-
turers
Willi Studer GmbH, Löffingen
(now: Studer Holding GmbH)

285 DUAL 1209 *automatic*
hi-fi record player
1968–69
Schima le Breux
DUAL Gebr. Steidinger, St.
Georgen (now: DUAL GmbH)

286 *Dynamic microphone
(German Federal "Gute Form"
Prize, 1969)
1969
Herbert Schnüll
Peiker acustic Heinrich Peiker
GmbH & Co., Bad Homburg*

287 HD414 de luxe *stereo
headphones (German Federal
"Gute Form" Prize, 1969)
1969
G. Rosenstand, G. Morgen-
stern
Sennheiser electronic KG,
Bissendorf*

288 _Home communications system (German Federal "Gute Form" Prize, 1969)_
_1969_
Burkhard Vogtherr
Photo: Willi Moegle

289 *Open-front table-top eccentric press ("Gute Form" exhibition, London 1965) 1961 Ulrich Burandt Helmut Hattler Maschinen- fabrik, Ulm*

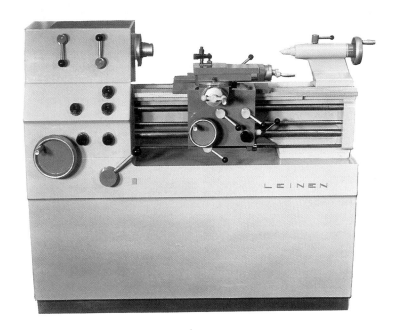

290 DLZ140 *lathe ("Gute Form" exhibition, London 1965)*
1961, 1963
Sheet steel
Erich Slany
Boley & Leinen, Esslingen (now: G. Boley GmbH & Co.)
Photo: Grünke

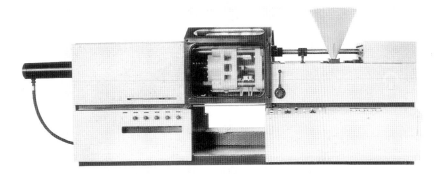

291 *Hydraulic injection-molding machine*
1965
Sheet steel, welded
Odo Klose and colleagues, Wolfgang Kramer
Salzgitter Maschinen und Anlagen AG, Salzgitter (now: Salzgitter AG)

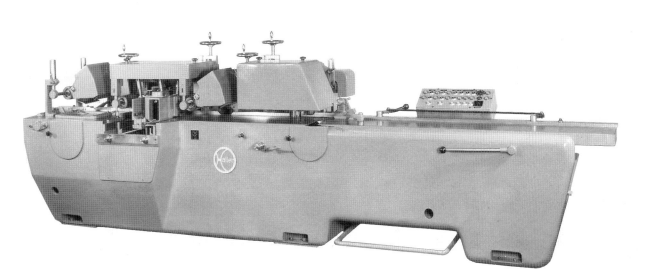

292 Heilbronn *six-spindle adjustable jointing- and molding-machine*
c. 1965
Designed by the manufacturers
Hermann Haller Maschinenbau, Nordheim
Photo: Haarfeld

293 B230G *articulated spindle drilling-machine*
c. 1968
Cast iron
Horst Hartmann
Burkhardt & Weber KG, Reutlingen (now: Burkhardt & Weber GmbH & Co. KG)

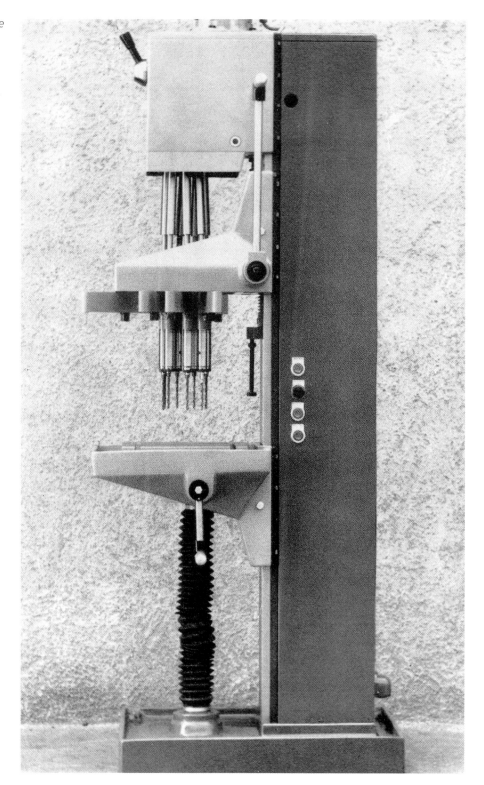

294 M670 *VDF standard lathe*
1964
Horst Hartmann
Gebr. Boehringer GmbH,
Göppingen (now: Boehringer
Werkzeugmaschinen GmbH)

295 Hanomag B16 *wheel loader*
1969–70
Steel
Designed by the manufacturers (W. Woyack)
Rheinstahl Hanomag AG, Hanover (now: Hanomag-Henschel GmbH)
Photo: R. Herbst

296 Hatra L700 *shovel dozer* ("Gute Form" exhibition, London 1965)
1963–64
Karl Ullman
Alfred Hagelstein Maschinenfabrik, Travemünde

297 Büssing *load-carrier*
c. 1965
form technik international (Louis L. Lepoix)
Büssing-Automobilwerke AG, Brunswick

298 14GT *mobile crane*
c. 1966
Friedrich Krupp Central Institute for Research and Development
Krupp-Ardelt, Wilhelmshaven (now: Krupp Industrietechnik GmbH, Duisburg)

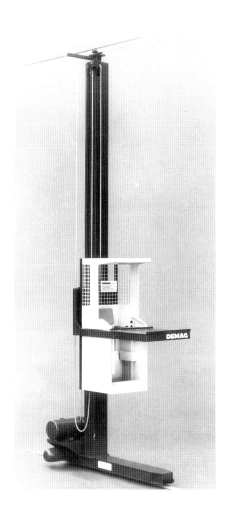

299 DEMAG DECOMBI *standard single-track shelf-stacker c. 1967*
Atelier Ernst Moeckl
DEMAG-Zug GmbH, Wetter
(now: Mannesmann Demag AG, Duisburg)

300 DEMAG DECOMBI *standard single-track shelf-stacker c. 1967*
Atelier Ernst Moeckl
DEMAG-Zug GmbH, Wetter
(now: Mannesmann Demag AG, Duisburg)

301 DG12 *diesel fork-lift truck 1966*
Horst Hartmann
SE-Fahrzeugwerke GmbH, Esslingen

302 STM M *motor-operator*
Before 1970
*Designed by the manufac-
turers*
*Gerhard Berger Fabrik elek-
trischer Messgeräte, Lahr
(now: Berger Lahr GmbH)*
Photo: Dieterle

303 AJ180L4R1 *three-phase
motor*
1968
*Designed by the manufac-
turers*
*AEG Allgemeine Elektricitäts-
Gesellschaft, Frankfurt (now:
AEG Aktiengesellschaft)* ▷

304 LA 3113, LA 3133 *three-
phase motor (size 90)*
1967
*Siemens-Design
Siemens AG, Munich* ▷▷

305 FHW 0156 *planet gear
motor ("Gute Form" exhibi-
tion, London 1965)*
1964–65
*Werner Glasenapp
Rheinstahl Hüttenwerk AG,
Werk Friedrich-Wilhelmshütte,
Mühlheim*

306 47D *gear motor*
1964
*Designed by the manufac-
turers*
Himmelwerk AG, Tübingen

307 2AD1, *portable water-
pumps*
c. 1962
*Siemens-Design
Siemens AG, Munich*

308 *Spiral bevel-gear motor*
1971
*Designed by the manufac-
turers*
*Michael Graessner KG Ge-
triebe- und Maschinenfabrik,
Steinenbronn*
Photo: Ceska

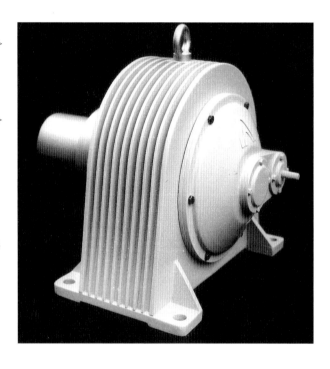

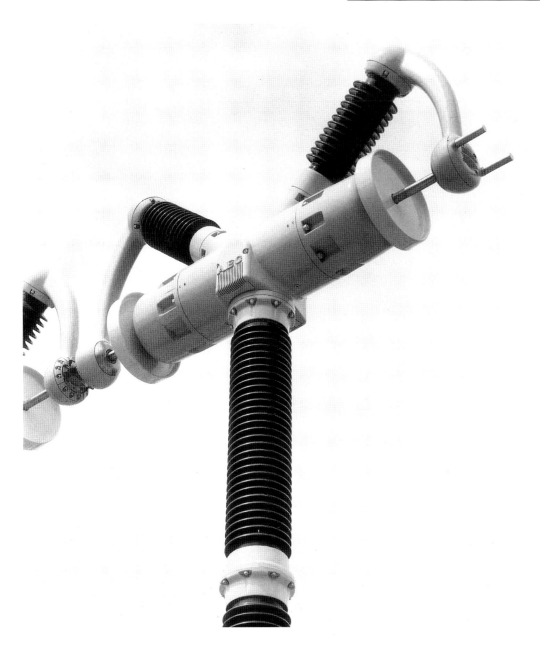

309 *High-power 220-kv free-jet breaker (demonstration apparatus for industrial-fair purposes)*
1966–67
Metal and plastic
Designed by the manufacturers
AEG-Telefunken, Frankfurt and Berlin (now: AEG Aktiengesellschaft, Frankfurt)

310 *F6 high-power circuit-breaker*
c. 1963
Metal and plastic
Siemens-Design
Siemens-Schuckert-Werke AG, Berlin and Erlangen (now: Siemens AG Leitungsbau, Erlangen)

311 *4/2 1/4" magnetic valves ("Gute Form" exhibition, London 1965) 1965 Erich Slany Robert Bosch GmbH, Stuttgart*

312 *Pneumatic roller-lever valves ("Gute Form" exhibition, London 1965) c. 1965 Erich Slany Robert Bosch GmbH, Stuttgart*

313 *4/2 1/4" magnetic valve ("Gute Form" exhibition, London 1965) 1965 Erich Slany Robert Bosch GmbH, Stuttgart*

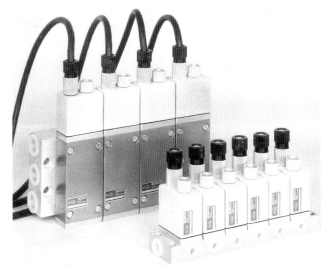

314 *Collection bases with magnetic valves ("Gute Form" exhibiton, London 1965) c. 1965 Erich Slany Robert Bosch GmbH, Stuttgart*

315 *Valves for automating machine tools ("Gute Form" exhibition, London 1965) c. 1965 Erich Slany Robert Bosch GmbH, Stuttgart*

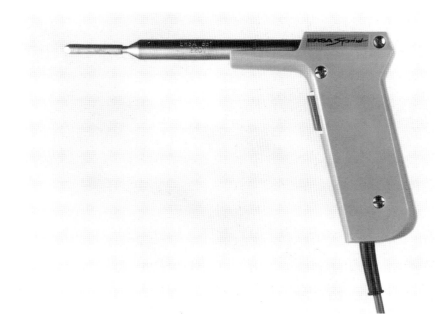

316 ERSA Sprint *solder-gun*
1968
Bernhard Schwann
ERSA Ernst Sachs KG, Wertheim (now: ERSA Ernst Sachs KG GmbH & Co.)

317 *Stage electric socket housing*
1967
Siemens-Design
GWR for Siemens AG, Munich

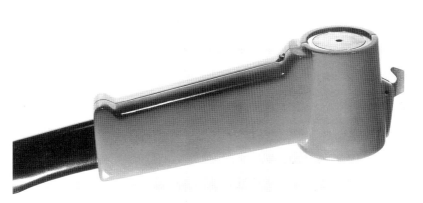

318 *Plasma-gun*
1963
Metal and plastic
Siemens-Design
Siemens AG, Munich

319 Saltus 5291 *ratchet spanner*
1963
Designed by the manufacturers
Saltus Werk Max Forst, Solingen (now: Saltus Werk Max Forst GmbH & Co.)

320 PKL6-60 W220/2 *fast-action auto-battery-charger*
1964–65
Metal casing
Erich Slany
Eisemann GmbH, Stuttgart;
Robert Bosch GmbH, Stuttgart

321 PKK 12/5 *battery-charger*
for home use
1969
Designed by the manufac-
turers
Eisemann GmbH, Stuttgart;
Robert Bosch GmbH, Stuttgart

322 G9E *miniature battery-charger ("Gute Form" exhibition, London 1965)*
1962
Plastic
Siemens-Design
Siemens & Halske AG, Munich
(now: Siemens AG, Munich)

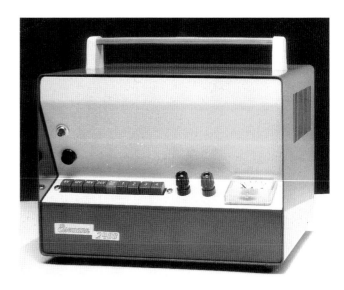

323 PKG 24/8 W220/1 *work-shop battery-charger*
("Gute Form" exhibition,
London 1965)
1961
Erich Slany
Eisemann GmbH, Stuttgart;
Robert Bosch GmbH, Stuttgart

◁◁ **324** 0.2 moving-coil instrument ("Gute Form" exhibition, London 1965)
1961
Designed by the manufacturers
AEG Allgemeine Elektricitäts-Gesellschaft, Frankfurt (now: AEG Aktiengesellschaft)

◁ **325** 0 471 101 *electronic dekatron*
1966
Designed by the manufacturers
J. Hengstler KG, Aldingen (now: Hengstler GmbH)

326 Multavi 10 *multipurpose measuring-instrument*
1965
Dieter Oestreich
Hartmann & Braun AG, Frankfurt

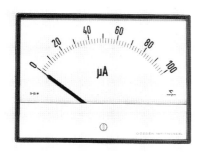

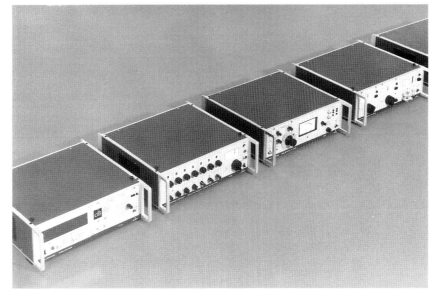

◁ **327** *Measuring-instrument ("Gute Form" exhibition, London 1965)*
c. 1963
Designed by the manufacturers
P. Gossen & Co. GmbH, Erlangen (now: Gossen GmbH)

328 *Measuring-instruments*
1967
Siemens-Design
Siemens AG, Munich

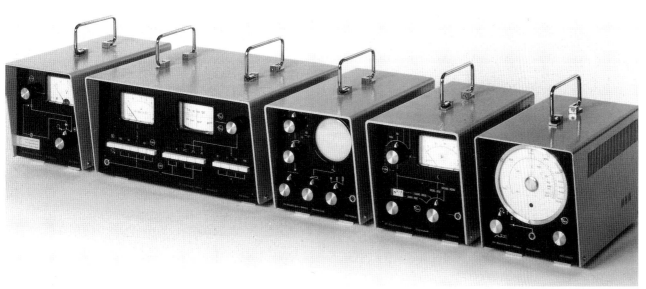

329 *Vibration meter*
Self-charging battery power-pack with panoramic monitor, cathode ray oscilloscope, portable balancing-machine, and high-speed flash stroboscope ("Gute Form" exhibition, London 1965)
1963–64
C. W. Voltz
Dr. Reutlinger und Söhne, Werkstätten für Schwingungstechnik, Darmstadt (now: Dr. Reutlinger + Söhne GmbH & Co. KG)
Photo: Friedrich Emich

330 AS *high-speed mixer for laboratory purposes ("Gute Form" exhibition, London 1965)*
1964
V4A steel
Klaus Fleischmann, Herbert Schultes
Turbo-Müller KG, Ottobrunn (now: Turbo Müller GmbH & Co. KG)

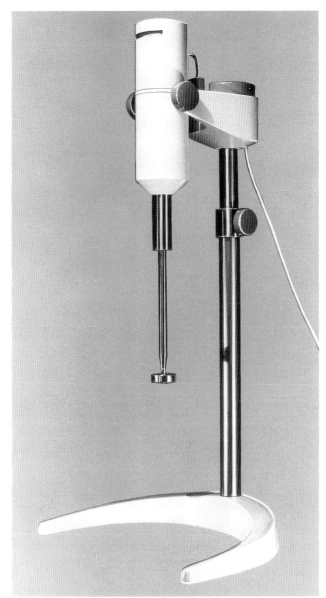

331 Skiascope *("Gute Form" exhibition, London 1965)*
1963
Metal
K. H. Wilms
Optische Werke Rodenstock, Munich
Photo: W. Anker

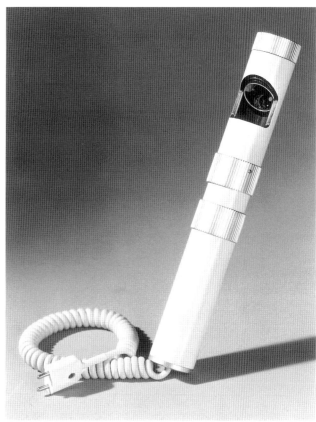

332 AXIOMAT NDC *research microscope*
1966
Kurt Michel
Carl Zeiss, Oberkochen
Photo: U. Furtwängler

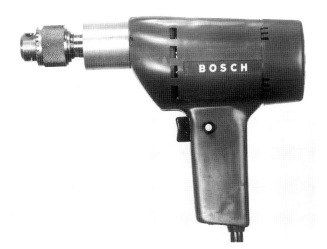

333 Combi E1 *drill ("Gute Form" exhibition, London 1965)*
1965
Erich Slany
Robert Bosch GmbH, Stuttgart

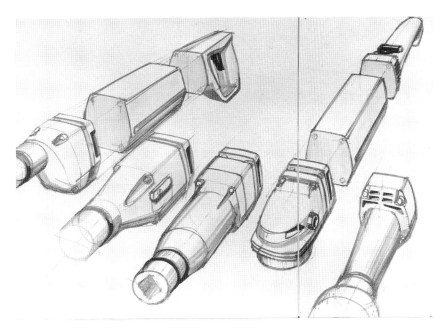

334 *Bosch drills: multicomponent modular system*
1959
Erich Slany
Robert Bosch GmbH, Stuttgart

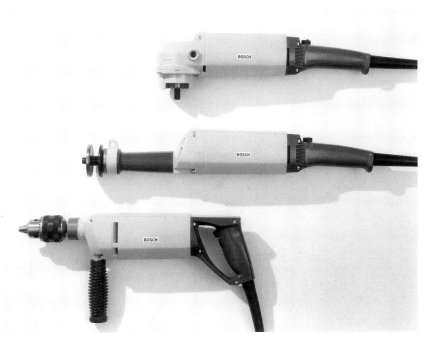

335 EW/UBJ *all-purpose drill ("Gute Form" exhibition, London 1965)*
1960
Erich Slany
Robert Bosch GmbH, Stuttgart

336 WS1 *switch-box ("Gute Form" exhibition, London 1965)*
1964–65
Designed by the manufacturers
Max Weishaupt GmbH, Schwendi

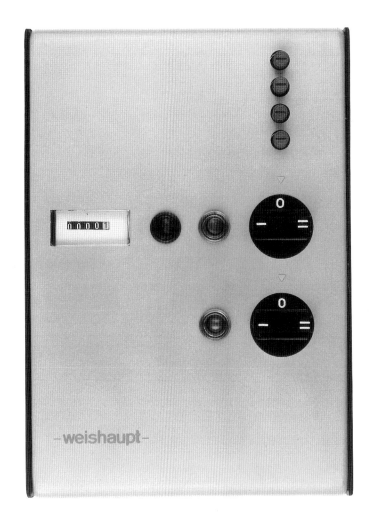

337 STF 3 *safety-switch for remote-controlled ignition ("Gute Form" exhibition, London 1965)*
1965
Metal
Bernhard Jablonski
Junkers & Co. GmbH, Wetzlar

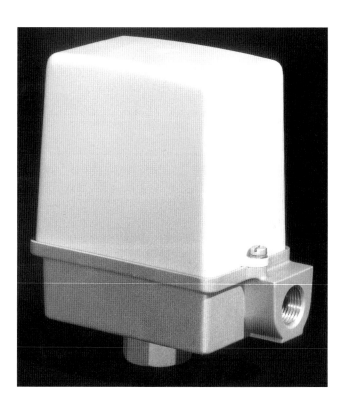

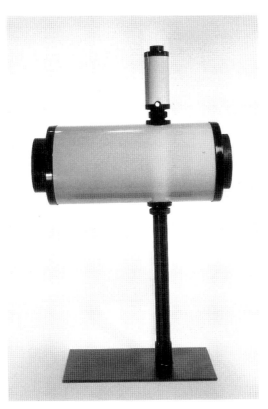

338, 339 B Series *heavy-duty boiler ("Gute Form" exhibition, London 1965)*
c. 1964
Steel
Günter Fuchs
Summa-Feuerungen GmbH, Schwarzenbach
Photos: Schwarzenbach

340 Lollar E87 *electric storage-heater*
1968
Cast iron, sheet steel casing
Rolf-Dieter Schiedrum
Buderus'sche Eisenwerke, Wetzlar (now: Buderus Heiztechnik GmbH)

341 Heinzelmann T20 *automatic heater ("Gute Form" exhibition, London 1965)*
1961
Sheet steel
Erich Slany
Witte Heiztechnik GmbH & Co., Iserlohn

342 H60 *towel-dryer*
1970
Sheet steel, plastic
Interform Wolfsburg
Stiebel-Eltron GmbH & Co.
KG, Holzminden

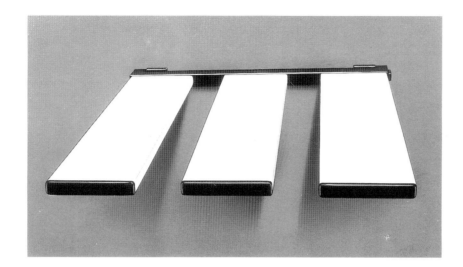

343 *Heat-storage plates*
1970
Duretan BKV and ceramic
fti design (Louis L. Lepoix)
Wigo Gottlob Widmann &
Söhne KG, Schwenningen

344 *Hotplate ("Gute Form"*
exhibition, London 1965)
1963–64
Metal and plastic
Interform Wolfsburg
ESGE GmbH, Neuffen (now:
ESGE electronic GmbH)

345 *Heat-storage plate*
1965
Metal and plastic
Designed by the manufac-
turers
Bauknecht Hausgeräte GmbH,
Stuttgart

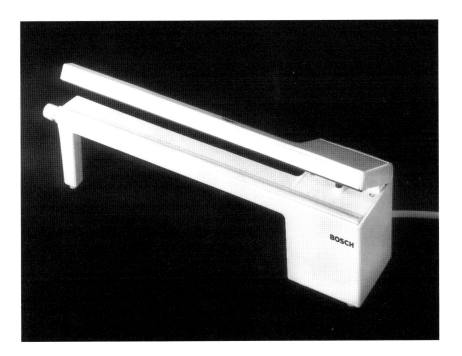

346 FG1 *foil seam welding*
machine (German Federal
"Gute Form" Prize, 1970)
1969
Rainer Patschull
Robert Bosch GmbH, Stuttgart

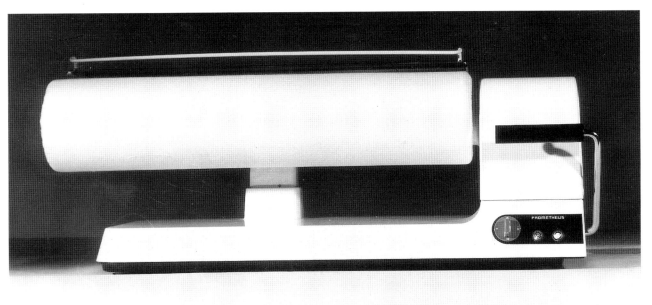

347 BM 40 *ironing-machine*
("Gute Form" exhibition,
London 1965)
1963
Die-cast aluminum casing
C. W. Voltz
Prometheus GmbH, Eschwege

348, 349 BL300 *UV lamp*
("Gute Form" exhibition,
London 1965)
1963
Sheet steel, injection-molded
aluminum, and aluminum
Dieter Oestreich
BBC Brown, Boveri & Cie. AG,
Mannheim (now: Brown Bo-
veri AG, Mannheim)

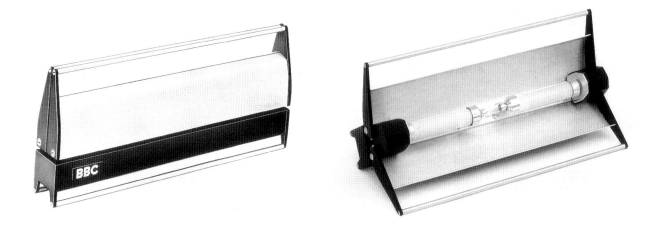

350 1125WG *waffle-iron*
("Gute Form" exhibition,
London 1965)
1960
Metal
Bernhard Jablonski
Grossag Elektrogeräte GmbH,
Schwäbisch Hall
Photo: Swiridoff

351 MX1000 *infrared grill*
("Gute Form" exhibition,
London 1965)
1963
Metal, glass, plastic
Rido Busse
Schmidt & Co. KG, Schwelm

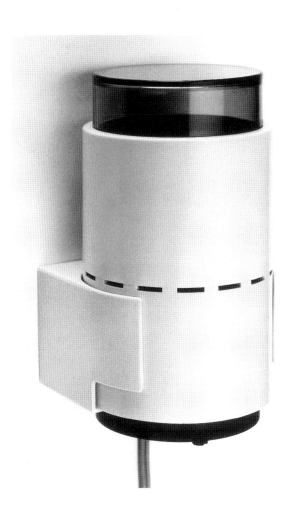

352 KM6 *wall-mounted or table-top coffee-grinder*
1966
Plastic casing
Rido Busse
EMIDE Metallindustrie Denkingen Gebr. Streicher, Denkingen

353 KM50 *electric coffee-grinder (German Federal "Gute Form" Prize, 1970)*
1969
Plastic casing
Designed by the manufacturers
Robert Krups, Solingen (now: Robert Krups Stiftung & Co. KG)

354 *Can-opener*
1965–66
Plastic casing
Designed by the manufacturers
AEG Allgemeine Elektricitäts-Gesellschaft, Frankfurt (now: AEG Aktiengesellschaft)

355 Multiwerk KM2 *kitchen-appliance system ("Gute Form" exhibition, London 1965)*
1964–65
Plastic casing
Braun Product Design (Dieter Rams, Richard Fischer)
Braun AG, Kronberg

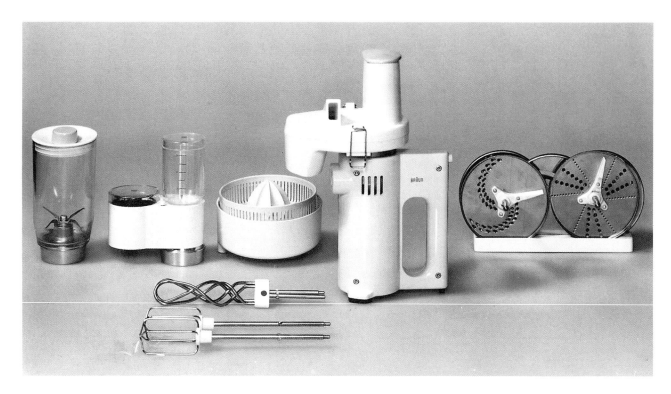

356 M140 *whisk (German Federal "Gute Form" Prize, 1970)*
1968
Braun Product Design (Reinhold Weiss)
Braun AG, Kronberg

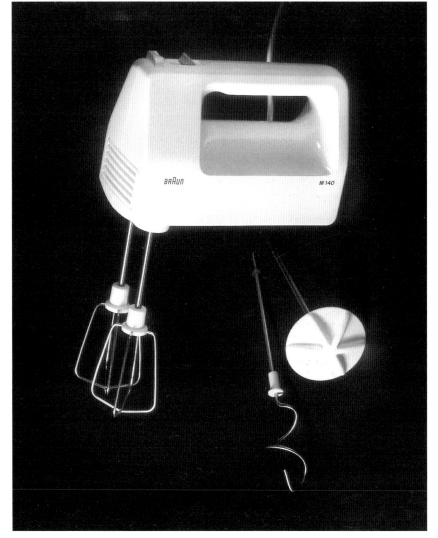

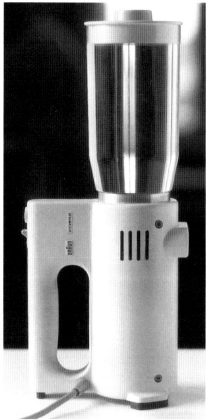

357 Multiwerk KM2 *kitchen-appliance system ("Gute Form" exhibition, London 1965)*
1964–65
Plastic casing
Braun Product Design (Dieter Rams, Richard Fischer)
Braun AG, Kronberg

358 *Mixer, basic unit with blender ("Gute Form" exhibition, London 1965)*
1960–61
Thermoplastic and duroplastic
Designed by the manufacturers
AEG Allgemeine Elektricitäts-Gesellschaft, Frankfurt (now: AEG Aktiengesellschaft Hausgeräte, Nuremberg)

359 *Mixer, basic unit with mincer*
1960–61
Designed by the manufacturers
AEG Allgemeine Elektricitäts-Gesellschaft, Frankfurt

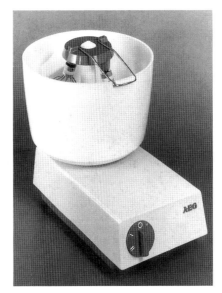

360 *Mixer, basic unit with whisk*
1960–61
Designed by the manufacturers
AEG Allgemeine Elektricitäts-Gesellschaft, Frankfurt

361 *Mixer*
1960–61
Designed by the manufacturers
AEG Allgemeine Elektricitäts-Gesellschaft, Frankfurt

362 *Mixer, basic unit with vegetable-grater*
1960–61
Designed by the manufacturers
AEG Allgemeine Elektricitäts-Gesellschaft, Frankfurt

363 T1000 *long-range radio receiver*
1962
Braun Product Design (Dieter Rams)
Braun AG, Kronberg

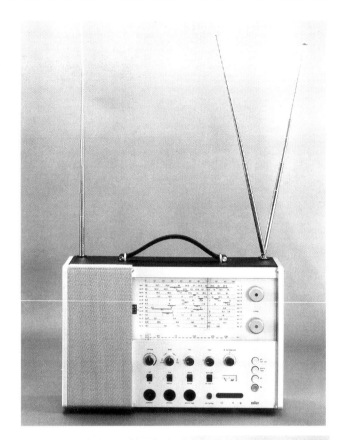

364 RT20 *radio receiver*
1961
Braun Product Design (Dieter Rams)
Braun AG, Kronberg

365 TG60 *tape recorder*
("Gute Form" exhibition, London 1965)
1962–63
Braun Product Design (Dieter Rams)
Braun AG, Kronberg

366 Audio 1/2 *equipment:*
Audio 1/2 combined radio and phonograph system, TG60 tape recorder, FS600 television-set, adjustable stand for audio and TV units ("Gute Form" exhibition, London 1965)
1962–63
Braun Product Design (Dieter Rams)
Braun AG, Kronberg

Dieter Rams

**Product Design
in the Sixties**

Although the sixties were marked by diversity and contradiction on the design scene, I can discern a clear line of development: the two poles are the almost euphoric feeling of a new dawn at the beginning of the decade, and the subdued pensiveness at its end. Of course, this view of things has been influenced by my own experience. At that time, I worked in West Germany – just as I do today – and I designed only Braun products and furniture for Vitsoe. Nevertheless, I think that others, too, will be able to relate to my impression of this decade.

In 1960, I started working on the Braun audio line. This product and design concept, and the way we worked – the very special atmosphere, the energy, the plans we had – all this seems characteristic of the early sixties to my mind.

The Braun Audio 1 receiver was an entirely modern product, newly developed from inside out, fully transistorized, with hifi quality, a breakthrough product that set standards. We had planned it as part of a complete system of audio modules, including a tape recorder, a television set, loudspeakers, and special stands. Our aim was that the user should be able to combine them and set them up as desired. They should also be suitable for installation in shelving systems by Vitsoe or Knoll International.

The design was consistently functional, very clean, well ordered, simple, and transparent. It was the embodiment of that practical, carefully planned humane design which had been postulated at the Bauhaus and the Hochschule für Gestaltung in Ulm (studies for a hifi module system had been developed by Hans

Gugelot and Herbert Lindinger in 1957/58 in Ulm).

"Modern" design – if I may use such a vague term (nobody would have questioned it at the time) – was displayed in store windows, attracted attention, was successful, won awards.

True, there were only a very few companies and designers that seriously and professionally endeavored to achieve a functional design embracing all facets of the product – basic concept, technical problems, even ways in which the user might wish to adapt it. But though few, there were more than ever before. And the small group of the avantgarde saw itself on an upswing. We saw our chance, we worked intensively and comparatively efficiently. Within the space of a few years, my staff and I created a whole range of products for Braun and Vitsoe: those were the days of the KM 2 kitchen appliances, the M 140 hand mixer, the sixtant electric shaver, the cylin-

367 Sixtant *shaving-blade
(close-up)*
*1962
Braun Product Design
Braun AG, Kronberg*

368 Sixtant *honeycomb
shaving-blade*
*1962
Braun Product Design
Braun AG, Kronberg*

369 Sixtant *electric shaver*
*1962
Braun Product Design
(Hans Gugelot, Gerd A.
Müller)
Braun AG, Kronberg*

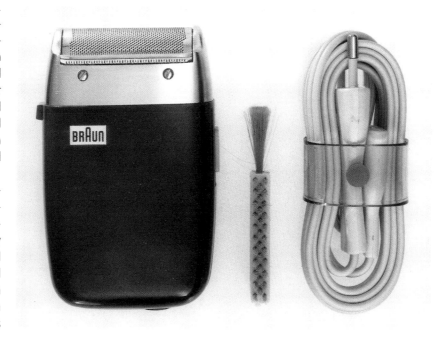

370 Sixtant *electric shaver,
with cable and cleaning-brush*
*("Gute Form" exhibition, London 1965)
1962
Braun Product Design (Hans
Gugelot, Gerd A. Müller)
Braun AG, Kronberg*

371 *Award-giving ceremony for the 1965 Berlin Art Prize (prize for "applied art," also given for design)*
1965
From left to right: Dieter Rams, Robert Oberheim, Jan Bontjes van Beek, Richard Fischer, and Reinhold Weiss

372 HL1 *table-top fan (German Federal "Gute Form" Prize, 1970)*
1961
Braun Product Design (Reinhold Weiss)
Braun AG, Kronberg

373 Cylindric TFG2 *table-top cigarette-lighter (German Federal "Gute Form" Prize, 1970)*
1968
Braun Product Design (Dieter Rams)
Braun AG, Kronberg

374 Multipress MP50 *centrifugal juicer*
1970
Braun Product Design (Dieter Rams, Jürgen Greubel)
Braun AG, Kronberg

dric table lighter, all for Braun, and the Vitsoe 606 shelving system and the 620 and 601/602 chair ranges. Many of these products – in some cases with improved technology and design – are still being manufactured today, more than a quarter of a century later.

The example we set stimulated and encouraged many a company; it may well have worried others. Interest in design grew, and the standards for assessing the quality of design changed radically. Naturally, most companies continued the way they had before. Careless, sloppy, naive, or deliberately showy was still the norm. However, it could no longer honestly be passed off as "good design."

During the first decade following the Second World War the German consumer goods industry had manufactured primarily for the domestic market to meet the enormous demand for restocking households. New markets opened up in the sixties, and with export opportunities came a new challenge and a testing-time for designers, too. We saw that modern design – the way Braun understood it – met with great acceptance on an international level, and this encouraged us.

And how did it end, this decade that had started off so confidently towards new horizons? It did not end in a nadir for design – but it did give way to a period of restlessness, questioning of current positions, criticism, and protest. For me, the student troubles in many Western nations are symbolic of this era. In Germany they were particularly vociferous and violent. And although on the face of it they caused very little change, they did in fact affect the intellectual and cultural climate, which strongly influenced the thinking and the work of designers, too. We were confronted with attacks on design, calling it "product aesthetics" which created no utility value and was nothing more than sales promotion. We had to listen to criticism of excessive production which wasted our resources and destroyed

our environment. The HfG was closed down in 1968. This was symptomatic of these years of sociocritical protest and the reactions to it.

In reality, the criticism confirmed our position. Our intention was and still is to make useful, longlasting products. We did not change our understanding of the duty of design; but we increasingly realized how demanding a task it was.

At the end of the seventies, more and more companies – convinced more of the marketing aspect than of the idea of functional design – were devoting attention to design. We, though, without the euphoria of earlier years, continued in our daily routine, seeking to improve the practical qualities of products through well-conceived, well-executed design. We are still doing this today.

Industrial design is after all still a very young profession. We are only at the beginning. In no product, in no detail, have we yet achieved the striking practicality of the "tools" natural evolution has designed for us: wing, hand, eye, skin, blossom, brain...

Technological progress is constantly picking up speed. The reality in which people live, their behavior, their attitudes and needs, are constantly changing. Thus, the context within which functional design is generated is constantly changing. New problems and new challenges await us. But what we have on our side is greater experience and more flexible technology.

We are confident that in the coming years we will be able to design products that serve their purpose better than those we have today. But we are also aware that we will never find the ultimate solutions.

375 Vitsoe collection: 601
armchair
1960
Dieter Rams
Vitsoe + Zapf, Kronberg
(now: Wiese Vitsoe GmbH +
Co., Frankfurt)

376 Vitsoe collection: 620
armchair
1962
Dieter Rams
Vitsoe + Zapf, Kronberg
(now: Wiese Vitsoe GmbH +
Co., Frankfurt)

377 Vitsoe collection: 606
shelf system, metal shelf va-
riant (German Federal "Gute
Form" Prize, 1973)
1960
Dieter Rams
Vitsoe + Zapf, Kronberg
(now: Wiese Vitsoe GmbH +
Co., Frankfurt)

378 Vitsoe collection: 606
shelf system (German Federal
"Gute Form" Prize, 1973)
1960
Dieter Rams
Vitsoe + Zapf, Kronberg
(now: Wiese Vitsoe GmbH +
Co., Frankfurt)

379 F1000 *flash installation for professional studios*
1966
Braun Product Design (Dieter Rams)
Braun AG, Kronberg

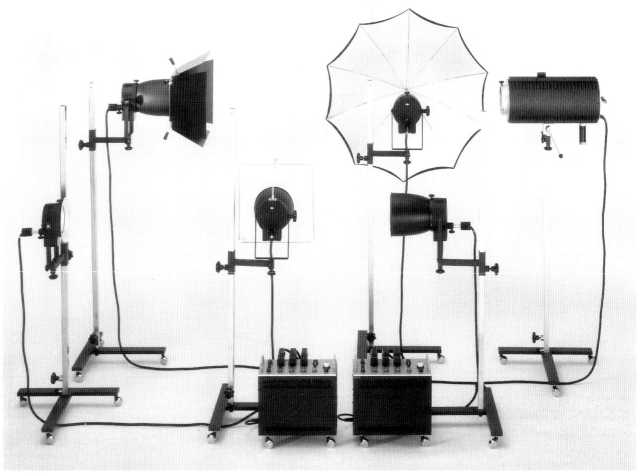

380 SB1 *film-viewer*
1968
Braun Product Design (Robert Oberheim)
Braun AG, Kronberg

381 Nizo S80 *amateur movie-camera*
1967–68
Braun Product Design (Robert Oberheim)
Niezoldi & Krämer GmbH, Munich

382 Combiscope D5 *viewer*
1962
Braun Product Design (Dieter Rams)
Braun AG, Kronberg

383 Rollei 35 *miniature camera*
1966
Designed by the manufacturers and Ernst Moeckl
Rollei-Werke Franke & Heidecke, Brunswick (now: Rollei Fototechnic GmbH & Co. KG)

384 Rolleiflex SL66 *camera*
1966
Designed by the manufac-
turers and Ernst Moeckl
Rollei-Werke Franke &
Heidecke, Brunswick (now:
Rollei Fototechnic GmbH &
Co. KG)

385 Kardan bi system
9 x 12 camera
1967
Light metal
Nikolaus Karpf
Linhof Nikolaus Karpf KG,
Präzisions-Kamera-Werke,
Munich (now: Linhof Präzi-
sions-Kamera-Werke GmbH)

386 Edixa 16 *camera ("Gute*
Form" exhibition, London
1965)
1962–63
Injection-molded aluminum,
brass, and glass
Designed by the manufac-
turers
Kamerawerk Gebr. Wirgin,
Wiesbaden

387 Trinovid *wide-range binoculars ("Gute Form" exhibition, London 1965)*
1962
Metal, glass, and plastic
Designed by the manufacturers
Ernst Leitz GmbH, Wetzlar

388 *Professional tubular tripod, with III patent socket head ("Gute Form" exhibition, London 1965)*
1961
Light metal
Designed by the manufacturers
Linhof Kamera Werke Nikolaus Karpf KG, Munich (now: Linhof Präzisions-Kamera-Werke GmbH)

389 AL41 *floodlight projector*
("Gute Form" exhibition,
London 1965)
1958
Anodized aluminum
Siemens-Design (Norbert
Schlagheck)
Siemens-Schuckertwerke AG,
Erlangen (now: Siemens AG,
Munich)

390 *Column floor lighting*
(German Federal "Gute Form"
Prize, 1972)
Before 1972
Zapfmöbel InDesign
Zapfmöbel InDesign Otto
Zapf, Eschborn

391 *Conductor rail system with spotlight*
1967
Designed by the manufacturers
Staff & Schwarz GmbH Leuchtenwerk, Lemgo (now: Staff GmbH & Co. KG)
Photo: Peter A. Schindler

392, 393 Staff Lite-Trac-System *with different spotlights*
Before 1968
Designed by the manufacturers
Staff & Schwarz GmbH Leuchtenwerk, Lemgo (now: Staff GmbH & Co. KG)

394–400 ERCO light-system *with different spotlights*
1967–68
Dieter Witte
ERCO-Leuchten Reinighaus & Co., Lüdenscheid (now: ERCO Leuchten GmbH)

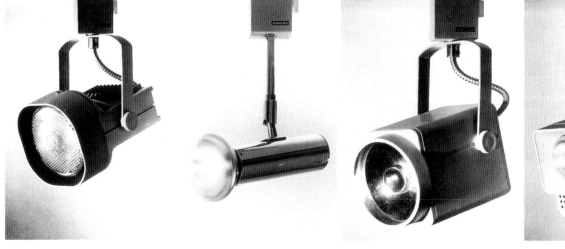

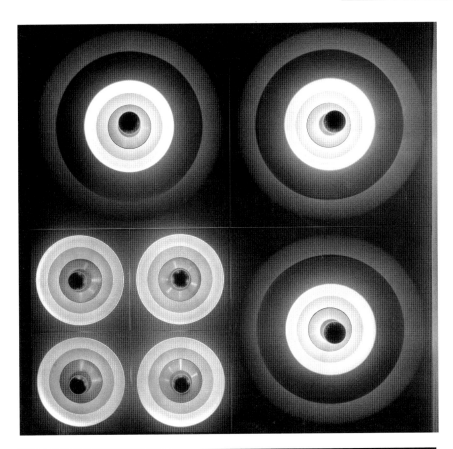

401 *04497 and 04498 wall light-sockets (German Federal "Gute Form" Prize, 1972)*
1971
Klaus Hempel
Gebr. Kaiser & Co., Neheim-Hüsten

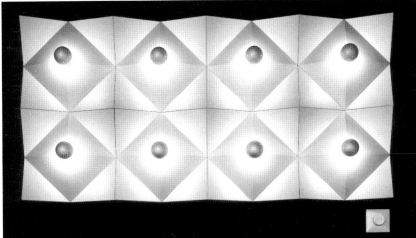

402 *1571 wall- and ceiling-lamps, units (German Federal "Gute Form" Prize, 1972)*
1971
Rolf Krüger
Heinz Neuhaus, Neheim-Hüsten

403 *Office swivel-chair (German Federal "Gute Form" Prize, 1969) c. 1961 Polyester molded seat Georg Leowald Wilkhahn Sitzmöbel, Eimbeckhausen (now: Wilkhahn, Bad Münder)*

404 *Stackable chair (German Federal "Gute Form" Prize, 1969) 1968 Plastic molded seat, steel tube frame Gerd Lange Drabert Söhne GmbH & Co., Minden*

405 mini 01 *children's chair and* mini 05 *table 1967 Special plastic, vacuum chrome-plated Luigi Colani Holzindustrie Kusch & Co., Hallenberg (now: Kusch & Co. Sitzmöbelwerke KG)*

406 16 *unit furniture:* 16/37 *stool,* 16/35-55-65 *armchair,* 41/11-41/12 *intervening sections*
1964
Flat oval anodized aluminum tubing, molded latex sections with springs, walnut, teak, palisander wood
Ernst Moeckl
Lübke & Rolf, Rheda (now: Lübke Möbelwerke GmbH & Co. KG)
Photo: Willi Moegle

407–410 15 *unit furniture:* 15/55 *armchair,* 15/37 *stool,* 15/65 *armchair,* 15/35 *armchair*
1964
Ernst Moeckl
Lübke & Rolf, Rheda (now: Lübke Möbelwerke GmbH & Co. KG)
Photos: Willi Moegle

411 1/14 *armchair and* 31/71 *table*
1963
Ernst Moeckl
Lübke & Rolf, Rheda (now: Lübke Möbelwerke GmbH & Co. KG)
Photo: Willi Moegle

412, 413 *Accordion cupboard-system (German Federal "Gute Form" Prize, 1973)
1966
Plastic and wood
gugelot design gmbh (Hans
Gugelot)
Wilhelm Bofinger Möbelwerk-
stätten, Ilsfeld*

414 *Accordion cupboard-
system (German Federal
"Gute Form" Prize, 1973)
1966
Plastic and wood
gugelot design gmbh (Hans
Gugelot)
Wilhelm Bofinger Möbelwerk-
stätten, Ilsfeld*

415 INwand *cupboard-system*
1961–62
Plastic-coated chipboard
Herbert Hirche
Christian Holzäpfel KG,
Ebhausen (now: Chr. Holzäp-
fel GmbH Möbelfabrik, Horb)

416 INwand *cupboard-system*
1961–62
Plastic-coated chipboard
Herbert Hirche
Christian Holzäpfel KG,
Ebhausen (now: Chr. Holzäp-
fel GmbH Möbelfabrik, Horb)

417 WUPPI *toy*
1973
Plastic, filled with water or
sand
Luigi Colani
Top System Burkhard Lübke,
Gütersloh (now: Kinderlübke)

418 Babbelplast *large and*
small inflatable toy-shapes
(German Federal "Gute Form"
Prize, 1971)
1970–71
Klaus Göhling
Klaus Göhling Babbelplast,
Düsseldorf

419 Siebensachen *cardboard*
building-blocks (German Fed-
eral "Gute Form" Prize, 1971)
1967
Peter Raacke
Waterproof corrugated card-
board
Papp Faltmöbel Ellen Raacke,
Wolfgang

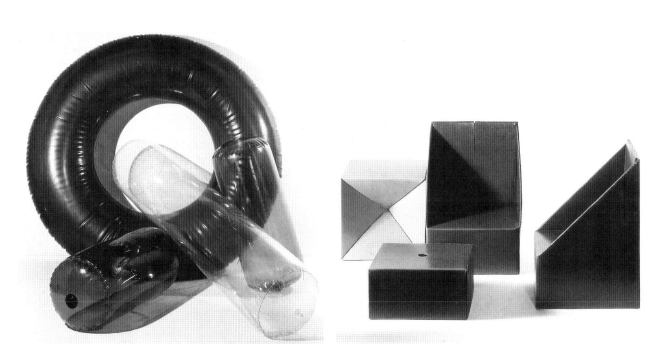

Bernd Busch   The Seventies

In times when all aspects of life are caught up in the vortex of the wind of change, the horizon on which the human use of things leaves its outline may also be transformed. The scenery of everyday life, cluttered with the paraphernalia of everyday culture, suddenly appears to have become a jungle. New demands and requirements disrupt familiar patterns, and the hectic spectacle of fashionable innovation starts to eat into the structure of things. Admittedly, shake-ups in the furnishing of everyday life, erosions of the material appearance of objects, the revolution in habits of living and familiar stylistic patterns, all this turbulence of the times initially poses questions and arouses curiosity.

In the wake of 1968, the hopeful slogans of a general change in the way we live gradually seeped into everyday life. At times they took the form of the cautious testing of new styles, while on other occasions they donned the treacherous cloak of commercial promises; in political debates sights were set high and hopes placed in change. The seventies are characterized not only by this fondness for experimentation but also by the fact that technological innovations and changing modes of production started to revolutionize working conditions and the whole world of objects. It was, in other words, a phase of radical change and experimentation that soon gave way to a generally more sober attitude — the burning questions as to the perspectives for human development in a highly technological society

seemed to be falling on deaf ears: it was business as usual again.

All of this affected and involved design insofar as designers saw themselves as the coiners of appropriate images for the reality of the object world. Design in the seventies was an expression of the overall awakening, of the search for a new, friendly quality of form; and it turned out to be an enormous productive force, whose increased commercial and social prestige had a strong impact on the world of objects. Yet design proved only rarely able to respond promptly to cultural and social changes by generating fundamentally new conceptions. And in those instances where thought had been given to potential problems and plans made, much remained at the level of unfulfilled ideas. Given the economic constraints of the day, designers were always forced to make compromises in practice, and the demands of production technology and marketing strategies came to influence development work to an even greater extent.

For this reason, the product catalog of the seventies displays no single trend: it is shaped in equal part by experimentation and monotony. What first strikes the eye is that the seemingly most tangible quality of objects tends to be drowned in the stormy tide of technological innovations. In the course of a mere five years, the most complex and bulky data-processing equipment has shrunk to negligible proportions, to small but highly efficient machines.

420 *Monorail system for commuter traffic (model)*
1973
Siemens-Design
Siemens AG, Berlin and Munich

421 4010 *long-range business-class seater*
Since 1983 (1986)
Horst Sommerlatte, Marlies Sommerlatte
Keiper Recaro GmbH & Co., Kirchheim

422 *Maglev trial vehicle*
1971–72
Neumeister Design
MBB Messerschmidt-Bölkow-Blohm GmbH, Ottobrunn (now: MBB-Verkehrstechnik, Schienenfahrzeuge und Zugsysteme, Donauwörth)

423 VW Golf
1970–74 (launched 1974)
Giorgio Giugiaro
Volkswagen AG, Wolfsburg

424 BMW 633 CSi A
1976
Designed by the manufac-
turers
BMW AG Bayerische
Motorenwerke Aktien-
gesellschaft, Munich

425 Mercedes-Benz
Unimog 1300
1974
Designed by the manufac-
turers
Daimler-Benz AG, Stuttgart

426 ALI *guidance and infor-*
mation systems for road-users
(in-car unit)
1983
Blaupunkt-Werke GmbH,
Hildesheim

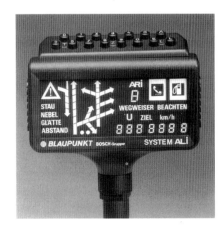

427 NSU Ro80
1967, reworked 1969
Designed by the
manufacturers (Klaus Luthe)
NSU GmbH, Neckarsulm
(now: subsidiary of Audi AG,
Ingolstadt)
Photo: Autopress

The technical innards no longer determine the shape of the exterior, namely that form which previously reflected the immaterial energies and invisible work processes for the operator. The relation between form and function has been gradually stripped of its material basis and becomes unstable. However, reduced to microscopic size, the functional elements suddenly allow for a relatively free design; they provide room for the deliberate planning of a "user interface." The example of VDU workstations, which began to invade the office world in the seventies, shows that the work-sphere, stripped of all bulky apparatus, has been given a new and rational organization, more rational modes of use. Design becomes the programmatic answer to the *horror vacui* left by the general disintegration of work traditions and work ethic. Ensembles that purport to be well suited to our needs replace the stabilizing and unifying force of a "morality of work" restored post-1949 and replace the conditions which had imposed these attitudes through power. The humanization of the world of work, one of the major tasks that design took on in the seventies, was at the same time the subtle integration of the psycho-physical characteristics of human beings into the world of production. This is true both at the micro-level of, for example, ergonomic workplaces and seating, and at the macro-level of the rapidly advancing process of interlinking individual tasks to form complex systems. And these radical technological changes also triggered off surges in rationalization that swept the newly designed workplaces clean of the people who were supposed to benefit from them. This, too, is the ambivalence of design in the seventies.

From the outset, however, the processes of change also extended to the details. In the minds of the designers and later in the hands of the users, the seemingly most simple things suddenly turned into the most complex structures. A chair, for ex-

ample, was no longer merely a cleverly designed object, the aesthetic appearance of which was intended to be linked to a function of the human body. Rather, the ergonomic chairs that forced their way onto the market were supposed to adapt to fit the body by virtue of their refined technological functions and mechanisms; they thus transpired to be sitting-machines, whose interior workings were concealed rather than visualized; by the design of the exterior. This understanding of the act of sitting or of seating comfort in terms of ergonomics was of course but one element of a more comprehensive setting, tested with respect to the various processes which went to make it up; philanthropic calculation came to set the standards that structured the professional workplace, offices and factories, housework, and even leisure time. Thus, new spheres of application for design constantly arose in which it could pursue its mission of taking on social responsibility and at the same time claim to remove both dangers and dysfunctionalities.

However, new forms of dysfunctionality emerged. In the seventies, for example, a type of kitchen began to take shape which was claimed for the first time to take women's work seriously in a major way and to liberate them by means of ever more ingenious aids from the burdens of manual work. Thus, with the best of intentions, housework was, as it were, industrialized. This rational planning of work in the home is the commercial answer to the desire for emancipation; instead of rethinking the relationship between the sexes, it is simply made more tolerable, and ways are sought to release time bound up in labor in the hope that such time, once released, can and will be used communicatively. In addition, the whole household starts to fill up with appliances, the scientifically investigated and justified handiness of which generates a plethora of operating controls, so that the housewife still has plenty to do. The most prominent feature of this industrialization of the household would seem to be not true labor-saving, but rather the transformation of physical work into tasks involving the operating of machines. And the "time thus gained" by this device is immediately occupied by other products clamoring for attention, first and foremost the messages of the media.

In the seventies, what was technologically feasible in product development not only set the standards of the day, it was also the decisive argument used by marketing, and a central element of everyday life. The fact that an ever-increasing number of companies had their products developed either in line with designers' recommendations or directly by their own design departments often let to a curious "standardization" in the appearance of things. Commodities became ever more alike on account of the technological "hardware" readily available, the widespread dominance of the ergonomic basis for product development, and the belief that a "hi-tech" look would convince anyone. This trend itself spawned a call for product differentiation, i.e. for design.

Nevertheless, the seventies did produce some characteristic and successful design solutions, be it with regard to reshaping the workplace or creating the wherewithal for new forms of life and communication. For the seventies were also an age in which design turned its attention to new, more complex tasks – seeking to develop new workplaces more suited to human beings, asserting its social responsibility, assuring itself of the mission given it by society, and at times also putting forward blueprints for new forms of social intercourse.

This is true, for example, of the seating and living scenarios that experimented with a more flexible ambience for a culture of the home seen as a sphere of experience. Much use was made of foam materials and plastics, which are very versatile, in the new world of forms that now took shape. Objects assumed bold colors; seating, entire living-room and bathroom interiors began to use shapes and colors that appealed to the senses. It is perhaps characteristic of the seventies that this new look of things evolved at the same time as the enormous advances in technology began to modify the fundamentals and the working conditions of design. One response to these changes was the increasing number of technological design utopias dreamed up in the seventies, drafts for a world in which what had once been science fiction would become reality. However, it is worthy of note that there were, not least in West Germany, designers and design groups who came out with provocative and unconventional proposals that cast doubt on the validity of the "morality of good form" in a brave new world. The "personal experience montages," unusual schemes for subway station design put forward by the Dreistädter Group from Cologne, broke with the prevailing understanding of functionality and good design just as "recycling design" tried to cast new light on the waste products of the throw-away society. Important impulse came from the creations of the Des-in group; yet these new approaches were soon overtaken by the alternative mass do-it-yourself movement.

Design shaped utopia and was the vision of new possibilities, the experimental field of new attitudes; a dimension of design could be conceived that was no longer shackled by commercial considerations. All this was to take on a more resolute shape in the eighties – in the seventies, such considerations were just a marginal phenomenon, however spectacular at times. But what is important is that they began to be formulated.

428 VSR 16000 *traffic computer*
1966
Siemens Design
Siemens AG, Berlin and Munich

429 *Central signal-tower, Munich station*
1974
Siemens Design
Siemens AG, Berlin and Munich

430 *Automatic train information service*
1964–65
Cast aluminum, sheet steel, electronic control system
Siemens Design
Siemens & Halske AG, Munich (now: Siemens AG)

431 *Carriers for electronic micromodules*
c. 1964
Siemens Design
Siemens Elektrogeräte GmbH, Munich

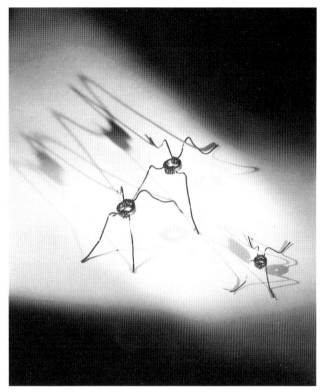

432 *Logic FZ 100 chips*
1970
Siemens Design
Siemens AG, Berlin and Munich

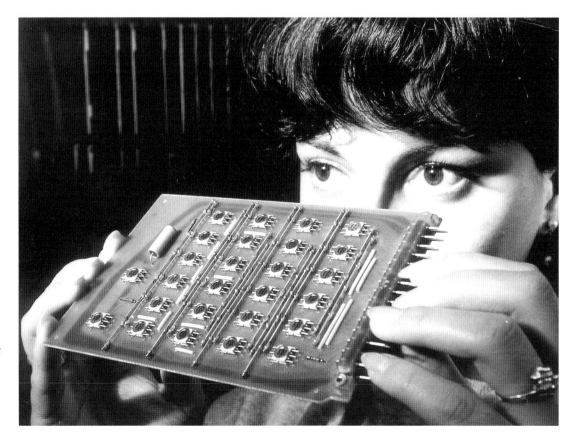

433 300 System *CPU integrated circuits with monolithic systems technology*
1965–66
Siemens Design
Siemens AG, Berlin and Munich

434 AVKOF outdoor current
and voltage transformer
c. 1974
Siemens Design
Siemens AG, Berlin and
Munich

435 Explosion-protected
switchboard plant (demon-
stration unit for fair-display
purposes)
1966–67
Designed by the manufac-
turers
AEG Aktiengesellschaft,
Frankfurt

436 *Control-panel for auto-mation of building-functions*
c. 1970
Designed by the manufac-turers
AEG Aktiengesellschaft, Frankfurt

437 8500 *data-terminal*
1968
Siemens-Design
Siemens AG, Berlin and Munich

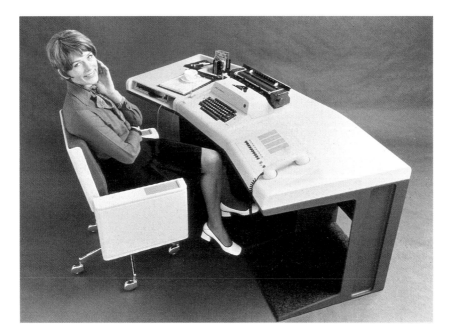

438 IBS 5000 *integrated workplace*
c. 1970
Olympia-Werke AG, Wilhelmshaven (now: AEG-Olympia Office GmbH); Mauser-Werke GmbH, Brühl

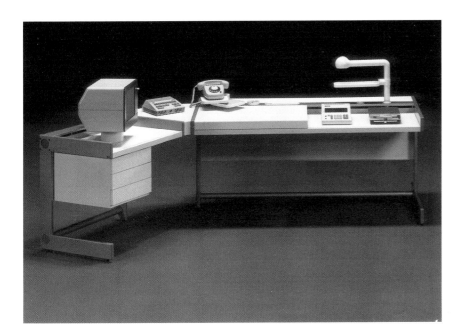

439 M.E.P. *workplace using Modular Elements Program*
1973
VOKO development team (Karl Dittert)
VOKO Büromöbelwerke, Giessen (now: VOKO Franz Vogt & Co., Pohlheim)
Photo: Walter von Deschwanden

440 DE 4800 *on-line counter terminal*
1970
Designed by the manufacturers
Olympia Werke AG, Wilhelmshaven (now: AEG-Olympia Office GmbH)

441 *Computer operator console*
1971
Siemens Design
Siemens AG, Berlin and Munich
Photo: Fössel

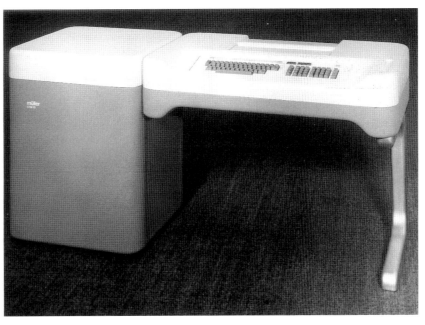

442 CTM 70 *middle-frame computer-system*
1972
Esslinger Design (Hartmut Esslinger)
CTM Computertechnik Müller GmbH, Constance

443 9007 *video workstation*
1982
Designed by the manufacturers and Schlagheck Schultes Design
Kienzle Apparate GmbH, Villingen (now: Mannesmann Kienzle GmbH)

444 DAP4 *visual display unit*
1980
design team moeckl (Ernst Moeckl, Jörg Stumpf)
Nixdorf Computer AG, Paderborn

445 6.611 *video computer with Siemens Systems Furniture desk top for VDU workstations*
c. 1982
Siemens Design
Siemens AG, Berlin and Munich

446 T4200/40 *text terminal text station with telex link*
1981
Siemens-Design
Siemens AG, Berlin and Munich

447 Durodet® standard base
1973
Designed by the manufac-
turers
Flachglas AG DELOG-DEFAG,
Fürth (now: Mitras Kunststof-
fe GmbH)
Photo: Keresztes

448 8809 LAMPERTZ-Data-
plan-LK *slide-top tab-system*
1965
Sheet steel
Ernst Moeckl
Otto Lampertz, Berlin (now:
Otto Lampertz GmbH & Co.
KG, Betzdorf)

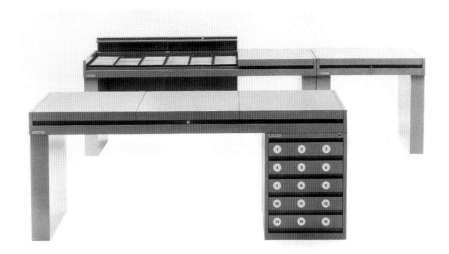

449 Kiel *office-furniture line*
1969
Klose & Partner
Studio für Industrial Design
(Odo Klose)
Arbeitsgemeinschaft Büro-
neuform e. V., Dusseldorf

450 VOKO A.C.M. M *work-*
place
1982
Karl Dittert
VOKO Franz Vogt & Co., Pohl-
heim

451 *Workplace unit (proto-type)*
1975
bader-design-concept (Wolf-gang Bader), Peter Engelhard

452 1200 *desk*
Before 1983
design team moeckl
Nixdorf Computer AG, Pader-
born

453 King alpha *office system*
1982
frogdesign
König & Neurath KG, Karben
Photo: Dietmar Henneka

454 *Manager's desk*
c. 1970
Polyurethane duroplastic
Igl-Design (Ernst Igl)
Wilhelm Werndl, Rosenheim
(now: Wilhelm Werndl Büro-
einrichtungen GmbH & Co. KG)
Photo: Roman Fink

455 dater *time-scheduler*
1971
Vacuum-preformed poly-
styrene
gugelot design gmbh
gugelot product gmbh
Photo: Wolfgang Siol

456 V *molded shelf*
1973
Günther Stark
Morphy Verlag Helga Kalvers-
berg, Wolfsburg

457 pac pic *organizational*
shelf
1971
Vacuum-preformed poly-
styrene
gugelot design gmbh
gugelot product gmbh
Photo: Wolfgang Siol

458 *Visual display telephone*
c. 1969
Siemens-Design
Siemens AG, Berlin and
Munich

459 Walther AE 33 *special-*
purpose computer for data
collection and forms
1983
Design Praxis Diener
Walther Electronic Vertriebs-
gesellschaft mbH, Gerstetten
(now: Walther Electronic-
Systeme GmbH)

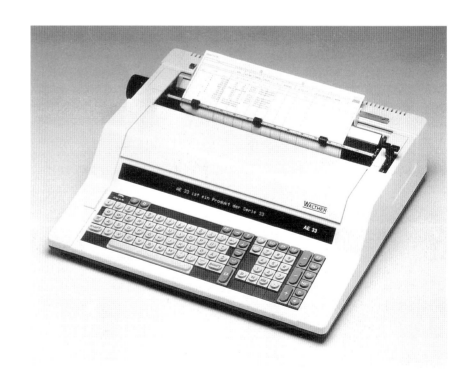

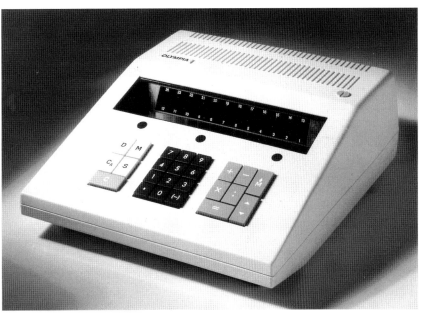

460 ET 66 *pocket calculator (based on the 1977* ET 22 *design)*
1987
Braun Product Design (Dieter Rams, Dietrich Lubs)
Braun AG, Kronberg

461 ICR 412 *electronic calculator*
1969
Designed by the manufacturers
Olympia-Werke AG, Wilhelmshaven (now: AEG-Olympia Office GmbH)

462 CD 200 *electronic calculator (display)*
1971
Plastic
Designed by the manufacturers
Olympia-Werke AG, Wilhelmshaven (now: AEG-Olympia Office GmbH)

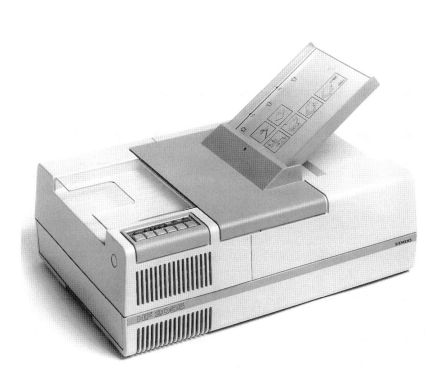

463 HF 2055 *facsimile unit*
1982–83
Siemens-Design
Siemens AG, Berlin and Munich

464 LGK 642, LGN 641 *lasers*
for laboratory purposes
1970–71
Sheet metal, electronic com-
ponents
Siemens-Design
Siemens AG, Berlin and
Munich

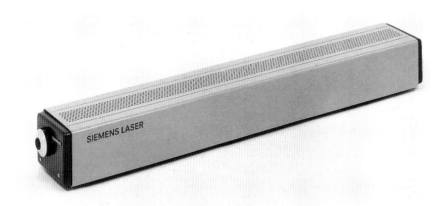

465 HFL 102 *high-frequency*
dynamic light-barrier
1969
Molded silumin
Siemens-Design
Siemens AG, Berlin and
Munich

466 Europac *magazine casing*
1973
Aluminum
Schroff Development Group
Schroff-Vertriebs-KG, Karls-
ruhe (now: Schroff GmbH,
Straubenhardt)

467 8151/52 *light-pen system*
1972
ABS – injection molding
Siemens-Design
Siemens-AG, Berlin and
Munich

468 *Supporting-plate for*
structural components using
the 902 insert system
1971–72
Aluminum and Makrolon RAL
7032
Siemens-Design
Siemens AG, Berlin and
Munich

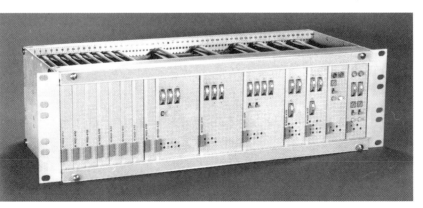

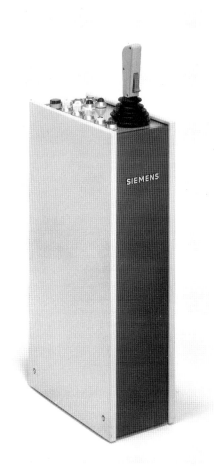

469 3SJ913 *steering-column*
1973
Sheet-steel body
Siemens-Design
Siemens AG, Berlin and
Munich

470 PL 80 *electric pulley*
1972
Aluminum and steel
Delta-Design (H. Grote)
DEMAG Fördertechnik, Wet-
ter (now: Mannesmann
Demag AG Fördertechnik)
Photo: E. Hanak

471 *Information-panel for*
environmental conditions
1974
Neumeister-Design (Alexander
Neumeister)
Messerschmidt-Bölkow-Blohm
GmbH, Environmental Protec-
tion Section, Munich

472 Panther E23 SBo
hammer-drill
c. 1974
*Slany Design Team (Erich
Slany, Helmut Scholz)
Robert Bosch GmbH, Lein-
felden*

473 *Hand tools and measuring-instruments (German Federal "Gute Form" Prize, 1975):*

OHO welding-equipment
(C. W. Voltz, Messer Griesheim GmbH)
Motor saw ax (Daniel Kremendahl,
Daniel Kremendahl)
Metal-cutting saw (C. A. Breger, Sand-
vik GmbH)
Ratchet screwdriver (Horst Holland-
Letz, Felo-Werkzeugfabrik KG GmbH)
Range of screwdrivers (Time and Mo-
tion Institute, Hermann Werner WERA-
WERALIT Schraubenwerkzeuge)
Kraftgrip range of pliers (Hardy Kol-
loch, Werner Möller KG)
Range of hammers (Johann Hermann
Picard, Johann Hermann Picard Werk-
zeugfabrik)
Screwdriver-set (Hermann J. Zerver,
HAZET-Werk)
Steel tape-measure (Ernst Moeckl,
Stabila Meßgeräte KG Gustav Ullrich)
2411 high-frequency automatic
screwdriver (Robert Bosch GmbH)
Dübelblitz 11205 hammer-drill (Slany
Design, Robert Bosch GmbH)
Panther E23 SBo hammer-drill
(Slany Design, Robert Bosch GmbH)
RX-55 electric hedge-shears
(Wolf-Design, Wolf-Geräte GmbH)
SPL welding-gun (Deutsche Hilti GmbH)

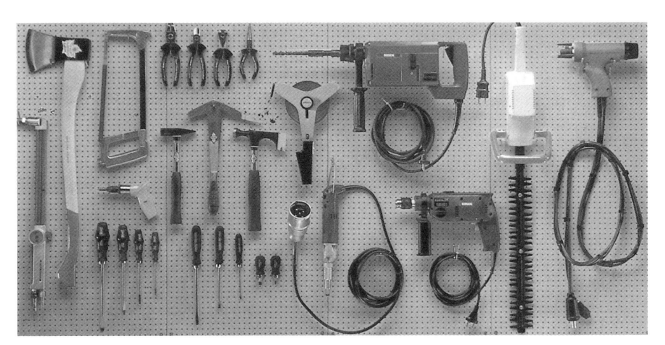

474 WS 700 angle grinder
1973
*Plastic body
AEG-Telefunken Institute for
Product Design
AEG-Telefunken, Winnenden
(now: AEG Elektrowerkzeuge
GmbH)*

475 TRAUB TD *automatic single-spindle lathe 1968–69 Erich Slany Hermann Traub Maschinenfabrik AG, Reichenbach/Fils Photo: Doris Hemminger*

476 60e *numerical steering-system for automatic milling and metalworking machines 1973 Erich Slany Robert Bosch GmbH, Industrial Equipment Department, Erbach*

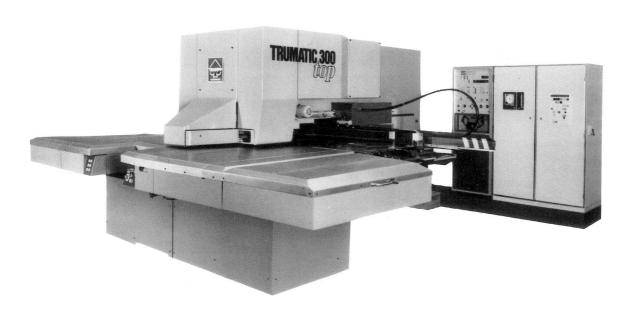

477 Trumatic 300 top *CNC sheet-metal-working machine 1977 Moll-Design Trumpf GmbH & Co. Maschinenfabrik, Ditzingen Photo: Andler*

478 *Pneumatic linear units for pick-and-place functions for handling-equipment*
1981–82
Slany Design Team
Robert Bosch GmbH, Stuttgart

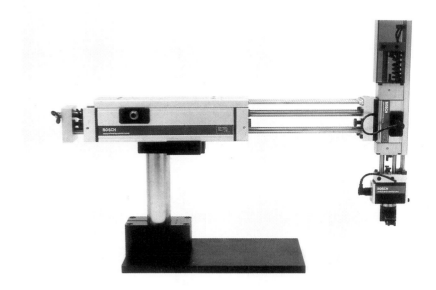

479 lambda 5 UV/VIS *spectrophotometer*
1979–81
Sheet aluminum, cast aluminum, and polyurethane
Design Bartlmae/Staudacher
Bodenseewerk Perkin-Elmer & Co. GmbH, Überlingen

480 SN 1000/16 M *oven*
1972
Product Design Working Group (Hartmut S. Engel)
Werner & Pfleiderer GmbH Lebensmitteltechnik, Stuttgart

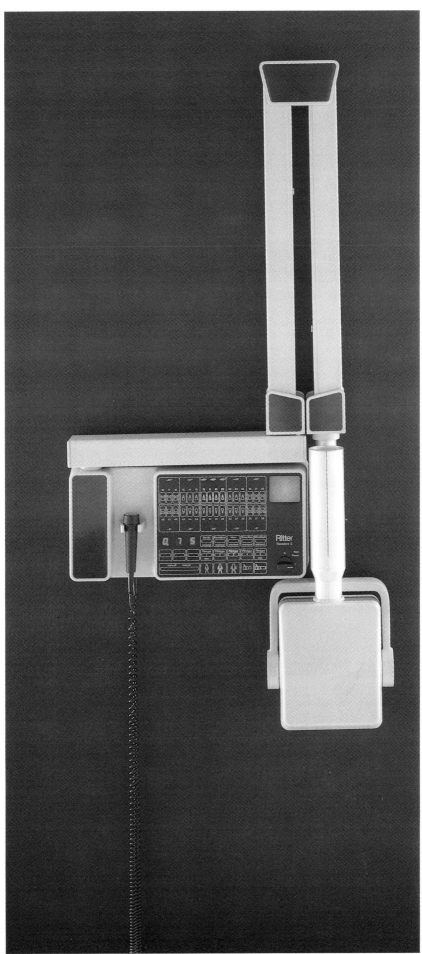

481 *Automatic telling-machine*
1979
Nixdorf Design Group
Nixdorf Computer AG, Paderborn

482 Transdent D 502 S *x-ray unit*
1978
Atv, Atelier C. W. Voltz
Ritter AG, Karlsruhe (now: Ritter GmbH)

483 SL *dentist's chair*
1970
Siemens-Design
Siemens AG, Berlin and
Munich

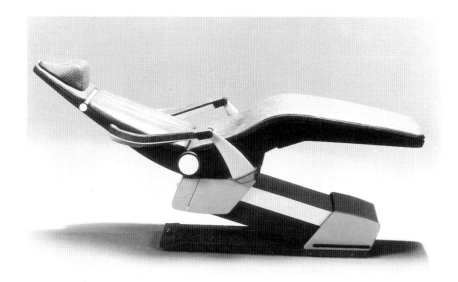

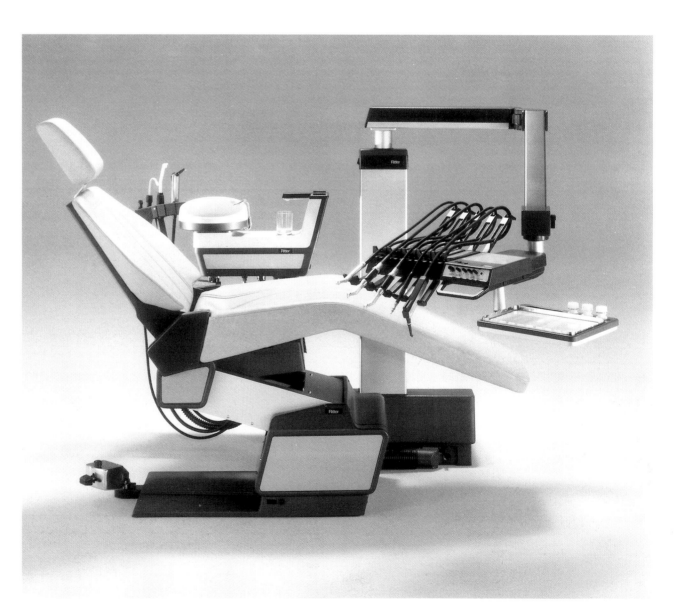

484 Ratiorest D 104 *dentist's*
chair with Dentana D 270
basin and water-glass system
1978–79
Atv, Atelier C. W. Voltz
Ritter AG, Karlsruhe (now:
Ritter GmbH)

485 WILA seat-rest
1976
Designed by the manufacturers (Brand/Häfner)
Heinrich Wilhelm Dreyer KG, Bad Essen (now: WILA Maschinenfabrik GmbH & Co. KG, Bad Essen-Wittlage)

486 Bima Profi *chair for industrial settings*
1978
Integral foam system and metal
D-Team (Dorothee Hiller, Rainer Bohl)
F. Biedermann GmbH & Co. KG, Hechingen

487 *Vitraviva 401622 office chair*
1978
Wolfgang Müller-Deisig
Vitra GmbH, Weil am Rhein

488 *Synchronic mechanism used in the* Vitramat 20 *and* 30 *chairs*
1978
Wolfgang Müller-Deisig
Vitra GmbH, Weil am Rhein

489 ergonom 190/ergomat
office swivel-chair
1978
hircheteam
Mauser Waldeck AG, Waldeck
Photo: Atelier Weber

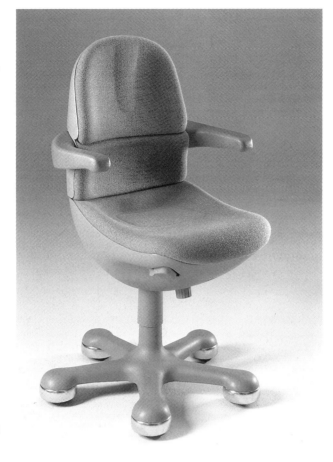

490 232 *office swivel-chair*
1971
Polyester reinforced with
fiberglass
Wilhelm Ritz
Wilkhahn, Eimbeckhausen
(now: Wilkhahn, Bad Münder)
Photo: Wolfgang Isser

491 S1 *swivel-chair*
1982
Arno Votteler
Martin Stoll GmbH, Waldshut-
Tiengen
Photo: Werner Bokelmann

492 Fröscher Consequo
552 42 *integral molded seat*
1974
Polyamide and pressure-cast
aluminum
Burkhard Vogtherr
August Fröscher KG,
Steinheim/Murr (now:
Fröscher Sitform KG)

493 S30 *chair*
1971
Hanno von Gustedt
Gebrüder Thonet AG,
Frankenberg

494 Binar 612/1 *chair*
1978
Reiner Moll
Wilkhahn, Bad Münder

495 Ergo-style DHL *swivel-chair*
1979
Burkhardt Vogtherr, using work by D-Team Design
Drabert Söhne GmbH & Co.,
Minden

496–499 Bofinger easychair
1974
Plastic, napa leather, alumi-
num
Bofinger Development
Department (Mehnert and
Valenta)
Bofinger Production, Ilsfeld

500 BA 1171 *plastic chair* ("Bofinger chair")
1966
Helmut Bätzner
Bofinger Production, Ilsfeld

501 Chair of nails *(designed for the 1971 "Bofinger chairs as* objets d'art" *campaign)*
1971
Günther Uecker
Photo: Frank Baresel-Bofinger

502 Bofinger with stilts *(designed for the 1971 "Bofinger chairs as* objets d'art" *campaign)*
1971
K. H. Hödicke
Photo: Frank Baresel-Bofinger

503 Black chair with hole, under it a glass filled with water *(designed for the 1971 "Bofinger chairs as* objets d'art" *campaign)*
1971
Joseph Beuys
Photo: Frank Baresel-Bofinger

504 CUMULI 840 *upholstered*
furniture
Before 1980
PER ProduktEntwicklung
Roericht (Hans Roericht,
Staubert)
Wilkhahn, Bad Münder

505 Pillorama *furniture suites*
1972
Otto Zapf
Zapf Möbel, Eschborn;
Knoll International, Murr

506 *The 28 unit seating furni-*
ture, seating unit
1972
Jürgen Lange
August Fröscher KG, Stein-
heim/Murr (now: Fröscher
Sitform KG)
Photo: Atelier Busche

507 *Tire sofa*
1974
Jochen Gros, "Des-in" Group

508 Canvas *stitched sofa*
1973
Canvas and inflatable plastic
filler material
Günter Sulz
Behr und Sulz, Bietigheim

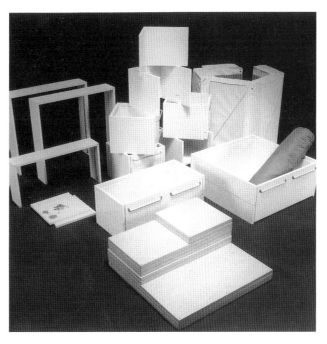

509 Podium 3 *unit furniture*
1973
Walter Müller
interlübke Möbelfabrik,
Rheda-Wiedenbrück

510 *Living room furnishing*
1971
Wil Eckstein
Rolf Benz GmbH, Nagold
Photo: Hendorfer

511 Apartment unit '80 *work-place*
1969–70
Arno Votteler
BASF Aktiengesellschaft, Lud-wigshafen

512 Funktionswand *multipur-pose wall fittings*
1978
hircheteam
interlübke Möbelfabrik,
Rheda-Wiedenbrück

513 *Container office (prototype)
1974–75
bader-design-concept (Wolfgang Bader), Peter Engelhard*

514, 515 *Container apartment (prototype)
1974–75
bader-design-concept
(Wolfgang Bader), Peter Engelhard*

516 Gardena Pipeline *tap and nozzle fittings*
1970
Franco Clivio, Dieter Raffler
Gardena – Kress+Kastner GmbH, Ulm

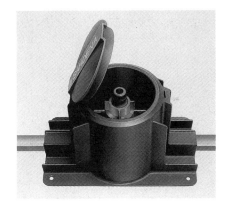
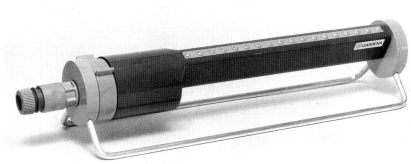

517 Gardena Pipeline *lawn-sprinkler*
1972
Franco Clivio, Dieter Raffler
Gardena – Kress+Kastner GmbH, Ulm

518 Gardena Pipeline *plug in hosepipe-connectors*
1967
Franco Clivio, Dieter Raffler
Gardena – Kress+Kastner GmbH, Ulm

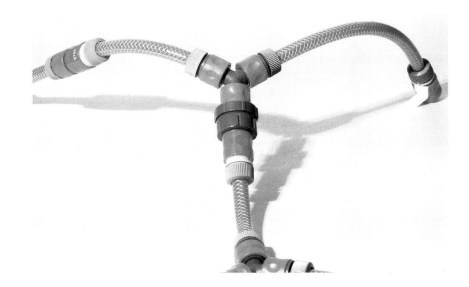

519 Gardena Pipeline *hose-pipe-set*
1970
Franco Clivio, Dieter Raffler
Gardena – Kress+Kastner GmbH, Ulm

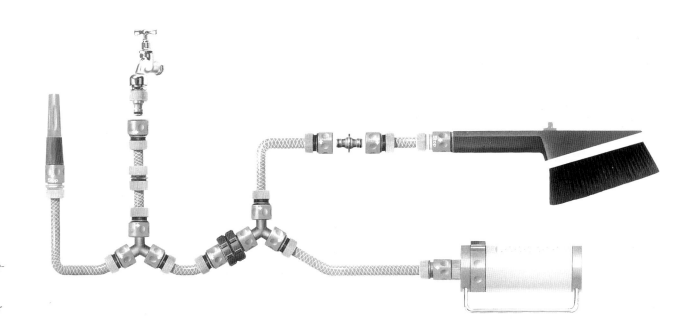

520, 521 *Ultrasonic remote control for lighting-purposes (a modular electronic system)*
1977
Jürgen K. Hölsken
Staff GmbH & Co. KG, Lemgo

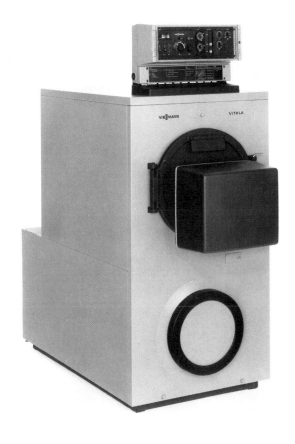

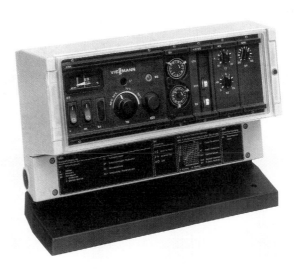

522, 523 *Vitola-s-e special purpose boiler (oil- and gas-fired) and control unit*
1976
Design Praxis Diener
Viessmann Werke KG, Allendorf/Eder

524 Nizo integral *sound-camera*
1979
Braun Product Design (Peter Schneider)
Braun AG, Kronberg

525 Bauer AF 2000 *movie-camera*
1978
Slany Design Team
Robert Bosch GmbH, Stuttgart

526 Agfa-Family 5190 *super-8 movie-camera*
1980
Schlagheck Schultes Design
Agfa Gaevert AG, Munich

527 HD44 *stereo earphones*
1973
Extruded plastic
Günter Nocon
Sennheiser electronic KG, Bis-
sendorf, Wedemark
Photo: Reinhold Lessmann

528 HD424 *headphones*
c. 1976
Sennheiser electronic KG, Bis-
sendorf, Wedemark
Photo: Reinhold Lessmann

528 HD424 *headphones*
c. 1976
Designed by the manufac-
turers
Sennheiser electronic KG, Bis-
sendorf, Wedemark
Photo: Reinhold Lessmann

530 M 412 N *dynamic direc-*
tional microphone
1973
Plastic, rubber
Dieter Auerbach
Eugen Beyer GmbH & Co.,
Heilbronn
Photo: Peter Zern

531 PS550 *record player*
1976
Braun Product Design (Dieter
Rams, Robert Oberheim)
Braun AG, Kronberg

532 Studio *hi-fi system: tuner,*
receiver Regie 510/520[1]
and TG1020[2] *tape recorder*
(1) 1972; (2) 1970
Braun Product Design (Dieter
Rams)
Braun AG, Kronberg

533 WEGA Concept 51K
compact radio-system
1975–76
Esslinger Design, frogdesign
WEGA-Radio GmbH, Fellbach
(now: Sony-Wega Production)
Photo: Dietmar Henneka

534 *Electronic baby scales*
1980
Interform Design Studio
Schönfeld
Seca, Vogel & Halke GmbH &
Co., Hamburg

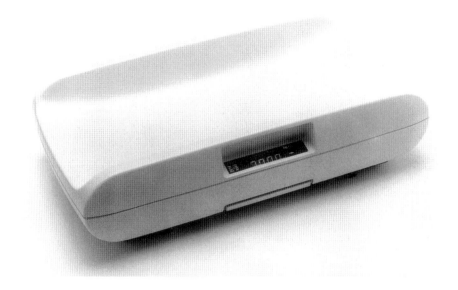

535 TK30 columbus *carpet sweeper*
1971
Plastic and cast aluminum
Rolf Garnich
G. Staehle KG, Stuttgart
Photo: Hans-Georg Jaehnike

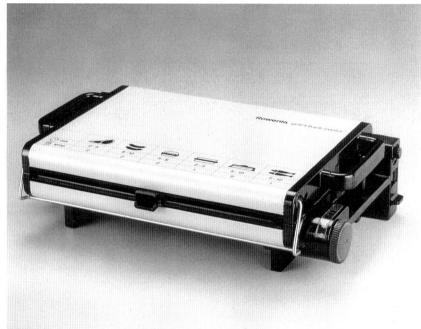

536 *The KG-63 grill and baking unit*
1979
Rowenta Design Department
Rowenta Werke GmbH, Offenbach

537 *Visotronic DN 50 table-top clock and alarm*
1979
Braun Product Design
Braun AG, Kronberg

538 *Miniature scales*
1972, 1976
busse design ulm gmbh
Soehnle-Waagen GmbH &
Co., Murrhardt

539 Aromaster *coffee-maker*
1971
Braun Product Design
Braun AG, Kronberg

540 THERMAT 8 *coffee-percolator*
1976
Designed by the manufacturers
Robert Krups Stiftung & Co. KG, Solingen

541 Coffina Super *grinder*
1974
Designed by the manufacturers
Robert Krups Stiftung & Co. KG, Solingen

542 MZE 4000 *electric toothbrush*
1981
Designed by the manufacturers
Robert Bosch Hausgeräte GmbH, Munich

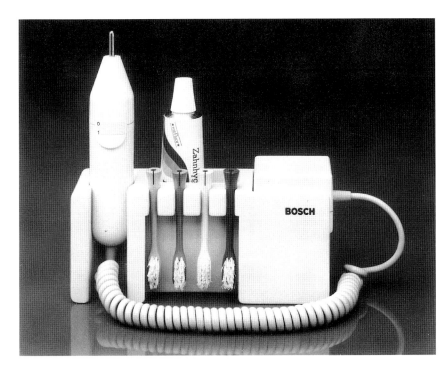

543 KG-72 *automatic egg-boiler*
1972
Franz Alban Stützer
Rowenta Werke GmbH, Offenbach

544 467 Solitär *hair-dryer*
1974
Designed by the manufacturers
Robert Krups Stiftung & Co. KG, Solingen

545 Lavett *washbasin*
1977
Herbert Hirche
PAG Presswerk AG, Essen-Bergeborbeck

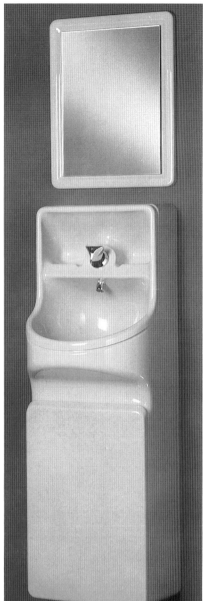

546 RS 2.77 *washbasin*
1977
Alape Produktbau
Alape Adolf Lamprecht KG, Goslar

547 Tri-Bel *handheld shower-unit*
1973
Designed by the manufacturers and frogdesign
Hans Grohe GmbH & Co.KG, Schiltach

548 NEF 1077. 23 LHCD-9 *electric cooker unit*
c. 1978
Armin Bohnet
Neff-Werke Karl Neff GmbH, Bretten

549 bomba *cutlery and crockery*
1972
Melamine
Helen von Boch, Federigo Fabbrini
Villeroy & Boch Keramische Werke KG, Mettlach (now: Villeroy & Boch AG)

550 drop *tea-service*
1970
Luigi Colani
Rosenthal AG, Selb

551 *Bulthaup cooking-surface unit*
1973–74
teamform design
Bulthaup Möbelwerke KG, Neumarkt (now: bulthaup GmbH & Co., Aich)

552 WK-Domina 909 com-
bined kitchen and living room
c. 1978
Dieter J. Reinhold
Gesellschaft für Wohngestal-
tung mbH, Leinfelden-Echter-
dingen

553 Poggenpohl CF 65/92
kitchen
1977–78
Günter Möllenberg
Poggenpohl Möbelwerke
GmbH & Co., Herford

554 Elektra Technovision
kitchen
1968–69
Metal, wood, plastic
Hasso Gehrmann
Elektra Bregenz GmbH and
Gruco Möbelwerke KG, Lauf

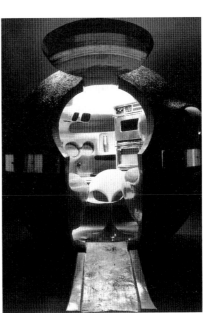

555 No. 1 *Bulthaup kitchen*
1969
Development Group for De-
sign, Ulm; Bulthaup KG
Bulthaup Möbelwerke KG,
Neumarkt (now: bulthaup
GmbH & Co., Aich)
Photo: Wolfgang Siol

556 Experiment 70 Küchen-
kugel *spherical kitchen unit*
(for demonstration purposes)
c. 1970
Plastic
Luigi Colani
Fr. Poggenpohl KG, Herford
(now: Fr. Poggenpohl GmbH)
Photo: Studio 63

557 *0.7 l returnable bottle for*
mineral-water (standard bottle
used by German Natural
Springs Cooperative)
1973
Günter Kupetz
Gerresheimer Glas AG,
Düsseldorf

558 Dynavit Meditronic *home*
trainer
1976
Richard Fischer
Keiper Trainingssysteme
GmbH & Co., Reckenhausen
(now: Keiper Dynavit GmbH &
Co., Kaiserslautern)

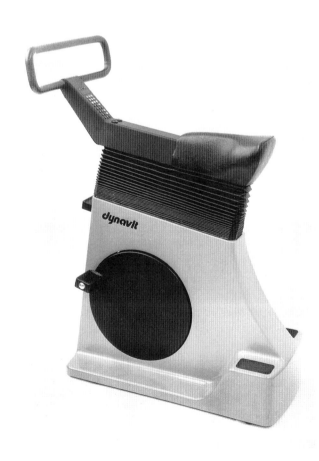

Gwendolyn Ristant **Corporate Identity**

What are today known not only in English-speaking countries but throughout the world as corporate image and corporate identity have a long tradition in a few German companies. One of the earliest examples was the Allgemeine Elektricitäts-Gesellschaft (AEG), for whom artist, designer and architect Peter Behrens developed a concept for a uniform product image between 1907 and 1914. Other features – from the factory architecture, the company logo, the company magazine, to brochures and advertising material (for which Behrens even designed a new typeface) – were gradually incorporated into this uniform design concept: AEG had created a recognizable public image. This was however an isolated, if unusually far-sighted, experiment.

Indeed, even after the foundation of the Federal Republic in 1949, companies that devoted serious study to the aptness and effectiveness of their overall image (as did the Braun Corporation, for example) were for a long time the exception. Things did not change until competition intensified owing to the fact that technical norms, quality, and functions had become standardized and costs and prices for mass produced items had leveled out. This competitive pressure in turn made it increasingly clear that to present the image of each individual company it had to be presented in such a way that it was internally consistent yet at the same time stood out – in other words, unmistakable. Horizons became broader. A company now needed a "philosophy," industry and the expanding service sectors were to be seen as "cultural" entities. Now it was no longer solely a question of the quality of the particular products and how these were presented to the public: comprehensive organization of the work process came to occupy the center of attention. As a concept, corporate identity was extended to embrace internal company structures, and these were understood to include not only forms of cooperation and communication but all kinds of activities both on and off the job where a "corporate style" might encourage and motivate the employees themselves to identify with "their" company.

Design has a special role to play in this development. For the first time, a broad awareness arises of the complexity of design, i.e. the all-embracing, interdisciplinary manner in which it shapes and organizes. The increasing relevance of graphic design and its integration in the design process as a whole is but one aspect of this. In an ideal situation, design synthesizes a company's internal and external image and is the structural interface of technology, production, marketing, distribution, and public relations. The company is no longer recognized solely as the manufacturer of certain products; rather, its entire "culture" shines through to the world outside. The company presents itself as a complex entity and as an overall image, and the products fit into this image. Individual material objects are transformed into almost

559 The Rosenthal Co.'s "Mirror House" in Selb Façade by Marcello Morandini 1986–87 In the background Otto Piene's "Rainbow" façade, 1972

560 The Rosenthal Co.'s Selb porcelain factory (new design for a concrete building) 1975 Friedensreich Hundertwasser, Rosenthal

561 *The Rosenthal Co.'s Amberg Glassworks, "Glass Cathedral"*
1968
Walter Gropius

562 *The Rosenthal Co.'s ceramics factory on the Rodach river; workplaces for handpainting of ceramics*

563 *The Rosenthal Co.'s Waldershof porcelain factory; first fluor filter plant in the porcelain industry*
1982

non-material components that lend expression to the company. Instead of simply selling lamps and lighting fixtures, Erco radiates light. Instead of simply supplying office chairs and tables, Wilkhahn organizes conferences. Instead of simply transporting passengers through the air, Lufthansa offers culinary delights and ego-trips. Messe Frankfurt is not simply an organizer of trade fairs, but rather a cosmopolitan meeting-place with an Italian flair. Deutsche Bank ostensibly deals in shares and foreign currencies only on the side; in public, it wants to be viewed as an institution geared to providing support for the arts and facilities for art exhibitions. The list is endless. Services, the visible and the invisible, the tangible and the intangible, merge to form an image – and design plays the most important role in shaping this no longer purely visual image. Design lays the foundations; it can no longer be conceived as mere packaging, but rather as a complex process, as a contribution to technological innovation, to ecology, to public confidence, as a challenge to production technology, training, marketing, advertising, and ultimately the end-user. This, incidentally, is true also of the service industries: here, too, there is a growing awareness of design as one of the outstanding market factors of the future, because in the long term design is the only guarantor that the company maintains its individuality in the market and its own corporate identity.

Corporate image and corporate identity provide new legitimation for the world of commodities; the manufactured objects themselves become part of the make-up of the company and this in turn constitutes a synthetic whole that shapes the forms of production, communication, and consumption.

Ein Fonds, der die Zinsvorteile internationaler Finanzmärkte nutzt.

Die Dresdner Bank zum An- und Verkauf von PKWs.

Die neue Quelle für eine hohe Rendite: DIT-LUX BONDSPEZIAL.

Auto, Motor und Geld.

Dresdner Bank Luxembourg S.A.

Dresdner Bank

564, 565 *Dresdner Bank AG brochures*
Hildmann, Simon, Rempen & Schmitz: SMS Werbeagentur

566 *Dresdner Bank AG window display: communications systems*

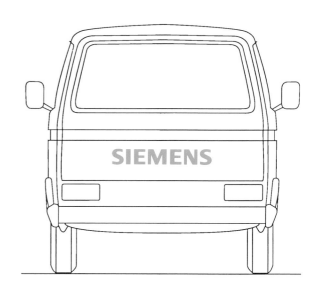

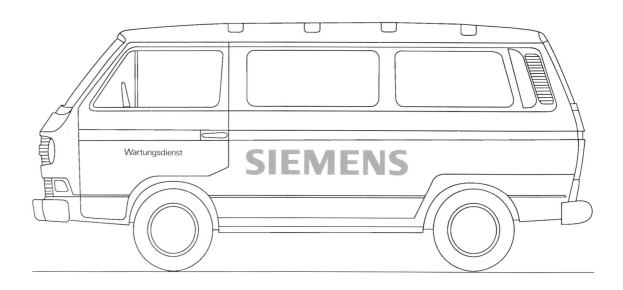

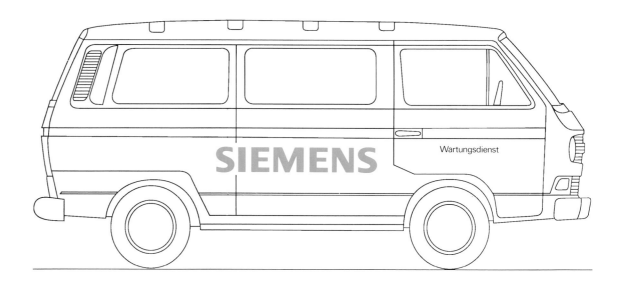

In 1989 the Siemens trademark was redesigned. The previous trademark had been in use unchanged for nearly thirty years. A new trademark design was necessitated by restructuring the enterprise. The six groups making up the enterprise were reorganized to form fifteen independently operating business sectors. This new overall structure was to be mirrored in a redesigned trademark. The previous trademark derived from a time that bore the stamp of mechanics. It embodied the weight and the power of the machine age. The new lettering is intended to symbolize the intelligence and dynamic force of the electronic age.

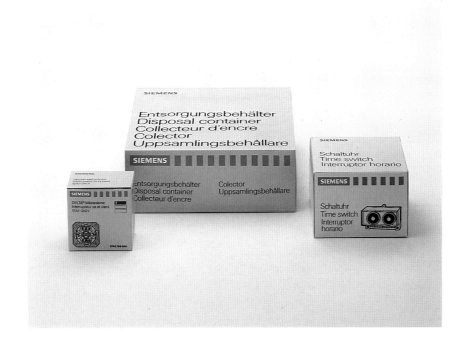

573 *Commerzbank branch in Villingen (building designated of architectural interest)*
1990
Photo: Wolfgang Brotz

574, 575 *Window display: communications systems*
Since 1989
Commerzbank AG
Photo: Marx Studios

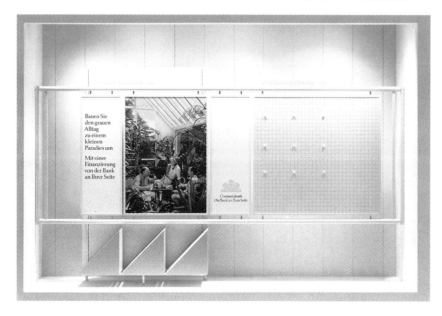

576 *Commerzbank headquarters in Frankfurt*

577 *Frankfurt Messe GmbH
(Frankfurt Fair Corporation)
logo
1984–85
Stankowski + Duschek*

578 *"Gatehouse": Frankfurt
Messe GmbH administrative
building
1984–85
Oswald Mathias Ungers*

579 *Graphic information
system
1986
Stankowski + Duschek, Anna
Christina Engels-Schwarzpaul
Photo: F. D. Deinhard*

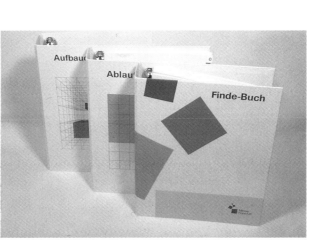

580 *Internal manuals used by
Frankfurt Messe GmbH
1985
Walter Stolz*

581 *Outdoor advertising used by BMW retailers*

582 *BMW: product launches*

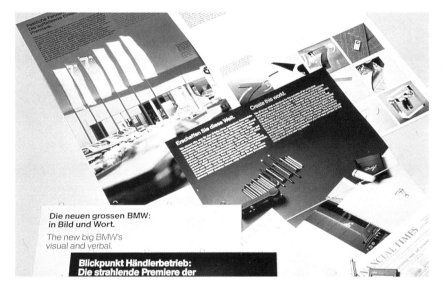

583 *BMW pavilion at Lenbachplatz in Munich*

584 *BMW: business letterhead series*

It is no accident that BMW have been so successful, and that a certain aura surrounds the company image; rather, it is the result of a strategy tailored to meet the needs of discerning customers. This focusses in equal measure on the management of development and production on the one hand and on logistics and distribution on the other. Corporate design in this context is viewed as a tool which, like a process, is gradually deployed to give the company and the brand image a clear, unmistakable profile that is shaped by special products and a distinctive environment. In this respect, the modular Corporate Identity Boxes have proven to be a substantial aid – they contain all the important materials to support decision-making, planning, design, and realization.

The examples show segments of the various subprograms at different stages of implementation. The optically dominant elements convey a lasting impression of transparency, spaciousness and clarity; backed up by bright colors, the functions and aesthetics generate the distinctive overall impression associated with BMW.

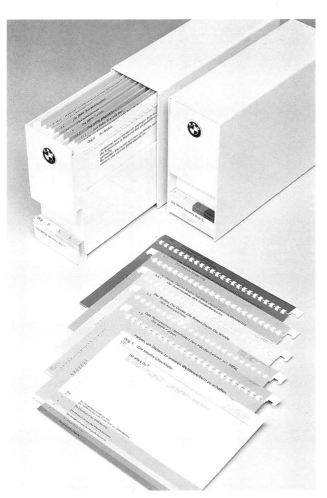

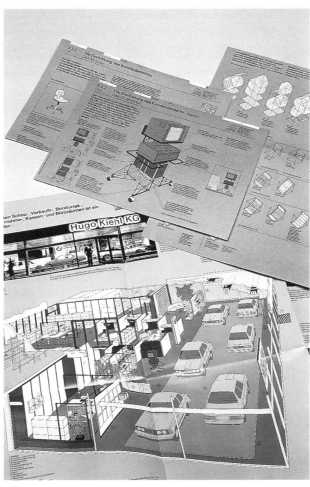

585 *BMW "Identity Box"*

586 *BMW: guidelines for design of customer services department*

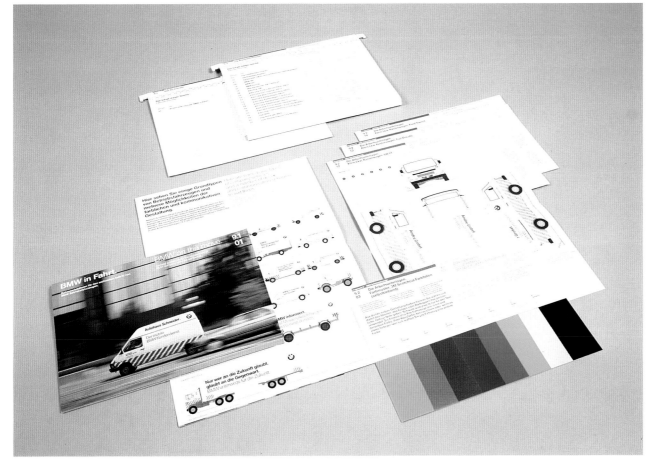

587 *BMW: markings for the company vehicle fleet*

588 *Vorwerk advertisement in consumer magazines*

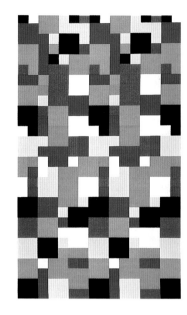

589 Dialog 2: 0341
Gerhard Richter

590 Dialog 2: 3625
Zaha M. Hadid

591 Dialog 2: 5675
Mimmo Paladino

592 Dialog 2: 5668
Sam Francis

593 Dialog 2: 1261
Sol LeWitt

594 Dialog 3: 1257
Roy Lichtenstein

595 *Wilkhahn exhibition-stand*

596 *Wilkhahn production-facilities and cutting-room in Bad Münder*

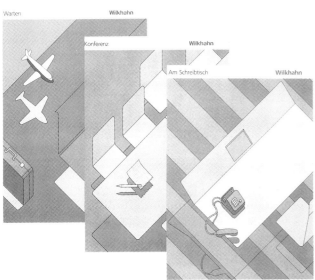

597 *Wilkhahn brochures and pamphlets*
Leonhard & Kern, Wilkhahn

598 *Brochures for staff*
Deutsche Bank AG

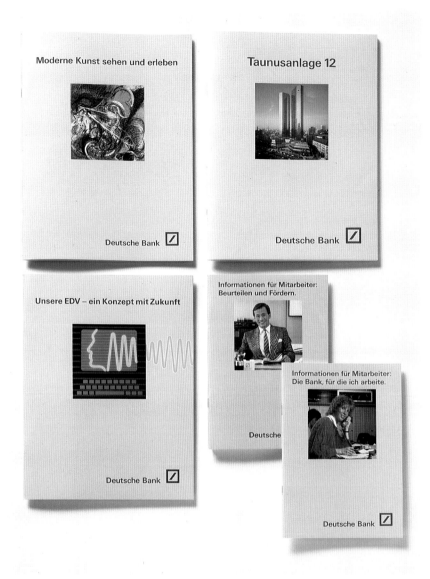

599 *Internal information system: information-stands*
Since 1985

600 *Letterhead for group companies*
1974
Stankowski + Duschek

601 *Deutsche Bank company logo*
1974
Anton Stankowski

602 *Window-display using repeated design elements*
Since 1980

603 E 111, E 103, and E 141
*electric locomotives with the
new color-scheme
1987*

604 *Electronic information
display in ticket-hall of Frankfurt station
1988*

605 401 Intercity Express (ICE)
*High-speed train
1989
Federal German Railways Design Center, Munich*

606 *Bistro in* Interregio *train
Presented in 1988
Federal German Railways De-
sign Center, Billing Peters &
Ruff*

607 *Packaging*

608 *Letterheads, envelopes, printed materials*

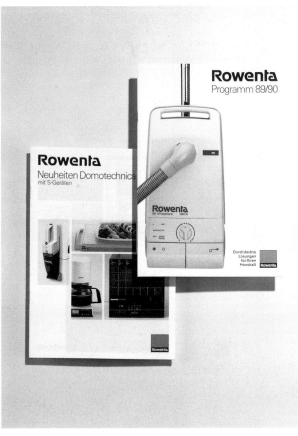

609 *Brochures, pamphlets*

610 *Outdoor advertising: flags*

611 *Outdoor advertising: electric sign in Frankfurt station*

612 *Image advertising*

613 *Standardized packaging*

The AEG Aktiengesellschaft corporation is a member of the Daimler-Benz group. Since its foundation over a hundred years ago, it has grown into a company with a worldwide presence, more than 76,000 employees in 110 different countries, and activities in the following areas:
— Industrial Automation
— Office and Communication Systems
— Electrotechnical Systems and Components
— Consumer Products
— Microelectronics
— Transportation Systems.
For all the diversity of its products, AEG sees itself as a working unit. This corporate understanding is mirrored in the image of itself that AEG conveys to the public, to staff members, and to clients, in Germany and internationally. All visual communications both inside and outside the corporation are therefore incorporated within a uniform framework that serves to lend formal and substantive expression to the corporation's consistent unity and overall aspirations.

In order to achieve a uniform appearance internationally, AEG insists that certain features must always be adhered to. These include recurrent basic design elements, such as:
— the logo, designed by Peter Behrens in 1912
— the name: AEG Aktiengesellschaft
— the color: warm red
— the typeface: Helvetica, preferentially roman typeface using both upper and lower cases.

614 *Trade advertising*

615 *Outdoor advertising: electric sign on building*

616 Modicon A 120 *automation equipment, with programmable logic controller*

617 *Outdoor advertising: nameplate*

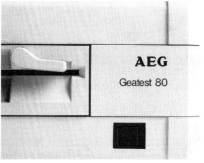

618 Greatest 80 *decentralized data-acquisition system*

619 *Maglev train system, Frankfurt Airport*

620 Öko-Lavamat *washing-machine*

621 Greatest 80 *motherboard*

622 *Folders, files, manuals*

Lufthansa Corporate Design, aircraft markings:

623 Logo, developed by Otto Firle in 1918, Deutsche Luft-Reederei 1919

624 Parabolic line used from 1957 until 1963

625 Logo with the blue and yellow color scheme, Deutsche Luft-Hansa Aktiengesellschaft 1929

626 Otl Aicher's concept, 1962 (taken as the basis for all further developments)

627 Lufthansa design department proposal, 1978

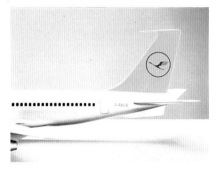

628 An alternative concept by Aicher used from 1963 until 1967

629 Scheme developed by LM 3 (Lufthansa design department), introduced in 1967

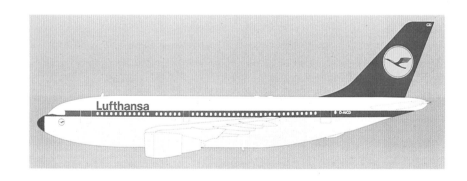

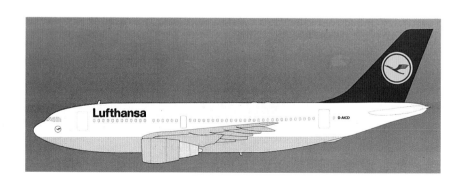

630 New concept, given the go-ahead in 1988

Gwendolyn Ristant Contemporary Design Trends

Fictitious Diversity

Design in the eighties found itself in a very different situation from that of the previous three decades. This is true not only of the status and the image of design, but applies also to the fact that structural changes in society have invaded the domain of design. Like many other areas, design is in a state of flux – the dogmatic precepts and clear categories are no longer to be relied on; various currents of design are developing alongside one another, others are converging. The situation has become more obscured, yet the possibilities more manifold. This new and at times confusing picture may to some extent, however, be the result of the vantage-point from which we study present-day trends. Whereas the other chapters adopt a retrospectively oriented stance and correspondingly take a valuative stock of the past, the present situation can be scrutinized only in terms of a still ongoing, still developing process.

The eighties seem to have produced a diversity of design processes. The decade saw a tremendous growth in design awareness among both producers and consumers. The intrinsic logic of the constant quantitative expansion of the world of designed commodities – be they technical appliances, capital goods, furniture, or services – leads of necessity to the individualization of products, for the consumer is indeed spoilt for choice. Not only are new paths being trodden; plentiful use is also made of

the historical repertoire of German design, features of which are adopted in new variations – occasionally this is also true of companies that made a substantial contribution to the establishment of functional and good design in West Germany.

Conceptual Design

The discussions of the eighties have brought change to specifically German positions that at times were stubbornly defended and rested on a conception of design both socially moralistic and apologistic. This has led to a broader notion of design. It has now become common, not only among young designers, to think about design in conceptual terms. Studies are being conducted on how we live and work at the end of the twentieth century; the problems of technologization and the intrusion of the media into our lives are being analyzed; and the changes in the design process itself and the results

631 BMW K100RS
1990 (basic K1 *model designed in 1983)*
Designed by the manufacturers
BMW AG, Munich

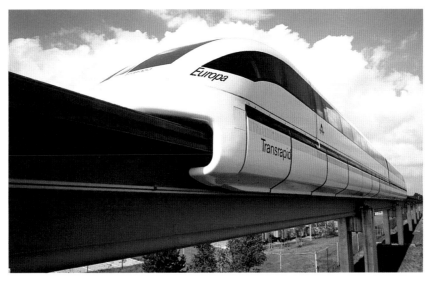

632 Transrapid 07 *maglev express-train*
1985–88
Neumeister Design
MVP Versuchs- und Planungsgesellschaft für Magnetbahnsysteme mbH, Munich
(German Federal Railways, Deutsche Lufthansa AG, and Industrieanlagen- und Betriebsgesellschaft mbH)
Photo: Stadler

633 Musculair I *muscle-powered aircraft*
1984
Günter Rochelt

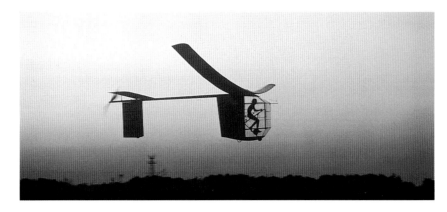

634 *Muscle-powered hydrofoil, model (3rd Prize in the 9th Braun Awards, 1989)*
1989
Thomas Fiegl, Achim Pohl

635 *Bridge-shaped coffin*
1989
Kurt Becker, Daniel Ludig
(master's degree project, College of Design, Offenbach)

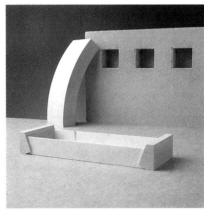

636 Kumpel II *table*
1986
Pickax-heads, wood, crystal glass
Axel Stumpf
Photo: Idris Kolodziej

thereof are also increasingly the subject of investigation. The task is seen to be more complex, so that far-sighted companies no longer simply call for the design of a new refrigerator, for example, but instead commission studies that aim to find a future-oriented solution to the problem of food storage in late industrial societies. Hardware design is becoming subordinate to the defining of function and the design of software and services. The concept of design is having to face up to new challenges now that computer technology has facilitated, modified, or abolished certain design processes, and CAD has opened up new possibilities for creating mini-series and for the individualization of mass production. These new tasks pose new problems for the designer, but also afford new opportunities. Design today must be capable of mediating material and immaterial conditions and interests, autonomous and mutually contradictory elements; it

must generate novel, non-hierarchical organizational structures, and not just new sets of norm values.

New Design

The eighties saw an unprecedented boom in design – and the word "design" finally became a part of the German language. The design which took center stage and was given a blaze of publicity in the media was totally different from that which had been evolving since the fifties, with its origins in Ulm and associated tendencies, its idealization as "good form," and its culmination in hi-tech euphoria. This new look in design had begun in Italy with Alchimia and Memphis, but it quickly spread to West Germany, where it was modified to become an independent, "new, young design" movement. Exhibitions such as "Möbel Perdu" (Hamburg 1982) or "Wohnen von Sinnen" (Düsseldorf 1986), and the presentation of this different kind of design at the 1987 "Documenta 8," the world's largest and most famous arts show, caused a sensation and divided the nation into enthusiastic supporters and outraged opponents. New design groups emerged (Bellefast, Pentagon, Ginbande, Stiletto, Möbel Perdu, Berliner Design-Werkstatt, Berliner Zimmer, etc.). The Italian models were not simply imitated: after a short period in which the provocative and spectacular predominated, the "virtues" of Germany were taken up again. Unlike the course of events in Italy, in Germany the emphasis on uniqueness and the stylization of the "artistic" component soon developed into a new attempt to come to terms with normality. Designers experimented with new concepts, new ways of looking at things, they re-analyzed objects and traditional ideas of function, they recognized the emotive relationship that exists between manufacturers and particularly consumers and the world of artefacts and sought to include this in their calculation. Thus it is that today the purportedly timeless codices of "good form" are being challenged by a generation of young designers, most of whom – significantly enough – were brought up on the orthodox Ulm diet. They exaggerate, they employ unconventional materials, their creations not only look different from what we have been accustomed to expect, they often function on novel principles as well; thus it is brought home to us that designed artefacts are anything but natural, self-evident, or logical. This is one of the keynotes of "New Design," the presentation of familiar things in an unfamiliar light, so that irritation will allow us to gain a new experience of objects. Another factor is the realization that objects always have psychological functions, too, acting as status symbols, expressing convictions, demonstrating allegiance to a particular group, or generating communication – "conversation pieces," as Tomás Maldonado, former president of the HfG, once aptly termed them. However, it is also true that these trends that rebel against "good form" appeal to a zeitgeist which encourages the expression of "individuality" through the acquisition and flaunting of extravagant material goods.

Yet these pointers provide only an inadequate characterization of the trends of design in the eighties. The focus on New Design belies the fact that, viewed quantitatively, this represents but a tiny segment of the broad range of design available, and its commercial importance is negligible compared with "classical" industrial design. Seen in perspective it is the nonconformist, provocative fringe, rather than a major rival in the product design, even though it undoubtedly has an impact on the latter. But we may safely say that the generally accepted notion of good design is now diversifying into a number of still far from completed processes. Contradictions and controversies will continue to enliven the design scene; the possibilities are boundless.

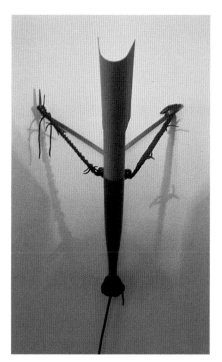

637 The Torch
1985
Aluminum, iron, ebony, and leather
Nicolas Anatol Baginsky

638 Comsumer's rest No. 11
lounge chair
1986 (prototype developed in 1983)
Disassembled supermarket trolley reformed by hammering, brazed, and varnished to create a golden metallic effect
Stiletto
Photo: Stiletto Studios

639 Aquarium
1985
Florian Aicher

640 Frankfurt skyscraper
cupboard
1985
*Outer surface: curled maple,
brass, gold leaf, Russian
jasper, lapislazuli, and plexi-
glass; inner surface: walnut
root, brier, curled maple,
ivory, and gold leaf
Berghof, Landes and Rang*

641 Black house chair *with*
house lamp *and* silhouette
1984
*Canvas painted with multiplex
on wood
Holger Drees*

642 Three ax tables *(stand, side-table, and coffee-table)*
1984–85
Ax-handles, galvanized sheet steel
Axel Stumpf

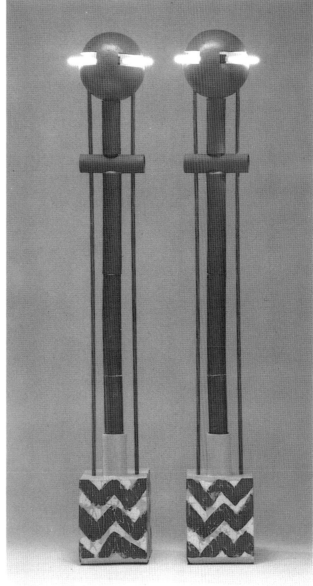

643 *Chair*
1983
Beech
Peter Strassl

644 Illuminations
1985
Glazed stoneware, unglazed oxydized copper tubing, electronics
Cocktail (Heike Mühlhaus and Renate von Brevern)
Photo: Idris Kolodziej

645 Mediengeil *copper televi-*
sion-set (makeup-mirror and
table-lamp)
1984
Copper, brass buttons, neon
tube, and brass
Rouli Lecatsa (Möbel Perdu)
Photo: Rainer Leitzgen

646 Blue armchair
1984
Waste materials and brushes
from carwashes
Ulrike Holthöfer, Axel Kufus

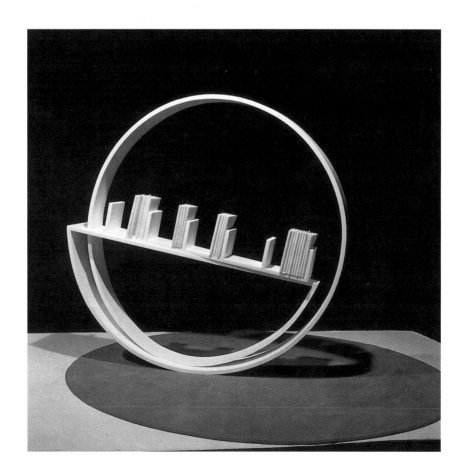

647 Balance II *bookshelves*
1985–86
Monika Wall
Photo: Peter Horn

648 Rabbit-ear cushion
1984
Brocade and PVC
Charly Hüskes (Kunstflug)

649 Sauvage *chaise-longue*
1985
A synthesis of two African materials: brass and zebra-skin
Schmid & Stemmann
Photo: Studio Eins

650 Hotel Ukraina
1985
Sectional steel tubing, viscose,
leather
Siegfried Michail Syniuga

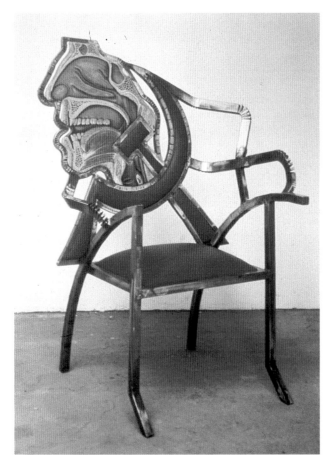

651 Family Flintstone *bar*
1982
Aluminium, polished or sand-
blasted
Michel Feith (Möbel Perdu)

652 *Collection of tables (din-*
ing-table-cum-desk, coffee-
table, side-table, bracket-
table, and café-table)
1983–84
High-grade steel, dyed metal
Thomas Wendtland
Photo: Reinhart Wolf

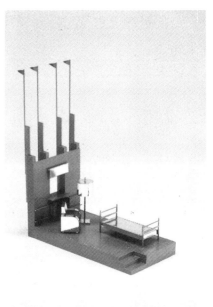

653 Parking and living space
1982, 1986
Hans Uwe Schultze, Wolfgang
Schulze

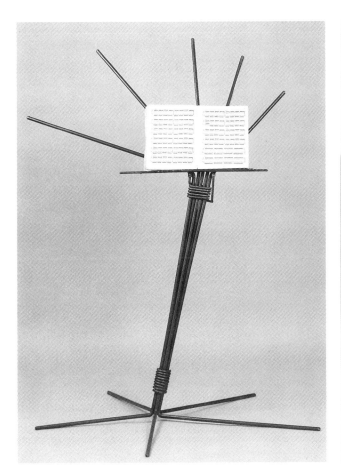

654 Music-stand
1984
Steel
Peter Schmitz
Photo: Dieter Schohl

655 Red-wedge shelving
1983
Lacquered wood
Peter Werner

What was once undoubtedly a fresh approach, namely "New Design," has since become jaded. Today, "art objects" are shunned from exhibition to exhibition without having an appreciable impact on industrial production. This gradually emerging trend — the autonomous development of design down a path to nowhere, back to the "arts and crafts" look of Art Deco — is hardly tenable in terms of social responsibility. For the free spaces remaining no longer embrace the flotsam that is carried landward, let alone process it.
Jörg Ratzlaff

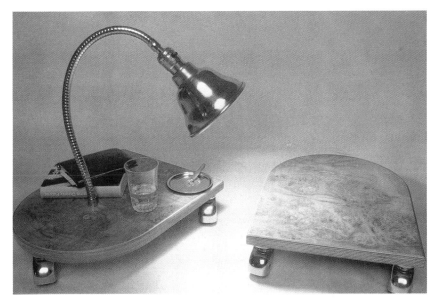

656 Gone to the dogs
1984
Root veneer on multiplex
Jörg Ratzlaff

657 *Table object*
1979
Steel, wood
Jens Peter Schmid

658 13 armchair
1985
Concrete, steel
Heinz H. Landes

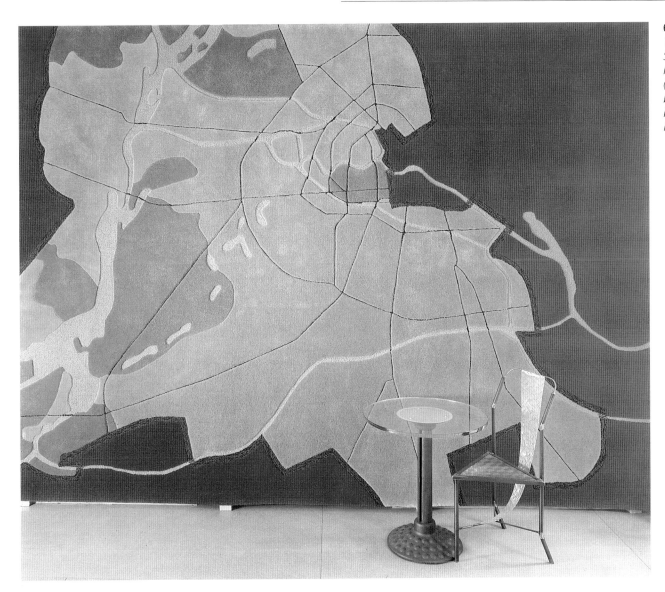

659 Berlin *floor carpeting*
1985
Superfine velvet
Herbert Jakob Weinand
(In the foreground a café-table
by H. J. Weinand and triangu-
lar chair by A. Kammermeier)
Photo: Idris Kolodziej

660 Ejector seat
1985
Aluminum, steel springs, foam
sandwich
Hermann Waldenburg

661 6C4 *computer workstation, height continuously adjustable;* Just-think *(screen mounting) desk with container drawers and trays;* Arena *variable space-defining elements*
1988
Berlinetta
Designwerkstatt Berlin
prototype
Photo: Idris Kolodziej

662 Filing Dungeon *cabinet;* Leaner *document storage facility with adjustable working-surface*
1988
Jörg Hundertpfund, Sylvia Robeck
Designwerkstatt Berlin
prototype
Photo: Idris Kolodziej

663 Tension *conference-table*
1988
Albert Langenmayr
Designwerkstatt Berlin
prototype
Photo: Idris Kolodziej

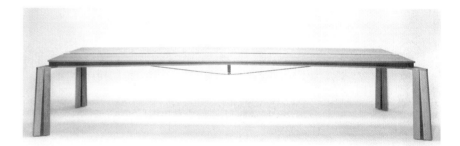

664 6C4 *computer workstation, height continuously adjustable*
1988
Berlinetta
Designwerkstatt Berlin
prototype
Photo: Idris Kolodziej

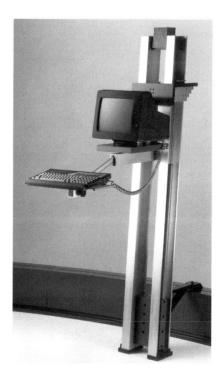

665 BT1 *interview-table;* GW1 *chair with headrest;* SK1 *chair*
1988
High-grade steel and lacquered wood
Joachim B. Stanitzek
Designwerkstatt Berlin
prototype
Photo: Idris Kolodziej

666 Nosechair *corrugated cardboard*
1988
Franz-Wolfgang Lorenz
Designwerkstatt Berlin
prototype
Photo: Idris Kolodziej

667 Threeswinger *conferencechair incorporating folding writing-support*
1987
Stiletto Studios
Designwerkstatt Berlin
prototype
Photo: Idris Kolodziej

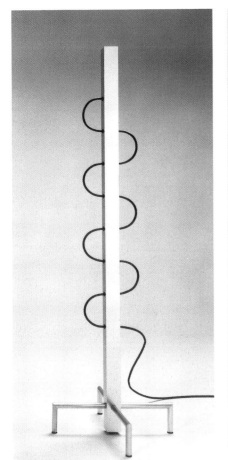

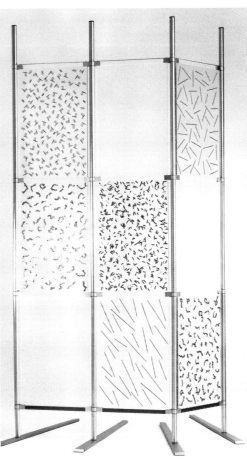

668 Hermes *standard-lamp*
1988
Axel Stumpf
Designwerkstatt Berlin
prototype
Photo: Idris Kolodziej

669 Fish'n Chips *dividing screen*
1988
Acrylic glass with magnetizable metal inserts
Ad Us
Designwerkstatt Berlin
prototype
Photo: Idris Kolodziej

670 LT1 *table-lamp*
1988
Joachim B. Stanitzek
Designwerkstatt Berlin
prototype
Photo: Idris Kolodziej

671 Karajan I *desk;* Karajan II
typewriter-table
1988
Herbert Jakob Weinand
Designwerkstatt Berlin
prototype
Photo: Idris Kolodziej

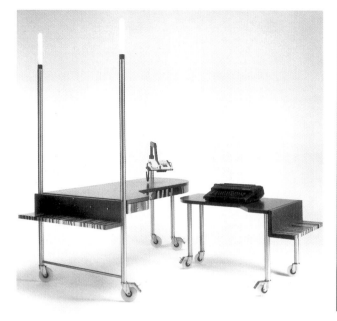

672 Standard office, garage,
computer container; support
for overhead cables; chair
1988
Andreas Brandolini
Designwerkstatt Berlin
prototype
Photo: Idris Kolodziej

673 Chameleon *divan, adjust-*
able in three positions
1988
Hermann Waldenburg
Designwerkstatt Berlin
prototype
Photo: Idris Kolodziej

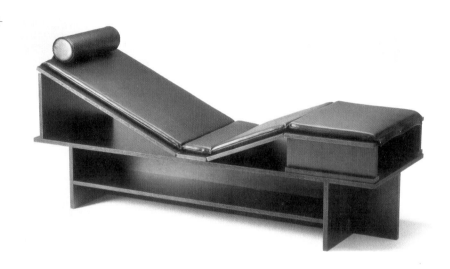

674 Rollo *swivel office-chair*
on castors
1988
Herbert Jakob Weinand
Designwerkstatt Berlin
prototype
Photo: Idris Kolodziej

675 Stork II *chair*
1988
Albert Langenmayr
Designwerkstatt Berlin
prototype
Photo: Idris Kolodziej

676 Precedent II *chair*
1988
Gabriel Kornreich
Designwerkstatt Berlin
prototype
Photo: Idris Kolodziej

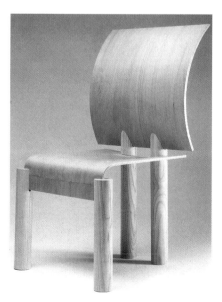

677 Tron *filing-unit and loose paper storage-facility*
1988
Jörg Hundertpfund, Sylvia Robeck
Designwerkstatt Berlin
prototype
Photo: Idris Kolodziej

678 Resi *conference-table*
1988
Andreas Brandolini
Designwerkstatt Berlin
prototype
Photo: Idris Kolodziej

679 Container *stackable filing-cabinet with drawers*
1988
Herbert Jakob Weinand
Designwerkstatt Berlin
prototype
Photo: Idris Kolodziej

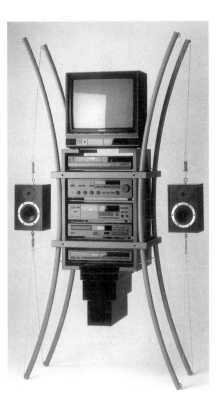

680 BG1 *rack for media equipment*
1988
Joachim B. Stanitzek
Designwerkstatt Berlin
prototype
Photo: Idris Kolodziej

681 Standard office, garage, *computer container*
1988
Andreas Brandolini
Designwerkstatt Berlin
prototype
Photo: Idris Kolodziej

682–684 Tabula rasa com-
*bined table and bench, slides
out from 0,5 m to 5 m
1987
Chipboard glazed black; ply-
wood with a colorless glaze;
bright galvanized steel
GINB*A*NDE Design (Uwe
Fischer, Klaus-Achim Heine)
Vitra-Edition, Vitra GmbH,
Weil am Rhein*

685 A59 *lamp-column
1983, 1988
Volker Albus
Photo: Felix Borkenau*

686 M20 *table, height adjustable*
1989
Volker Albus

687 Weaner Blut *chandelier*
1987
Volker Albus
Photo: Bernhard Schaub

688 Römerberg *seating suite*
1987–88
Volker Albus
Photo: Felix Borkenau

689 Dish
1988–89
Sheet steel, steel, high-grade
steel sphere
Ralph Sommer (Pentagon)

690 Sulky
1988
Right-angled tubing, sheet
steel, sulky
Reinhard Müller, Meyer-
Voggenreiter (Pentagon)

691 Little Sisters *seating, com-*
missioned by Philip Morris for
the 1989 Art-Frankfurt-Fair
1989
Andreas Brandolini
Photo: Wilmar Koenig

692 Living-room, *at*
documenta 8, Kassel
1987
Andreas Brandolini

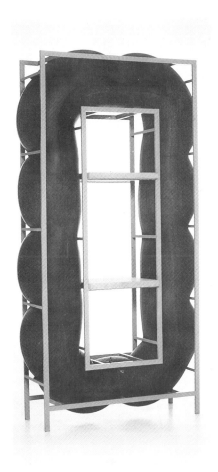

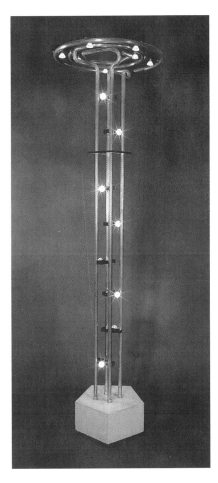

693 Chambre A Air
1987
Steel, tractor-tires, stone floor
Reinhard Müller (Pentagon)

694 Suspended shelf
1985
Steel, steel cable
Wolfgang Laubersheimer
(Pentagon)

695 Pentagon standard-lamp
1989
Steel tube, concrete, halogen,
magnets
Gerd Arens (Pentagon)

696 Pentagon Casino, *Installa-*
tion at documenta 8
1987
Pentagon Group

697 Crazy modular packaging
(for body-hygiene products)
1988–89
Yellow Design
MODIMA SA, Switzerland

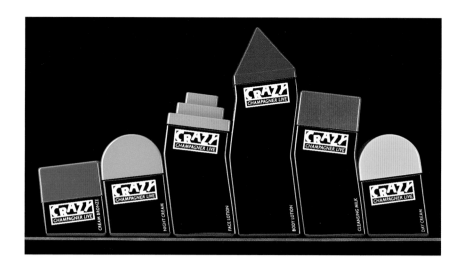

698 Lagoon packaging
1988
Yellow Design
Blendax GmbH, Procter &
Gamble Group

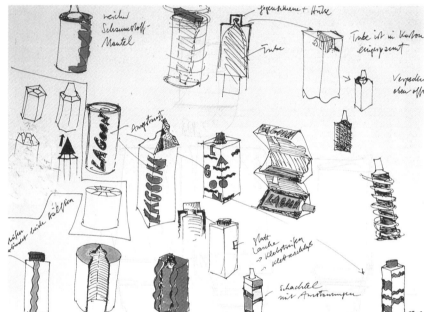

699 Lagoon packaging
designs (studies)
1988
Yellow Design
Blendax GmbH, Procter &
Gamble Group

700 Jug-shaped condensed-
milk package
1987
Yellow Design
Südmilch AG
Photo: Aktiv Team

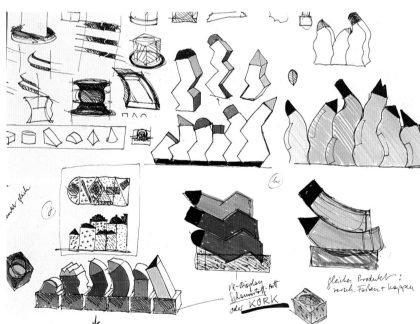

701 Crazy packaging for a
body-hygiene product-line
(studies)
1988–89
Yellow Design
MODIMA SA, Switzerland

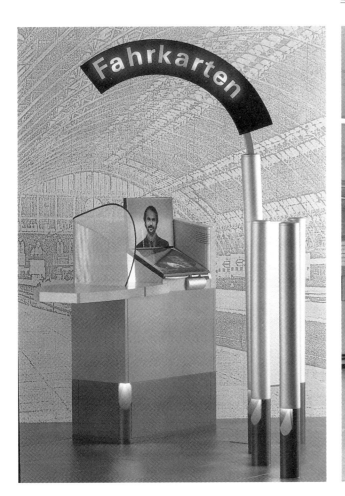

702 *Ticket machine
(Draft Design Award of the
North-Rhine-Westfalian State
Prize, 1987)
1987
Kunstflug (Charly Hüskes, Har-
dy Fischer, Harald Hullmann,
Heiko Bartels)
Photo: Klaas and Adams*

703 *Automat for rapid-transit
information with print-out,
Dusseldorf Airport
1988–89
Kunstflug (Charly Hüskes, Har-
dy Fischer, Harald Hullmann,
Heiko Bartels)
Photo: Klaas and Adams*

704 *Electronic hand calculator
for the German Architecture
Museum, Frankfurt
1987
Kunstflug (Charly Hüskes, Har-
dy Fischer, Harald Hullmann,
Heiko Bartels)
Photo: Walter Vogel*

705 The Offshore Solar Hydrogen Farm *(Grand Prize: Prime Minister's Prize, 4th International Design Competition, Osaka, 1989)*
1989
Holger Drees; co-producers: Ulrich Reif, Martin Kuhles

706 *Sketch of the whole Offshore Solar Hydrogen Farm (1) Sun, (2) Breakwater atoll, (3) Second drive system, (4) Drag anchor, (5) Solar Farm with modular pontoon units, 3 km³, (6) Floating hydrogen production plants*

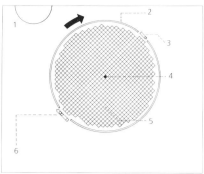

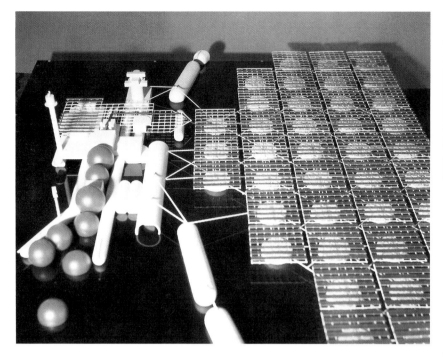

707 The Offshore Solar Hydrogen Farm: *Several floating units working together*

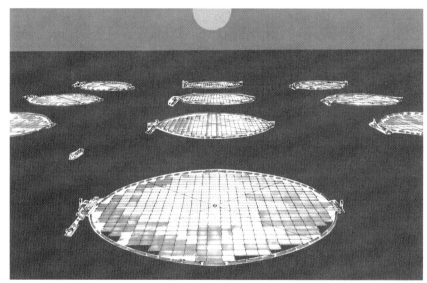

708 *Aircraft carrier transformed into a Solar Hydrogen Farm*

The Offshore Solar Hydrogen Farm

Internationally, hydrogen is regarded as the environmentally sound energy resource of the future. At some point, it will replace coal and mineral oil, and thus put a stop to the greenhouse effect caused by carbon-dioxide emissions; nuclear power stations will then also be superfluous.

Unlike ideas to date, which involve using installations in desert areas, the OFFSHORE SOLAR HYDROGEN FARM will produce hydrogen on the open sea. A large number of pontoon modules with solar-cell surfaces generate electricity, which is used for electrolysis, thereby separating water into hydrogen and oxygen.

The floating farm has substantial advantages, not least its mobility. The farms can rotate 360° each day, following the path of the sun. They can also turn further, changing their position at sea.

Shipping the liquid hydrogen worldwide will be effected using returnable spherical tanks. Also — and this is an important feature of the concept — aircraft-carriers could be refitted to serve as bases for the floating farms, which would then serve to further international disarmament.

When used as fuel, the hydrogen combusts with the oxygen in the air and turns back into water. Thus, the sun's fire is used to fuel fires on earth via its interim storage in the shape of hydrogen.

Holger Drees, January 31, 1990

SIEMENS

Design Process Prototyping

The Hicom communications terminal was developed using the prototyping process.

With this rediscovered method of product development one proceeds as follows: first of all a team of specialists is selected to work on the project in question. The only criterion for the choice of the team members is their relevant technical know-how. The normal department hierarchy does not apply in this case. A project manager is nominated and is provided with a fixed budget (time and money). The project manager is responsible for defining the objective.

On the basis of the definition of the overall objective small groups with specific objectives are formed; these groups organize themselves and present the results of their work on scheduled dates. The individual results are coordinated by the project manager, integrated and processed to a model. User tests are then performed on the working model. The findings from the user tests serve as a basis for developing a prototype.

Objective:
To develop a communications terminal which is optimally designed with regard to operation and integration.
Solution:
A modular system in which the central feature is the design of the user surface.
Planning and laboratory set-up:
Basis of all planning and constant criterium for all decisions are the user requirements: the concrete situation

709 *Distinguishing design features are the compact telephone component and a surface that can accomodate arbitrary functions Siemens-Design (Tönis Käo, Axel Loritz)*

710 *One of the possible product variants: a soft-key telephone*

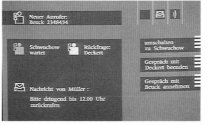

711 *Here, the software layout makes the telephone visible on the display Siemens-Design (Anette Schwuchow)*

is simulated in a laboratory set-up and a user test performed. The results of this test are integrated in the planning and the software is developed accordingly.
Construction:
The housing comprises a plate and a trough. All the technical components are accommodated on the plate. This means the device can easily be built in and avoids tolerance problems during assembly.

712, 713 Rollei SL2000 cam-
era
*1977–78 (draft design)
Dieter Mankau
Rollei fototechnic GmbH & Co.
KG, Brunswick*

714 *Pneumatic ski (private
project)
Since 1983
Dieter Mankau*

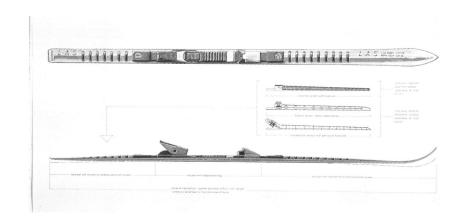

715 *LCD-transmitted light
projection (large picture),
time-moved pictures at
documenta 8 (sketch)
1987
Dieter Mankau*

716 *LCD-transmitted light
projection (large picture) at
Multi Mediale, Karlsruhe
1989
Dieter Mankau*

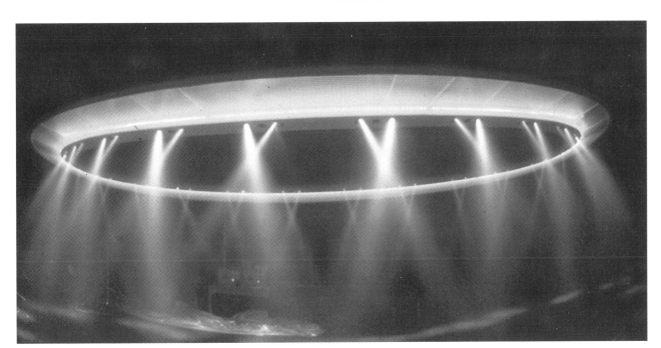

717 *Conference-lighting for Hongkong and Shanghai Bank 1985*
ERCO, Claude R. Engle
ERCO Leuchten GmbH, Lüdenscheid

718 *Conference-lighting for Hongkong and Shanghai Bank 1985*
ERCO, Claude R. Engle
ERCO Leuchten GmbH, Lüdenscheid

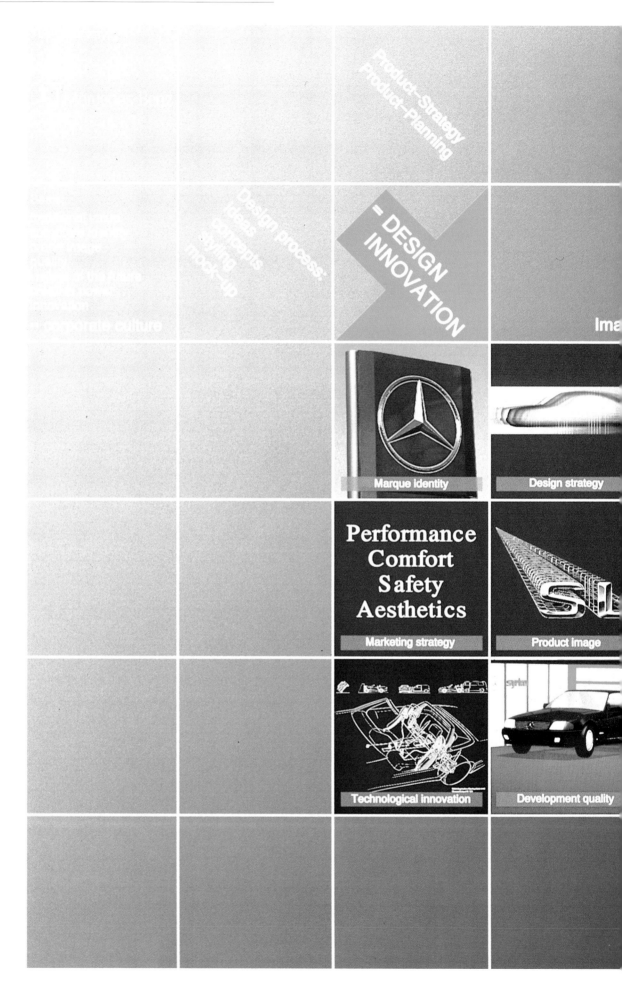

Product-Strategy
Product-Planning

Design process:
Ideas
Concepts
Styling
mock-up

= DESIGN INNOVATION

Corporate culture

Ima

Marque identity

Design strategy

Performance
Comfort
Safety
Aesthetics

Marketing strategy

Product image

Technological innovation

Development quality

ntrolling

Design philosophy

Design quality

oduct benefits: sociological, economical, ecological

Functionality

RESULT

Production quality

Material quality

A quality product with a high level of distinctiveness, emanating the typical marque characteristics and long lasting value retention

719 Studies, MacScripts, *pub-lications of project work ProduktEntwicklung Roericht*

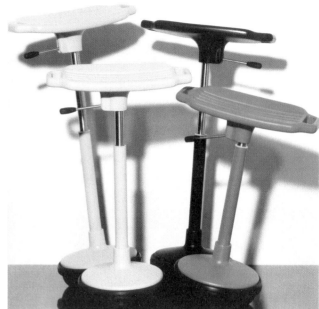

720 Stitz
*1973
ProduktEntwicklung Roericht
(Hans Roericht)
Distributed by Ingo Maurer,
Munich*

721 *Survey of work by Hans Roericht and ProduktEntwick-lung Roericht*

In recent years, ProduktEntwicklung Roericht has drawn up numerous design research studies on behalf of various clients. The result of intensive and complex work, these studies contain proposals for a sometimes radical redefinition of products and suggestions on how new fields could be accessed and how far-sighted requirement planning could be implemented. They are often the result of long workshop sessions, and are an expression of interdisciplinary teamwork, based on the international cooperation of the company's partners in London, New York, and Tokyo.

The following studies are among those prepared to date:

Study 410/10.80, "Corporate Identity Program" for Heinle-Wischer und Partner, Stuttgart

Study 800/85, "Space" (office scenarios) for Dyes, Bad Münder

Study 660/84, "The Future of PC" for NCR, Augsburg, FRG, and Dayton, Ohio

Study 660/85, "Why Building-Blocks?" for NCR

Study 660/7.86, "The Responsive (Computer) Environment" for NCR

Study 660/10.87, "Input Devices" for NCR

Study 300/9.88, "Conferring" for Wilkhahn, Bad Münder

Study 600/9.88, "New Interfaces in Commodity Trade" for Nixdorf, Paderborn

Study 680/4.88, "Multitel: Hardware and Software Concepts" for Loewe, Kronach

Study 700/12.87, "Table-Top Sink" for Bosch/Siemens Hausgeräte (BSHG)

Study 700/3.88-1, "Warm Water: Decentralized and Location-Related" for (BSHG)

Study 700/3.88-2, "Table-Top Sink" (supplement) for BSHG

Study 700/6.88-1, "Built-in Heating-Appliance" for BSHG

Study 700/6.88-2, "Built-in Heating for Kitchens" for BSHG

Study 700/11.88-1, "Air-Conditioned Storage" for BSHG

Study 700/11.88-2, "Cool Storage" for BSHG

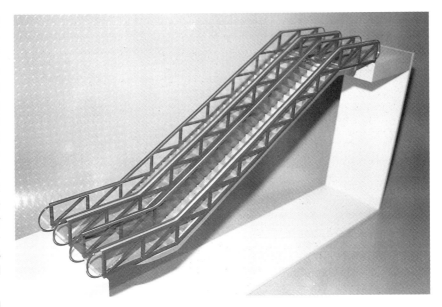

722 *Escalator (model of there-and-back system)*
1989–90
Johannes Geyer (master's degree project)

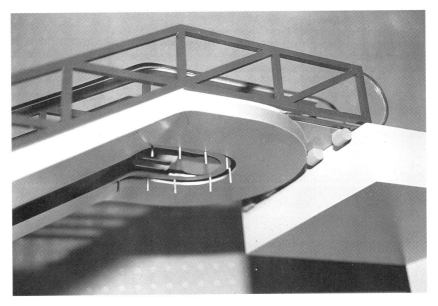

723 *Escalator (model of there-and-back system): escalator band mechanism*
1989–90
Johannes Geyer

724 *Draft of a new tramcar with a dropped frame (model)*
1988–89
Wolfgang Hasenauer

725 Minipack 900 *packaging plant*
1987
Lotsch & Partner
Benz & Hilgers GmbH, Dussel-dorf

726 Leybold L560 UV *thin-film research plant*
1988
Designed by the manufac-turers (Diethard Wenz)
Leybold AG, Hanau

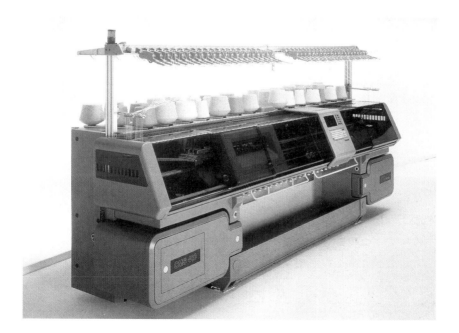

727 CMS 400 *flat knitting-machine*
1988
Rudolf M. Wieland
H. Stoll GmbH & Co., Reut-lingen

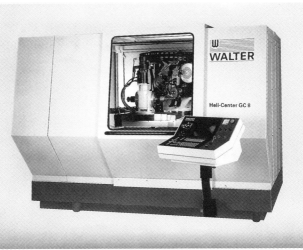

728 MH1000C *all-purpose milling- and drilling-machine*
1989
MAHO Aktiengesellschaft, Pfronten

729 Heli-Center GC8 CNC *grinding-machine*
1988
Designed by the manufacturers and Team Industrieform Günter Horntrich
Montanwerke Walter GmbH, Tübingen

730 FES *flexible deburring-system*
1987
Slany Design Team
Robert Bosch GmbH, Stuttgart

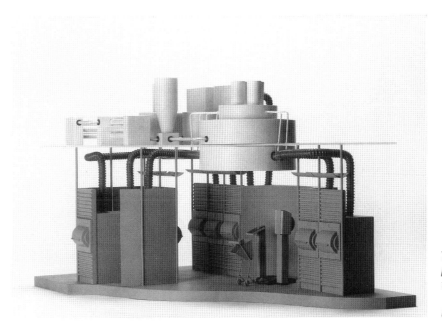

731 Laundrette *with integral purification plant (2nd Prize in the 9th Braun Awards, 1989)*
1989
Peter Eckart, Jochen Henkels

732 Kombitast-R *control-switch with* Krabt *switch-panel*
1986, 1987
design-praxis diener
Georg Schlegel GmbH & Co.
Elektronische Fabrik, Dürmen-tingen

733 *Control and regulator modules*
1988
Interform Design-Studio Schönfeld
W. C. Heraeus GmbH, Hanau

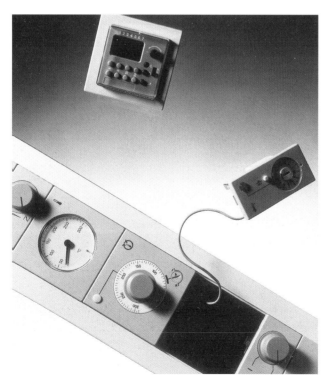

734 μKRoS316 *high-position accuracy robots with integrated image processing*
1987
frogdesign (Hartmut Esslinger)
Bodenseewerk Gerätetechnik GmbH, Überlingen

735 KCH 100 *HDTV-camera*
1988
Slany Design Team
BTS Broadcast Television
Systems GmbH, Darmstadt

736 M Solar Power Pack
1987
AEG Industrie-Produktgestal-
tung (Gerhard Röhrer)
AEG Aktiengesellschaft Raum-
fahrt, Neue Technologien,
Wedel

737 POLCID® DC *process*
control system
c. 1984
Schlagheck Schultes Design
Krupp Polysius AG, Beckum

738 *Spherical loudspeakers
(modular system)
c. 1989
Lotsch & Partner
Trinity, Dortmund*

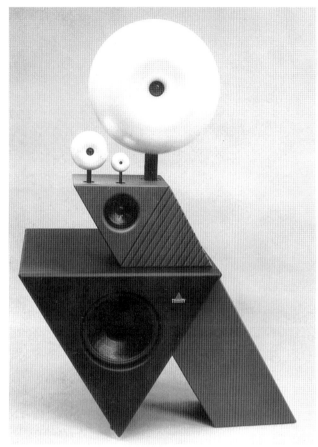

739 tele-scope *(prototype)
1985–86
Aluminum sheet and contin-
uous tube
Bernd Meurer*

740 Geha top vision portable E
*overhead projector
1988
Geha Product Design
Geha-Werke GmbH, Hano-
ver
Photo: Zimmermann*

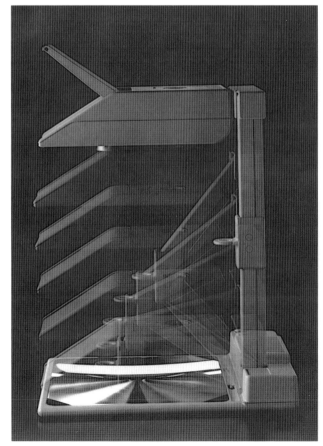

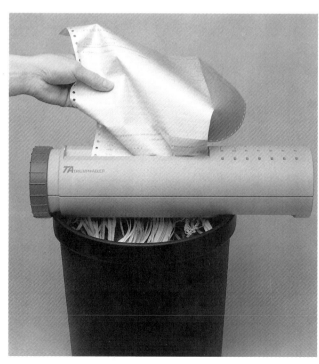

741 SECRET STAR *shredder
1989
TA-Design (K. D. Krause,
F. Stolzenberger)
TA Triumpf-Adler AG, Nurem-
berg*

742 Aachener Kopf *artifical measurement system*
1988
Development Group of Technical University Essen (Stefan Ambrozus, Michael Hosenfeld, Volker Knauff, under the direction of Friedbert Obitz)
HEAD acoustics GmbH, Aachen
Photo: Jürgen Jeibmann

743 igus 15 *energy chain*
c. 1987
igus-Team
igus GmbH, Bergisch-Gladbach

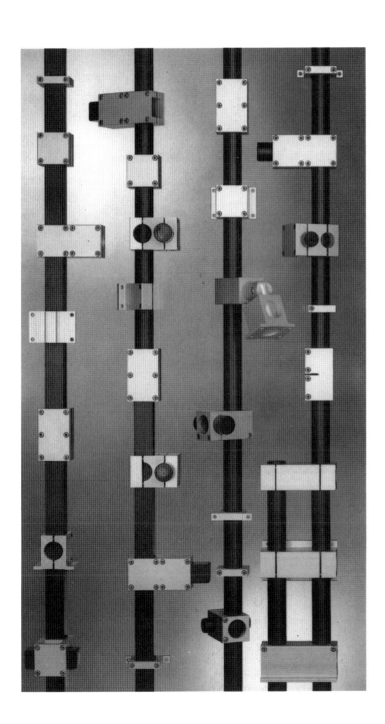

744 Baco *mounting-system*
1988–89
Frank Bahr
Rose & Krieger GmbH & Co. KG, Porta Westfalica

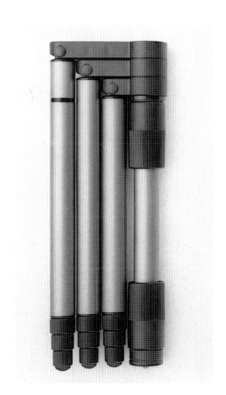

745 Magic 1 *tripod for cameras and video-cameras*
1987
Pelzel & Zaliukas
Cullmann GmbH, Langenzenn

746 Stratos *sanitary wares*
1988
frogdesign
Villeroy & Boch, Mettlach
Photo: Villeroy & Boch

747 7663/01 edelweiss
Magnum
WC sanitary wares
1987
frogdesign
Villeroy & Boch, Mettlach

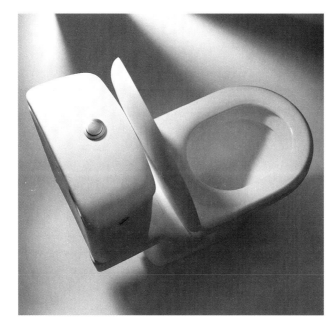

748 Magic Line *pans*
Launched in 1989
frogdesign
Fissler GmbH, Idar-Oberstein
Photo: M. Wozny

749 Küchenwerkbank pur
kitchen workbench
1988
Bulthaup-Werksdesign-Team
Bulthaup GmbH & Co., Aich
Photo: Rudolf Schmutz

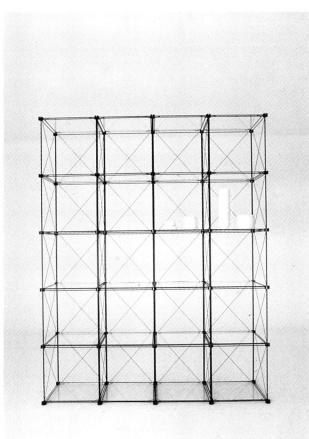

750 Leitner 6 *shelving-system*
1980
Burkhardt Leitner
Leitner GmbH Ausstellungs-
systeme, Waiblingen

751 kitchen tree *kitchen unit*
1983
Stefan Wewerka
Tecta, Lauenförde

Design-Orientated Companies
in the FRG

AEG

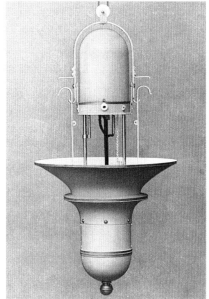

752 Ultralux Strato *spotlight for rail and direct ceiling fixture; switchable spot and flood modes.*
Design: Mercedes Design, 1987/88;
launched on the market in 1989

753 *Arc light with direct current supply for indoor lighting with indirect illumination, especially of factory halls.*
Design: Peter Behrens, 1907

754 *Rechargeable torch.*
Design: AEG Formgestaltung, Peter Sieber, c. 1955

755 *Control panel for airport firing with light wires (Hamburg Airport).*
Design: AEG Industrie-Produktgestaltung, Gerhard Röhrer, 1988;
launched on the market in 1989

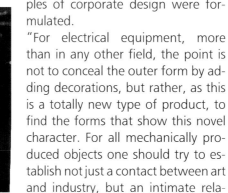

The AEG company has a long tradition in design. Peter Behrens, who was art advisor to AEG from 1907 to 1914, is considered to be the first German industrial designer. A freelance artist and architect, he not only designed buildings for AEG, but also developed products, posters, brochures, and even the typeface of the company logo which is – slightly modified – still used today. It was in his design office that the basic principles of corporate design were formulated.

"For electrical equipment, more than in any other field, the point is not to conceal the outer form by adding decorations, but rather, as this is a totally new type of product, to find the forms that show this novel character. For all mechanically produced objects one should try to establish not just a contact between art and industry, but an intimate rela-

tionship.... The design should be appropriate to the materials used and should lend itself to efficient construction and proper functioning; rather than seek to catch the eye by just being different, it should embody the good taste of the day." (Peter Behrens, 1910)

Due to wars and economic crises, it was no longer possible to adhere to these principles. A new start was made in 1953 with the setting-up of the central design department. Under the direction of Peter Sieber and his successor Eberhard Fuchs well-designed consumer goods and also capital goods – such as engine and high-voltage switches – were developed that possessed a distinctive identity. The rechargeable torch, for instance, which is still produced today, has found a place in the Museum of Modern Art, New York. Since 1986, when AEG was incorporated in the Daimler-Benz group, the company, under the influence of the central marketing department, has been promoting a new, consistent image based on Peter Behrens's principles. Product design receives new impulses through central design coordination, in cooperation with internal and external design offices, impulses which are translated into innovative product lines.

● *BLAUPUNKT*

Living with the Media

Design, taken seriously, is never supplementary to but always an integral part of the entire solution. Form expresses ideas; it's not packaging but soul. Design mediates the philosophy behind the objects. At every stage it must resist the temptation to present merely the naive pose of a pleasing appearance, because at the end of the "right" path there is always a succinct solution: a self-evident product. For functionality is not just restricted to mere functioning – to handy operation, for instance – but likewise appeals to all the senses; also (or especially?) when everyday things are fundamentally re-examined, for example a television set. Blaupunkt has taken up the challenge to find solutions for living with the media, which – by themselves – are an expression of the accentuated will for forms, and which may even prompt change in the complex "technology and dwelling" with similarly logical and sometimes surprising impacts.

With TV Modular this means, for example, that the monitor can be turned and inclined. This provides for the optimum viewing angle from various positions, allows the realization of spontaneous ideas about how to use and lay out one's rooms, and banishes all the restraints imposed by the traditional TV corner. Now it's the viewer who decides the most favorable place to watch TV at home – and not the TV set.

TV Altro stands for TV receivers with interchangeable front panels. The television set becomes a variable object, its freely selectable "looks",

ever new and fundamentally different responding to different moods and ambiences and aquiring a new quality.

With the Portable PS 45-29, Blaupunkt goes one step further in the classical design of mobile media electronics: clearly ordered lines with special emphasis on the vertical harmonize with the strictly geometrical structure of the rear panel.

Good form means appreciating the principle of "lifestyle." We take the wishes of our customers seriously.

756 TV Altro 5540 VTM

757 TV Modular MS 70–109

758 TV Portable PS 45–29

BRAUN

759 Braun Aromaster
10-plus KF45
1984
*(Colors: white, red/gray,
black)*

760 Braun Citromatic MPZ 2
1972
(Color: white)

761 Braun micron vario 3
universal cc.
1988 (basic design, 1984)
(Color: gray/metallic)

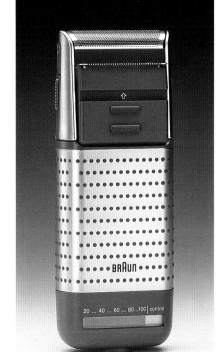

Braun Aromaster 10-plus KF 45

Automatic coffee machine for ten cups, with swing-out filter-funnel, automatic drip stop when jug is removed, "plus" switch for longer brewing time with small quantities, water container with measuring scale, cord storage space. The basic design consists of two cylinders: the cold water container at rear intersects the second cylindrical complex of filter-funnel, jug, and hotplate. This arrangement insures a closed, very compact design of small base surface. The design is intentionally restricted to only few design elements. For maximum convenience the coffee machine can be operated with one hand from one side. The sequence of the procedure is not fixed. The swing-out filter-funnel and the lids of the cold water container and the jug can be operated with a flick of a finger. Cleaning presents no problems.

Braun micron vario 3 universal cc.

Electric shaver, cord/rechargeable unit. Attachable, full-width extendable long-hair trimmer. Short-hair system and long-hair trimmer can be used simultaneously. Microcomputer-controlled charging display. Soft case, including mirror. The appliance supplements Braun's universal shaver line. Its most significant user advantage is that it can be used alternatively as a cord or rechargeable shaver. As a novelty, the universal cc has an LCD display showing the status of its rechargeable batteries. The shaving system and design of the appliance correspond to those of the Braun micron vario 3, which was launched in 1984. Characteristic features are the slim, handy basic design, the completely closed metallic housing with its rows of knobs made of soft, non-slip material, and the long-hair trimmer extendable in two steps, which can be used together with the short-hair system.

Braun Citromatic MPZ 2

Electric citrus press with drip-lock spout. Juice flows directly into a glass or other receptacle placed underneath the spout in the housing recess. The special feature of this citrus press is that the spout folds up to avoid dripping. The cone is removable and easy to clean. After use, a transparent lid protects the citrus press against dust.

ERCO

Light and Design

By redefining their corporate policy and objectives, the ERCO company have contributed to a major change in the "light-consciousness" of architects and their clients, lighting engineers, and consumers over the past twenty years.

Whereas twenty years ago – apart from prices, of course – purely aesthetic criteria played an important role in purchasing luminaires, nowadays the planning of lighting installations is mainly guided by formal, functional, light engineering considerations.

Twenty years ago, we decided to sell light instead of lights – which made it necessary to develop products in keeping with the specific light functions as we defined them.

We have developed a wide range of products, which at present comprises well over a thousand items; for these, completely new forms had to be developed. These forms, which were so different from ordinary chandeliers or freestanding luminaries, first had to be interpreted to the consumers and to architects and lighting engineers.

Now, what's so special about the attitude adopted by ERCO towards design? Design is generally understood as the aesthetic appearance of products. This results either from an aesthetic endeavor and thus constitutes an effect, or from a constructional option to solve a technical problem.

The effects resulting from aesthetic endeavors would be better termed "fashion." For it is only the shaping of constructional options in order to solve a technical problem that brings about design. Hence, new designs come into existence only on the basis of innovations, namely new solutions to a task.

The design solutions developed within a specific sector of industry form a code which is particularly evident in certain fields, such as entertainment electronics or household appliances. Such form codes may not be used in other industries since their way of thinking is different.

Thus, design results from a way of thinking, an attitude. If an attitude is applied properly, it should consistently produce designs that take account of technical requirements and possess the aesthetics of the "technically correct."

762 Gantry
Lattice beam with tracks designed by Roy Fleetwood and Eclipse spotlights designed by Mario Bellini

763 Eclipse
Fresnel spotlight for tungsten halogen lamps designed by Mario Bellini

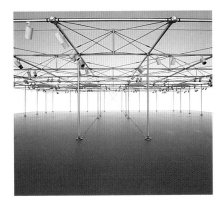

764 Axis
Wide-span light structure designed by Mario Bellini

Franz Schneider
Brakel GmbH + Co

FSB

About rgs

765 rgs 1
rgs 2
rgs 3

with Rams, is proud to present a selection of fittings whose simplicity is all the more crisply distinctive given the stylistic bedlam elsewhere. Strikingly styled and technologically innovative, these handles are adaptable to doors and windows of every description. Their plainness is startlingly novel and yet somehow familiar. The initials rgs stand in German for Rams, gray and black. All components in the rgs series are manufactured in die-cast aluminum and thermoplastic. Robust metal for the working parts, synthetic material reinforced with glass pellets for gripping areas. The technique of jointing aluminum and thermoplastic that FSB has developed is innovative and protected by patent. The rgs range is notable for its striking combination of black and gray. It is the silvery gray sheen of die-cast aluminum that makes it so distinctive. Rams and FSB deliberated at great length over the right alloy. Above all, it needed to be metallically pure and natural in appearance. The perfect answer was the form of pure aluminum with a high proportion of silicon. The choice of silicon was not accidental. No element except oxygen is present in greater abundance in the earth's crust. It is retrieved in pure form from quartz through a process of reduction with aluminum. The rgs range consciously bucks current trends in interior furnishings, offering a real alternative to flashy colors and brassy eclecticism and signaling a whole new approach. Stylistically, rgs is set to hold its own well into the next century.

766 *Detail* rgs 1

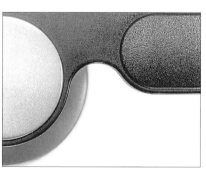

Convinced that every epoch is entitled to devise its own forms, FSB asked Dieter Rams, probably Germany's number-one designer at present, to come up with a few doorhandles. Rams accepted the challenge on one condition, to wit that he be permitted to produce not just one-offs but several entire series of fittings. He christened them rgs 1, 2, and 3. One thing led to another and he ended up with a collection comprising 27 separate items. As well as the three doorhandles, there are two window-grips, two doorhandles for narrow frames, roses, narrow backplates, broad backplates, fittings for lavatory doors, a furniture-grip, and two doorstoppers. FSB, in conjunction

767 *Detail* rgs 3

GERMAN WINES

Deutsches Weininstitut GmbH, Mainz

Careful research is necessary for good creative design in advertising. The German wine industry conducted extensive research among wine drinkers and discovered that German wines were misunderstood by both consumers and the wine trade. A communications campaign was needed to enhance the image of today's German wines and to convey the message that they are light, elegant, and fashionable. A series of impressionistic advertisements in a colorful aquarelle style were created for upscale consumer and trade publications. The handwritten text works together with the advertisement's subject matter and style to deliver a straightforward message and an overall impression of elegance, contemporary style and lightness. Initially three themes were introduced: wine with contemporary cuisine; wines for relaxed, summer enjoyment; wines for the festive holiday season. Each asked the reader a simple question about wine and provided the response: "The perfect answer is German wine".

To extend and reinforce the campaign, the aquarelle style was adopted for a wide range of promotional materials, including scenic posters, educational booklets, menu and winelist covers. In both promotional materials and advertisements the consistent style and message help to create and reinforce a new and appropriate image for German wines in the English-speaking world.

Which wine tastes light enough to enjoy before meals, but bold enough to serve with them? The perfect answer is German Wine.

GERMAN WINES
LIGHT AND ELEGANT
naturally

Both the contemporary artwork and copy of this new advertisement for German wine delivers the message that German wines are light, elegant and appropriate with food.

Garden Technology with System

769 GARDENA V12 *accu-system: A single high-perform-ance power-pack for a wide range of units.*
Design: Franco Clivio.

GARDENA's exemplary success story began more then twenty-five years ago with the invention of the waterhose click-system. These products were something completely new, in concept, in construction, and in design. Close cooperation with graduates of the Hochschule für Gestaltung in Ulm gave GARDE-NA its unique reputation: unconventional garden equipment with technically sophisticated standards and yet a highly attractive appearance! Durable products, which make high-quality plastics presentable; solid in appearance and easy to use.

Product development continues consistently and intensively using new technology and ideas, such as computer-controlled irrigation systems or the new V12 accu-system, with which a wide range of units can be operated without cables by a single power pack.

GARDENA products are developed and manufactured in the company's own production plants, exactly designed down to the last detail and presented to the trade in an extraordinary manner.

GARDENA products are known today throughout the world for their trend-setting technology, equipment, and design. They figure at the top in consumer tests and continually receive prizes for design. These awards are recognition of the high investments in product development, material research, and manufacturing technology and evidence of GARDENA's accomplishments in the field of garden technology with respect to design.

770 GARDENA *irrigation technology: Computer-controlled irrigation systems for the hobby gardener.*
Design: Franco Clivio.
771 GARDENA 850e *electric pump:*
In 1989 it was awarded first prize in the competition for design with respect to non-polluting products.
Design: Franco Clivio.

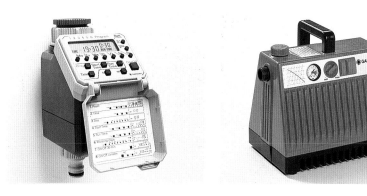

HEWI

Today, HEWI hardware has attained a significant place in the international market. This is due to product development that is distinguished by creative design and the use of appropriate material. HEWI design results from the search for clean, simple, functional form. This principle gives the HEWI program its consistent style, with all parts complementing one another. The cornerstone of HEWI style is the 111 lever handle, with its U-shape and round cross-section that reduces the design to its clearest geometric form. With this style established, other product programs were developed, such as pulls, hooks, hinges, bathroom accessories, and the railing system.

As important as effective design are the internal characteristics of the product. High-quality materials and carefully developed technology assure a high level of function. All HEWI products benefit from the qualities inherent in the material nylon: it is visually brilliant on the surface, easy to care for, and strong. The texture of nylon is similar to that of wool and silk, and it always feels pleasantly warm.

HEWI's 13 colors also are an important design element, allowing personal accents in decor.

The HEWI program enables a uniform design theme to be used throughout the house from the entrance, via the staircase and closets, to hardware for bathroom cabinets and accessories.

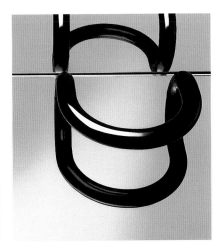

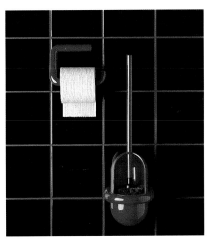

778 Krups Espresso Novo Plus

779 Krups CompactAroma 10 Luxe

780 Krups 3 Mix 4004

Tasteful, distinctive design has always been a characteristic of Krups products. The very first model of the Krups 3 Mix series blended efficiency with functionality and ergonomics.

In today's age of corporate identity, product design has acquired prominent status as a blend of performance, appearance, and "philosophy." For Krups, design is an expression of corporate culture and underlines both the aesthetic and the social orientation of its products.

Aspects such as utility, visual appeal, distinctiveness, and emotiveness are product design criteria that unite the practical, the aesthetic, and the symbolic.

Unique product design gives Krups a competitive edge. Clearly defined, positive associations based on a limited range of striking, typical design features come to symbolize quality, innovation, modernity, functionality, and product benefits. Such features therefore facilitate recognition, help the user to identify the product, and promote brand loyalty.

Krups product design adopts an international outlook, presenting Krups as a lifestyle brand for the serious cook. The company sees itself as a top-grade manufacturer and quality leader in the premium market, offering everything from coffee and espresso machines to kitchen aids.

LAMY

Writing by hand

Situated in the beautiful city of Heidelberg the firm of Lamy sees its main task as developing, manufacturing and selling the best handwriting tools.

C. Josef Lamy GmbH has, in fact, made a whole science out of studying how different writing methods should affect the design of the instruments used. As a guideline for the activities of the company, its "Mission Statement" says that Lamy products should be:
— Function-oriented, fulfilling every requirement of handwriting tolls.
— Innovative, intelligent and aesthetic — a high quality solution to the problem of writing by hand.

Continuity and development
The company was founded in 1930 by C. Josef Lamy. Dr. Manfred Lamy, son of the founder of the family-owned company, created a new product design concept in 1966 by adopting the Bauhaus idea, embodied in the statement "form follows function." The result was a product that triggered off an entire design development programme.

In the late 60s he set up a design team with a group of freelance product and graphic designers, the company's engineers and marketing people, and himself as chairman. In 20 years, using the same designers, Lamy created not only a strong product family but also a strong product and company image. Both design and technical innovation were the result of Lamy's consequent product strategy. Examples are the solid, spring-operated stainless steel clip of

781 *Heidelberg production facilities*

the product families LAMY 2000 and cp 1, the brush finishing of plastic and stainless steel (again 2000 and cp 1), and the injection moulding of two different materials in one operation (LAMY white pen).

The Lamy visual identy
The visual identity of Lamy has developed in stages. The Lamy logotype was used for the first time in 1952. With the commissioning of Gerd A. Müller in 1966 the house colours were established as being black and silver and with the launching of the LAMY white pen in 1982, white was added to the graphic colour scheme. "Physical form and graphics come gradually," says Dr. Lamy, managing director since 1974, "but they do not come haphazardly; the product criteria were set down at an early stage, and we were one of the first German companies to launch a design manual."

782 Lamy unic

783 Lamy 2000

784 Lamy white pen

LOEWE.

High-Tech Made in Germany

785 Loewe Concept
Innovative design, the newest digital technology as well as functional detail make the "Concept" range appeal to a young target group, who get enjoyment out of technical sophistication and design.

786 Loewe Art 95 Sat
When Loewe conceived its first television of the new type, the intention was to create a television that reflects state-of-the-art technology. The harmony of technical, functional and design quality has won this television numerous design prizes.

Loewe was one of the first German companies to be active in the electronics industry. Founded in Berlin in 1923, Loewe played a major role in the technical development of radio and television; numerous inventions are associated with the name Loewe. In 1931, for example, the company presented the first electronic television set fitted with a tube. In 1981 Loewe was the first company in Europe to produce a stereo color television set.

The company's trailblazing work in the field of development and its ability to keep coming up with new ideas are reflected time and again in its creative range of products. The quality and performance concept of Loewe's products is consistently geared to buyers who demand high standards and who are looking for alternatives to mass products that lack a distinctive image. Loewe supplies high-tech products with its Art Sat range. Integrated direct satellite reception, multistandard compatibility, including the D2-Mac standard, and thus a further improved quality of picture and sound are the characteristics of this range of television at the top of the market.

With its Concept television range, Loewe again demonstrates its ability to come up with intelligent ideas for products. Various systems offer the television, video, and hi-fi enthusiast optimal audio and visual conditions. Innovative design, the latest digital technology, and uncompromising functional detail are the hallmarks of the Concept range.

In the future, too, Loewe will strive to be first on the market with new high-quality products that stand out from the rest through up-to date design.

meroform®

Each time a designer embarks on a new project he faces a problem. The problem Max Mengeringhausen solved with his "tube construction" (MERO stands for MEngeringhausens ROhrbauweise, i.e. tube construction) can be well described by a quotation from Walter Gropius: "I believe that a new way has to be found to express also in architecture the vast changes of our time." (*Architektur*, Frankfurt/Hamburg 1956) Mengeringhausen's solution was the tube and node system. Derived from nature, this system could and still can be industrially mass-produced, can be applied to buildings of various purposes, and allows for variable design and later expansion of the buildings.

The basic principle of the tube and node system is "variety of application." Architects, engineers, and interior designers all over the world rely on tubes and nodes for building a hangar of several hundred meters' span, just as exhibition designers do when planning an imposing fairstand. The MERO construction kit is extremely simple – just a set of tubes and nodes of different sizes and diameters; over the past forty years its versatility has been increased through detail improvements and the provision of a large number of useful accessories.

Thus, the user in the field of fairs and exhibitions (M12 construction system) can choose from a variety of light fittings, display programs, decorative elements, dome or tunnel vaults, and multistory stands.

For several years now the indus-

trialized countries have been aware of the necessity to protect the environment. MERO has been able to improve the tube and node system in the area of environmental technology. One example is that it is possible to integrate solar panels into the system.

MERO's plans for the future are to enter new spheres of applicability for the MERO system. The priorities hereby are that the products must be ecologically beneficial and meet MERO's high standards in design.

Mercedes-Benz

The Mercedes-Benz-Design Philosophy and a Few Typical Applications

790 *Mercedes-Benz SL-Range*

As part of the "Designed in Germany" exhibition Mercedes-Benz is offering interested visitors an inside view of the company's design philosophy.

SL-Range

The new Mercedes-Benz SL design is intended both to set a real example and to stand the test of time. Exotic formal ornamentation, which experience shows soon loses its attraction, is not compatible with such a philosophy: the brand identity and the SL's image would inevitably be forfeited.

The SL's unmistakable appearance is characterized by exceptional design features: an extended hood with the SL radiator grille, which has evolved over the years, a short and robust roof structure, and compact tail dimensions. Building on these underlying elements, the new version is a "typical SL."

Mercedes accordingly produced the new roadster in two versions with identical lines – either as a true convertible (with a cloth roof which can be fully lowered automatically) or with one of two roofs (cloth-based or hardtop).

The SL's external appearance also radiates a sense of tradition, of enduring values, of great prestige, of safety, comfort, and high performance – the result of a complex and acutely sensitive design process.

And only one name can be associated with the individual design stages and this unique combination of formal attractiveness and perfect functionality: the Mercedes-Benz SL. Indeed, the new SL emphasizes the leading role Mercedes-Benz design plays in the automobile industry. In other words, despite the common brand image they share, each model has its own formally substantive individual character.

792 *Mercedes-Benz* T-*Range*
Mercedes-Benz CE-*Range*
Mercedes-Benz 300-*Range*

CE and T Ranges

The CE and T models, two medium-size Mercedes automobiles, as well as the limousines not shown here, all have a common denominator in formal terms, namely the uniform front hood components typical for Mercedes cars and fenders that function as integrated front cowlings. The fender and apron systems were also designed to constitute formal unity.

CE-Range

The new Mercedes 300 CE coupe rounds out the line of medium-size Mercedes automobiles by successfully combining the formal elements typical of the 124 line limousines and a completely distinct design unique to the coupe. The front of the vehicle in particular fits naturally into the formal design pattern set for the car as a whole. In contrast to its predecessors, however, the new coupe has an even more distinctive overall image of its own owing to the use of unique formal elements and special bodywork details.

Smooth surfaces and generously designed side cowlings made of metallic-colored thermoplastic polyurethane, combined with fender coverings that also use the metallic contrast colors, set this coupe off visually from the other Mercedes models.

The overall impression of the coupe is also distinctive thanks to the extremely harmonious proportions and the soft, flowing lines of the roof and tail.

More favorable proportions, combined with an innovative roof design and rear window shape, made it possible to lower the upper edge of the trunk by 35 mm, while retaining aerodynamic holding every bit as good as that of the limousine.

T-Range

The T series is just as homogeneous in overall design, with a front-to-mid section identical with the lines that have meanwhile become associated with the 124 series limousines, illustrating the fact that the five-door version was integrated at an early date into the formal development concept used for the medium-size Mercedes models. This symbiosis of functionality and aesthetics comes to light in exquisite stylistic features – the functional hatchback, complete with electromechanical locking mechanism, which merges harmoniously in formal terms with the taillights, and a new roof railing that is incorporated smoothly into the lines of the roof.

190 Range

The Mercedes-Benz 190 has now been available for five years and its success set the tone for up-market compact cars. An important new feature was its tail design, which has

since become a hallmark of the series. The 1989 model incorporates a whole range of detail modifications that further refine the 190 model and integrate it more strongly into the Mercedes-Benz family.

The changes that most meet the eye are the new front and tail aprons, the added door scuffplate cowlings, and the smooth-surface side paneling – all of which are harmoniously color-coordinated to match the color of the body. There are now 12 colors to match the selection of 24 body colors available.

The dropped tail apron also has aerodynamic advantages. The side paneling made of high-grade glass-fiber-reinforced synthetic material affords further side shielding characteristics and, in the case of more severe damage, significantly reduces service time and repair costs as whole sections can simply be replaced at once.

793 *Mercedes-Benz*
190-*Range*

Miele

794 *Design is art made practical. Objects that look good not just today, but will be the classics of tomorrow.*

795 *The Miele Black Diamond is extremely mobile with three castor wheels effortlessly guiding it around the furniture.*

796 *Several attachments available to suit almost any type of surface and need are easily accessible in the integrated tray.*

The Top Class of Vacuum-Cleaners: Miele Black Diamond

Miele-design for the things you use every day. Good looks which stand out from the crowd. Concentrating on essential functions emphasizes the level of technology used in Miele appliances. Elegant, simple and charming: the Miele Black Diamond. The vacuum-cleaner that leads the way with the best of design not only in appearance but also in operational features. Superb performance and good looks – Miele's up-to-date household technology with character.

New developments coupled with reliable design have led to the production of the Miele Black Diamond. Miele's answer to the needs of smaller households. A compact vacuum-cleaner, now with a new look. Top-

rate technology has led to the creation of a small vacuum-cleaner without having to make any compromises in design or features. Well-known Miele perfection coupled with even greater maneuverability. You can see the perfect union of quality and performance in an elegant form.

Performance: electronic suction-power regulation from 250 to 1,100 W. Easily accessible integrated accessories for cleaning different surfaces – flooring to soft furnishings and curtains to books. A holder for the suction tube and hose enables easy storage.

Maneuverability: the Miele Black Diamond is extremely mobile with three castor wheels, rotating 360° to take the cleaner around any corner. A buffer strip gives the cleaner and furniture added protection. Even the suction hose rotates 360° in its socket for extra mobility. The telescopic suction tube can be adjusted easily to the correct height for easy cleaning.

Superb cleaning performance: with multiple protection to ensure that only clean air is expelled from the cleaner. The double-layered dustbag keeps the dust in and lets the air out. The motor is protected by a filter to protect it from dirt and the "air-clean" exhaust filter thoroughly cleans the air as it is expelled. It even retains microscopically small dust particles and pollen to leave the air 99.9 % particle-free.

Rowenta

The Old And The New

Rowenta filtermatic® thermo FK-70S

An Example of Rowenta's Design Philosophy

Rowenta is known and accepted worldwide as a producer of small electrical appliances with manufacturing plants in West Germany and France, subsidiaries in Europe and overseas, and agencies all over the world. Rowenta belongs to the SEB Group (Ecully-Lyon, France). Other members of the group are CALOR, SEB S.A., TEFAL, and VOGALU. Rowenta owes its present top position in the market both to the outstanding design level of its products and to its uncompromisingly high level of production quality. The realization of ideas for the future is one of Rowenta's main principles and an integral part of its design objectives. This is proved by the high number of awards given to Rowenta by design juries in West Germany and abroad. The FK-70S coffee machine was selected from the enormous range of Rowenta products. In over a century of corporate history, special attention has always been given to coffee preparation. The first coffee machine for domestic use appeared in the Rowenta catalog in 1919.

The pleasure of drinking coffee, known in the past only to very few nations, has in the meantime conquered the whole world. The reviving cup of coffee "in between" is just as satisfying as the contemplative pleasure of a cup of coffee at a beautifully laid table.

The Rowenta Filtermatic has especially been designed for this reason. It is a logical development of the well-known coffee machine, incorporating novel features. The design does not aim to be spectacularly modern, with the risk of soon becoming outmoded: it symbolizes and represents long-term quality.

The primary requirements of a coffee machine, e.g. technical safety, are complemented by unique special product functions such as automatic power cut-off when the coffee is ready, good overview of operating elements, detachable water-tank with water-level indicator, insulated pot with high resistance to breaking, pouring without spillage. Comfortable handling proves the ease of use. The aesthetically pleasing appearance, perfectly smooth and soft forms, well-balanced proportions and careful detailing make for the distinctive overall appearance. Therefore, the FK-70S filtermatic® thermo meets the requirements. This product guarantees long life quality. Rowenta-Werke GmbH, Offenbach/Main

F.A. Stützer (Head of Design Department)

797 Rowenta filtermatic® FK-70
Coffeemaker for 2–8 cups with shock-resistant thermal jug, removable water-tank with water-level gauge, illuminated on-switch, automatic switch-off at the end of brewing, cord storage.

798 *The aesthetically pleasing appearance and perfectly smooth and soft forms characterize this shock-resistant thermal jug.*

SCHOTT ZWIESEL

Schott – Zwiesel – Glaswerke AG

799 Geometria
Design: Rolf Krüger
1989

800 Teapot
Design: Wilhelm Wagenfeld
1932, modified 1958

801 Malmö
Design: Heinrich Löffelhardt
1967

Schott:
Designing for a Special Material

There's no challenge in designing a practical drinking-glass, a vase, or a bowl. You can drink perfectly well from almost any kind of glass; drinking-glasses have satisfactorily fulfilled functional requirements for centuries. This is perhaps the reason why only rarely do the industrial design experts come up with new ideas. Wilhelm Wagenfeld is one of the few exceptions – in 1932 he designed a tea service made from heat-resistant glass.

Glass is a unique substance. The oldest man-made material known, it has a comparatively high density and weight. It is impervious to liquids and gases but at the same time transparent – very real and yet also spiritual. Glass is like no other substance: you don't just look at the surface, you take in the whole essence of the object – you can always see the back of a glass.

The real challenge in designing a glass is to ensure not its functional, but rather its aesthetic quality. This explains why glasses come in all shapes and sizes. The real priority in designing with glass is not just to create a practical vase or wine-glass, but to incorporate shape, light, and color into the design.

That's the difference between glass design and other product design. Glass-designers should be aware of these special creative requirements.

MODelec® – Modular System:
Prize-Winning for Design
and Innovation

802–804 Modular System
MODelec®
Design and development:
Siegfried Schulte

Electric motors and machines no longer need to be supplied with feed-cable connected, but can be used with separate plugs and/or cable systems. Due to the different technical and national requirements (110, 220, 240, 380 V, 2-, 3-, 4-, 5-poles, VDE, SEV, UL; with/without switch; motor protection on/off, emergency stop; plug right or left or integrated; with/without screw terminals, etc.) many problems requiring costly individual solutions have occurred for manufacturers and craftsmen: prototypes for large series production or short runs, or one-off jobs cannot be made in a short time. Approved component assemblies have been possible only with high costs for tooling and testing in line with customer requirements. Even major manufacturers cannot afford to keep stocks for all necessary functional options and feature positions.

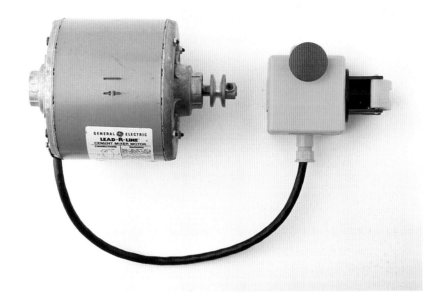

The basic housing of our MODelec® modular system incorporates all elements: plugs for all voltages and configurations, different-diameter cable glands, capacitor housings, etc. Wiring-connections are built directly into the housing with self-locking 6.3 spade or screw terminals.
MODelec® has self-locking covers with additional safety-catches. It can be extended with low development and tooling costs to provide individual solutions for customers. It achieves an enclosure rating of IP 55 without

separate gaskets for seals. Each self-locking module can be assembled in four 90°-rotated positions. Modules can be made to suit customer and national requirements. MODelec® is an international system with inductive switching capacity for connecting electric motors and appliances.
MODelec® was awarded the First State Prize of North-Rhine-Westphalia for design and innovation and the prize of the 1988 Hanover if'88 for good design; it was selected to represent the Federal Republic of Germany at the 1st International Design Show 1988 in Singapore and at the World Design Exposition 1989 in Nagoya, Japan.

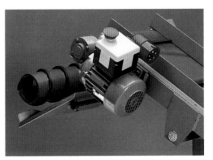

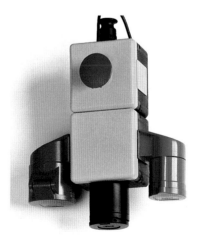

SIEMENS

805 *Office Communication Terminal* Complus
Design:
Siemens Design
Harry Hentschel

Complus is a compact apparatus for speech, text, and data communication. It comprises a 10-inch screen and a freely movable keyboard which, when not in use, can be "parked" between screen and screen base. The optimal ergonomic design of the keyboard and the use of windows render the machine extremely user-friendly: clearly arranged menus can be superimposed on the information on the non-reflecting flicker-free screen.

With the addition of a printer, Complus can also be used as a typewriter. Additional facilities include

– on-hook dialing
– register for max. 120 entries
– register dialing
– noting-function and automatic redialing
– preparation of texts for videotex communications
– videotex-telex and letters (one DIN A 4 page)
– operational and register protection through use of password
– macromemory with simple learning function for fully automatic access to often-needed applications
– database destination register for fully automatic call set-up, including all line parameters and identifications.

VIE⌇MANN

Good Design: An Important Corporate Task

"The performance of a corporation and the quality of its products can only be effectively portrayed using a consistent visual image and good design. As I see it, good design is an ongoing task because it supports my efforts to familiarize the public with high-grade technology. It is important to introduce and maintain a consistent line and not allow oneself to be diverted by temporary, fashionable trends. Anton Stankowski's principle of 'concentration through omission' applies to graphics as well as to the design of technical products. Working intensively with design gives me valuable ideas on how to implement new product ideas and techniques – corporate performance and aesthetics have to go hand in hand in order to give a corporation its own unique identity. The recognition that Viessmann products enjoy today is attributable not least to our efforts to achieve good design." (Hans Viessmann)

A Brief Profile of the Viessmann Werke

In 1917, the Viessmann Werke, then a small mechanical engineering company, was founded in Hof (Saale).
Group sales in 1988 amounted to DM 825 million. Approximately 5,300 people are employed in its eleven production facilities and branches, both in Germany and abroad.

Viessmann is the world's largest producer of steel heating-boilers.
The Viessmann group is, moreover, one of the leading European manufacturers of walk-in freezers, refrigerators, and coolers.

Vitola-Biferral-SR: A New Generation of Heating-Boilers

The new technology can already be seen in the external form of the boiler: the body and the combustion area form a vertical cylinder – the burner is placed on top. Like all Vitola-Bifferal boilers, the SR also has the tried-and-proven dual-shell com-

pound heating-surface made of two ferrous materials, namely cast-iron and steel. The bottom of the combustion chamber is also based on a dual-shell design and thus does not cause condensation of the combustion gases. A favorable distribution of heat is thus insured, which serves to counteract any condensation of the heating-gases. When equipped with the corresponding pressure-jet gas burner, the Vitola-Biferral-SR fulfills all the requirements of the Blue Angel environmental protection seal for low emission levels and energy-saving operation, even without an exhaust recovery system.

VORWERK

Teppichboden

Creativity instead of Monotony

The present carpeting market is characterized by uniformity and homogeneity. The product has declined to become a uniform article, a "commodity product." After all elements of an interior have been chosen, decorators chose a matching carpet, usually beige or gray.

With its new carpeting collection Dialog, Vorwerk aims to put carpeting back in its role as one of the most important design elements in a room.

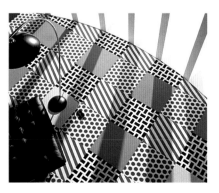

Dialog with Artists and Architects

Together with 16 international artists and architects Vorwerk Teppichwerke has developed the new Dialog collection. This collection is not a signed, limited edition at artificially inflated prices – it is not a substitute for art, but rather a mass-production article at a reasonable price for home and business use.

The artists and architects have created 46 designs and 80 different color combinations; these designer carpets are matched by a line of single-shade carpets, opening up a vast range of creative carpeting solutions.

Carpeting Can Communicate

Carpeting provides the link between floor and furniture. It is the go-between for walls. It meshes with neighboring carpet designs and other floor-coverings in a dialogue of color and form. Today's trend in interior decorating is towards wider spaces with clear lines and less furniture, making floor design more conscious and more important. "Creative floors" has been Vorwerk's motto for a number of years, standing for practicality combined with high aesthetic standards. The new Dialog collection is its logical continuation.

Artists and Architects

Hans Ullrich Bitsch, Norman Foster, Sam Francis, Michael Graves, Milton Glaser, Zaha M. Hadid, David Hockney, Arata Isozaki, Sol LeWitt, Roy Lichtenstein, Richard Meier, Jean Nouvel, Mimmo Paladino, Gerhard Richter, Matteo Thun, O. M. Ungers.

Wilkhahn

The company was founded in Bad Münder in 1907 by two master carpenters, Christian Wilkening and Friedrich Hahne. Initially, Wilkening & Hahne manufactured sturdy, good-quality chairs in keeping with the bourgeois tastes of the day. It was Fritz Hahne who prompted the firm's reorientation after World War II. Under his management, Wilkhahn became a pioneer of state-of-the-art furniture design. Georg Leowald, an architect and designer, played a key role in this change, designing the first seating using glass-fiber-reinforced plastic for Wilkhahn. The sixties saw fruitful and intensive collaboration between the company and the Ulm Hochschule für Gestaltung, efforts that have had a lasting impact. The result was something which would today be called corporate design, namely the congruent interlinking of product design and product communication. At the same time, a long-term strategy was developed, in line with which the company concentrated forthwith on furniture for offices and commercial premises.

In 1971, under the direction of Klaus Franck, an in-house design department was established, which was also to coordinate links with outside designers. Since 1986, this department has been operating independently under the name of "Wiege" (Wilkhahn Entwicklungs-Gesellschaft), also working for third parties. Alongside product design, its activities include – and here it cooperates with the marketing department – preserving and further

810 *Bad Münder production facilities, designed by Frei Otto*

developing Wilkhahn's visual image. Wilkhahn can also look back on a tradition of close ties to freelance designers, such as Herbert Ohl and Nick Roericht. The company's efforts to manufacture well-conceived products that have a profile of their own have been accorded recognition in the shape of numerous German and international awards. Wilkhahn's corporate philosophy rests not only on a design policy that knows no compromises but also on a notion of social culture. This is expressed in a cooperative style of management that is based on a sense of fairness; and, since 1971, on a staff profit-sharing scheme. The firm has been managed since 1982 by Theodor Diener; under his careful eye the marketing department has been systematically expanded with a view to the planned internationalization of the company's activities. Its clear sense of orientation, its efficiency, and its unbroken tradition have made Wilkhahn an international market leader. Today, the company has 500 employees and subsidiaries in France, Great Britain, Japan, Spain, and Switzerland; its products

are manufactured under license in Australia, Brazil, and the USA; and it has representatives in thirty other countries. Sales volume in 1989 was approximately DM 105 million, half of this being accounted for by exports – proof of the worldwide acceptance enjoyed by Wilkhahn products with their exemplary design.

811 *"P" Office-chair line, designed by Franckl Sauer*

Since 1853, WMF company policy has been strongly influenced by the determination to provide an extremely varied and demanding public with the best possible solutions for table and kitchen problems. The company has repeatedly set standards of innovation in function and design without having in the least jeopardized the consumers' acceptance of WMF products. For decades now, WMF has led the cutlery market in Germany, has been one of the most important manufacturers of cooking-utensils, and has played a leading role in the production of commercial coffee machines. WMF products are exported all over the world.

The WMF Design Workshop, started in 1985, carries on a tradition which began in the twenties. In 1927, in fact, the "New Handicrafts Department" was established in Geislingen — a metal workshop outside the traditional production area, but still within the organization. This department set the trend for the firm's metalware program, shifting the emphasis of the product program from fashionably acceptable mass production towards artistic and experimentally oriented craft. In addition to WMF employees, such well-known craftsmen as Richard Riemerschmid, Paul Haustein, and Fritz August Breuhaus, figured amongst the designers.

The fifties saw the beginning of the Wagenfeld era. Similarly to the way in which Breuhaus had worked with silver-plated metal, Wilhelm Wagenfeld, strongly influenced by the Bauhaus, used the effects of the pure surfaces of Cromargan. His clean shapes exploit the play of light on the intensely differentiated curved and plane surfaces.

The latest designs by Matteo Thun (Milan) and Jo Laubner can only be interpreted against this background and tradition. The designs achieve additional effect through the reflectiveness of the base-mounts, handles, and knobs. Characteristic of the late eighties is the intensified endeavor to create an emotional bond between user and object, to endow surface and shape with new excitement and new energy. This is a new form of communication, the acceptance of which is based on a successful relationship between function and fiction.

West Germany

The Pyramids of Zeiss: The New Geometry for Microscopes

For more than 140 years, Zeiss has been in the forefront of the industry with innovations in microscopy.
Ernst Abbe's work on image formation in the microscope, which still serves as the basis of modern microscope optics, the development of Köhler illumination, phase contrast, antireflection coating, and Plan-Apochromat objectives – these are all advances that have changed the course of microscopy and were realized industrially by Zeiss.
In 1986, another chapter in the history of Zeiss microscopy began with the "pyramids of Zeiss." A new generation of highly versatile microscopes with infinite image distance now makes it possible to perform all microscope techniques with exceptional ease.
The pyramids of Zeiss ideally combine state-of-the-art technology and an aesthetic, functional design. Versatility of application and perfect ergonomics are further outstanding features which set these microscopes apart in a class all of their own.

ICS optics: All microscopes feature advanced, newly computed optics which Zeiss has named ICS optics (Infinity Color-corrected System). It guarantees brilliant, aberration-free images over an exceptionally wide field with all available techniques.
SI design: The innovative, system-integrated architecture of the new Zeiss microscopes permits incorpora-

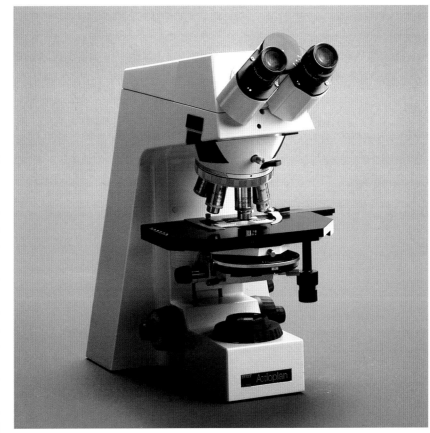

tion of all illuminating and contrast-enhancing techniques without impairing the integrity of the total system.
A well-devised ergonomic design, utmost reliability, long-term performance, and optimum value further characterize the "pyramids of Zeiss," and point the way to the future.
But don't just take our word for it – see for yourself what an important difference the new Axioplan universal microscope from Zeiss can make in your research.

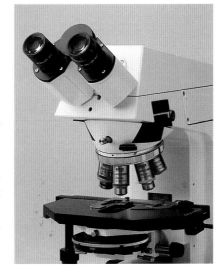

einrichtung

817 "Quadrondo", *designed by Erwin Nagel.*
Two tables in one: with just a few movements of the hand the round table top can be converted into a square one.

manufacturer of products designed for a much broader scope of cultivated living.

A dialogue between function and esthetics

The trend toward individuality is changing our lives, our attitude towards our surroundings. External impulses, particularly from art, are helping to reshape our environment. It is Rostenthal's endeavor to combine the creativity of art with the functionality of things of everyday use.

World-famous artists have been commissioned by Rosenthal to design furniture which achieves a perfect synthesis of art and function, of esthetic appeal and practicality. The Rosenthal furniture program covers three main themes:
— Furniture for living and working environments.
— Furniture for hospitality.
— Furniture which combines art and design.

818 "Corner", *designed by Marcello Morandini.*
A shelf system based on the parallelogram – functional furniture and work of art rolled into one.

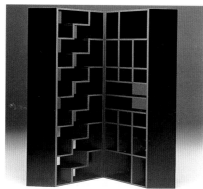

"Design for living" – by Rosenthal

Rosenthal has been writing its own chapter of German design history since the middle of the 50s. In close teamwork with famous artists and designers Rosenthal manufactures products for the cultivated dining table which convince by their highly esthetic quality and contribute — each in its own right — to the culture of our time.

Anyone who, like Rosenthal, sees design as part of our culture and whose entrepreneurial motives are guided by a cultural responsibility can easily think in terms much broader than those dictated by specific materials or applications. Thus it was a logical step for Rosenthal, in 1972, to introduce its first furniture collection, completing a process of development from a manufacturer of porcelain through to a

819 "Life Service", *designed by Jochen Flacke.*
The mobile sideboard system with the flexible interior.

Appendix

The following appendix presents important West German designers, design-related institutions and design awards. It also enumerates important journals that regularly report on design in Germany and, in addition, provides a select list of recommended further reading to the individual chapters of the present book. When compiling this information, we were of necessity forced to restrict ourselves to a modest number of entries; the choice made therefore should not be understood as a value judgment on the part of the editors. This is particularly true of the profiles of designers. It was not possible to include numerous important designers and design studios for the simple fact that space constraints compelled us to limit ourselves to 25 profiles, which at the same time had to provide a representative section spanning 1949 to the present day. Should you wish to have more detailed and extensive information, we would like to recommend *Industrie-Designer. Portraits und Profile*, a constantly updated handbook issued by the Verband Deutscher Industrie-Designer e. V. (VDID), Altestadt 8, D-4000 Düsseldorf 1, Federal Republic of Germany.

Designers

Kerstin Bartlmae was born in Stockholm, Sweden, in 1941. In 1956 she underwent practical training in a ceramics workshop in Stockholm, and from 1957 onward she attended evening classes at the Stockholm College of Art. In 1958 she commenced studies at an Italian art college in Florence, and three years later qualified as an industrial ceramicist, going on to work for Swedish companies. In 1962, she went to the HfG Ulm to study product design, graduating in 1967; in 1965/66 she had done work for a design studio in Milan. From 1968 to 1969, Bartlmae worked under Herbert Lindinger at the Institute for Product Design in Ulm, before setting up her own design studio in Ulm in 1969.

Since 1959 she has received numerous awards for her products in industrial design, technical consumer goods, and home and office furniture. Kerstin Bartlmae has worked (in collaboration with Volker Bartlmae) for firms such as Soehnle, Faber-Castell, Fröscher-Sitform, Casala Möbelwerke, and Bodenseewerk.

She was a visiting professor at the State Institute for Architecture in Antwerp, Belgium, from 1970—80, and at the Stuttgart College of Printing in 1983.

Since 1987 she has been operating a second design studio in Varese, Italy, and teaching package design at the Istituto Europeo di Design in Milan. She lives in Ulm and Varese.

Wilhelm Braun-Feldweg was born in Ulm on January 29, 1908. In 1922 he began an apprenticeship as a steel engraver at the Oskar Fischer metal-works in Brackenheim, qualifying as a craftsman in 1925. After further vocational training as a silversmith and engraver he entered the Department of Graphic Arts and Book Production at the Württemberg State College of Art in 1927. From 1928 to 1935 he studied painting at the Academy of Fine Arts in Stuttgart, and also qualified for the graduation diploma he had failed to make at school. While working as a professional painter, he started studying the history of art at the universities of Stuttgart and Tübingen, where he gained his doctorate in 1938. His career was interrupted between 1938 and 1948 by war service, when he was taken prisoner.

In 1949 he was appointed lecturer in the history of art, drawing and painting at the State Higher Technical College for Precious Metal Work in Schwäbisch Gmünd. With the opening of new glass factories in Schwäbisch Gmünd it became necessary in 1950 to set up a Department for Glassworking at the college.

Braun-Feldweg took charge of the classes in "Design and Development of Industrial Products." His first glass designs date from 1952/53. In 1958 he was appointed to the newly created chair of industrial design at the Berlin Academy of Visual Arts; he was simultaneously active as a designer in a variety of fields. His work includes designs for glass series, glass for everyday use, lamps, metal goods, doorhandles, slide projectors, adding-machines, photocopiers, photocomposers, and electronic measuring instruments for firms such as Seibel, BEKA, Peill & Putzler, Ruhr AG, WMF, Wehag, Berthold, Landis + Gyr, and Wiesenthalhütte.

Most of his publications on industrial design date from the fifties.

He left teaching in 1973, but continued to work as a designer. In 1976 he moved to Würzburg to devote himself exclusively to painting.

Rido Busse was born in Wiesbaden on August 14, 1934, and studied industrial design at the HfG, Ulm. In 1959 he set up busse design ulm, a company which organizes the complete process of product development, from the initial design work, through models and prototypes, until the product is ready for mass production. busse design ulm concentrate mainly on technical equipment, such as measuring instruments, household appliances, and saws. The firm has successfully developed products for companies like BBC Brown Boveri, Braun, Klöckner-Möller, Osram, Pelikan, Siemens, Soehnle, Vaillant, and Stihl.

Busse has founded two design awards. The Busse Longlife Award is presented triennially for products which have enjoyed a long-standing success on the market. The Plagiarius award is Busse's way of drawing attention to products copied from others by manufacturers who hope to cash in on the success of the original design. Rido Busse lives in Elchingen near Ulm.

Luigi Colani was born in Berlin on August 2, 1928. He began his studies at the Berlin Academy of Visual Arts, but then moved to Paris to study aerodynamics at the Sorbonne. While still at university he designed a shoe collection for Christian Dior which was soon being sold in major fashion outlets. After Colani had completed his studies he was persuaded by Douglas, the aircraft manufacturers, to do research work in California in the field of high-speed aerodynamics. He returned to Berlin in 1954 and concentrated on work for the automobile industry. Colani's designs for Fiat, Alfa Romeo, Lancia, VW, and BMW provided all these companies with important insights into aerodynamics which they applied in their own development work.

In 1968, Colani shifted his attention to furniture, setting up a design team in Westphalia which produced successful designs for the industry. In 1972, he and his team moved to Harkotten Castle, where they worked for companies like Thyssen, Villeroy & Boch, Rosenthal, Pelikan, Boeing, VW, BMW, and Rockwell (on a NASA project). In 1979, Japanese companies first entered into contact with Colani, and in 1982, he moved to Japan, designing highly successful products for Sony, Yamaha, Seiko, Hitachi, Nissan, and Canon.

1986 saw the foundation of the Colani Design Center in Berne, Switzerland, and in 1987 he was awarded an honorary professorship by the Bremen Academy of Music and Visual Arts.

The range of products Colani has designed is exceptionally wide, including crockery, ballpoint pens, sanitary china and accessories, fashionwear, spectacles, headphones, and much more. Besides his mass-produced articles, Colani is the kind of designer whose ideas have prompted — and continue to prompt — product design to adopt new directions. His work has set trends, for example, in office workplaces and kitchen fittings, and in aerodynamics for the automobile and aviation industry.

Karl Dittert was born in Mährisch-Trübau in Austro-Hungary in 1915. After leaving school he started training at a silverware and metal works, for whom he was later active designer.

Until 1943 he attended the Berlin Academy of Visual Arts, but military service interrupted his studies several times. He resumed studies from 1945—48 at what was then the State Higher Technical College for Precious Metal Work in Schwäbisch Gmünd. On graduation, Dittert was offered a teaching position at the college in 1951, and was appointed head of metalwork instruction. At the same time he set up his own design studio and began working freelance for companies such as Württembergische Metallwarenfabrik (WMF). In 1961, the Schwäbisch Gmünd college appointed him professor, and he assumed responsibility for industrial product design classes, expanding them to form an autonomous degree course in industrial design. In 1970 he was made principal of the college, which under his leadership was upgraded to a College of Commercial Art and later transformed into a Higher Technical College for Design. He was appointed rector in 1972, a position he held until he retired in 1979.

Dittert's main design interest focussed on the world of work, be it in the home or the office. He collaborated with Ritterwerk, Munich, on designing kitchen appliances, and became consultant for VOKO, Pohlheim, where he was able to realize his ideas for office workstations. He continues to work for VOKO.

Besides teaching and his own design work, Dittert has also written books and articles, has sat in an advisory capacity on many committees and juries, and was one of the founder-members of VDID, the Association of German Industrial Designers.

The products developed by Dittert have received numerous international awards, have been shown in exhibitions, and figure in various design collections. Karl Dittert lives in Schwäbisch Gmünd.

Heinz H. Engler was born in Biberach an der Riss on June 5, 1928. After graduating from high school in 1949 he began training as a potter, followed by a period as a student at the Higher Technical College for Ceramics in Höhr-Grenzhausen. In the fifties he started designing glass and chinaware for companies such as Arabia (Finland), Wiesenthal Glashütte, Porzellanfabrik Weiden Gebrüder Bauscher, and Stölzle Glasindustrie.

Engler designed numerous series of drinking-glasses, crockery for everyday use, and individual items such as vases. Probably his most famous work is the Bauscher B1100 crockery system, which he developed in 1960. This stacking crockery, highly practical and with a wide range of possible combinations, was truly trend-setting in the manufacture and design of canteen and hotel crockery. Products designed by Engler were on show at numerous exhibitions both in Germany and abroad between 1955 and 1984. He also received many awards for his designs.

In 1957 the Hamburg Academy of Visual Arts appointed him Professor for Ceramic Design, and in 1981 Professor of Industrial Design. The Vienna College of Applied Art offered him a professorship of Ceramic and Glass Design in 1977. Engler accepted all these appointments, but never actually did any teaching. He died in Biberach an der Riss in 1986.

Hartmut H. Esslinger was born in Beuren in the Black Forest on June 5, 1944. He studied electrical engineering from 1966–67 at Stuttgart Technical University and from 1968–70 read industrial design at Schwäbisch Gmünd Technical College. He has worked as a freelance industrial designer since 1969 and founded his own company, frogdesign, headquartered in Altensteig in the Black Forest. In 1982 he opened a frogdesign office in California, where he provided consultancy services on design questions as well as acting as corporate manager of design at Apple Computers. Frogdesign has also had a Japanese office since 1987. Hartmut Esslinger and frogdesign work internationally, predominantly designing technical products, such as computers, TV

and hi-fi systems, cameras, and household appliances, and also lamps and bathroom ceramics and fittings for such companies as WEGA, Polaroid, Sony, Erco, Olympia, Texas Instruments, AEG-Telefunken, Apple, Hansgrohe, and Villeroy & Boch.

In 1985 Hartmut Esslinger started the "frogjunior" design competition, which is held annually in the USA and FRG. Design students and design colleges compete for the awards. Hartmut Esslinger lives in the USA and in West Germany.

Hans Gugelot was born in Makassar, Indonesia, on April 1, 1920. He studied architecture at Lausanne Technical College and Zurich Technical University from 1940–46. From 1948 onward he worked in various architects' offices, among others for Max Bill, before going freelance in 1950.

It was then that he created his first furniture designs for the Zurich firm "Wohnbedarf" and started experimenting with furniture systems. In 1956, Gugelot was appointed professor at the HfG Ulm, where he taught until 1965, mainly in the product design department. In 1958 he was put in charge of the "Development Group II" at the HfG.

From 1954 to 1958 he developed a completely new series of radio, hi-fi, and TV systems for Braun – these were a spectacular success, and highly significant for the future course of design. In his M 125 furniture system Gugelot pressed ahead with his notion of modular systems; the Wilhelm Bofinger company put the range into large-scale production in 1956. The 1963 Kodak "Carousel" slide-projector attests to Gugelot's interest not only in innovative design, but also in new ways of using objects. Between 1959 and 1962 Gugelot, Herbert Lindinger, and Helmut Müller-Kuhn developed the Hamburg subway system. In the 1950s, together with Otl Aicher, he drew up the general design guidelines for Braun and thus shaped the company's overall image. In 1961 he was a consultant for the team planning the Ahmedabad Design Insitute in India, where he was guest professor in 1965. In 1962 he set up his own project planning company independent of the HfG, gugelot design gmbh. In addition to the products mentioned above, he designed sewing-machines, cameras, household appliances, photocopiers, radial drills, and oil burners. The companies he worked for include Braun, Telefunken, Pfaff, Lumoprint, Agfa, Girards, and Weishaupt. His designs received various awards, and numerous exhibitions have featured them.

Gugelot died in Ulm in 1965. gugelot design gmbh continued to exist until 1974.

Herbert Hirche was born in Görlitz, Silesia, in 1910. Between 1924 and 1929 he completed an apprenticeship as a joiner and spent some time as a traveling journeyman. In 1930 he began to study at the Bauhaus, where he remained until 1933. He then worked for Mies van der Rohe and Lilly Reich. Following a year of freelance work, he joined Egon Eiermann, with whom he collaborated from 1939–45. For the next three years, the Berlin City Council appointed him a member of the building directorate for reconstruction and the Hans

Scharoun planning-group responsible for replanning Berlin. From 1948–50 Hirche taught at the Weissensee College of Applied Art in Berlin, where he was made professor in 1949. In 1950 he again worked with Egon Eiermann in Karlsruhe. From 1951 to 1952 he planned the establishment of a design college in Mannheim, and was then appointed lecturer in interior and furniture design at the State Academy of Visual Arts, Stuttgart; from 1969 to 1971 he was rector of this institution.

Hirche has worked as as freelance architect and designer since 1948. He has designed mainly furniture and furniture lines for firms like Christian Holzäpfel, Akademie-Werkstätten Stuttgart, Walter Knoll, Wilde + Spieth, Wilkhahn, Mauser, and Interlübke. The products he has designed have been shown in many exhibitions and special presentations. Together with Claus-Peter Klink and Karl-Georg Bitterberg, he founded the Hircheteam in 1970.

Hirche has been responsible for planning various exhibitions, an early example of which was the 1949 "Wie wohnen" exhibition in Stuttgart. He lives near Stuttgart.

Stefan Lengyel was born in Budapest, Hungary, in 1937. After graduating from high school he studied at the Budapest Design College. In 1961 he gained a degree in industrial design, as well as a master's in philosophy and art, going on to work from 1962 onward as instructor at the Budapest College. In 1964 he was offered a post of assistant professor at the HfG Ulm, and it was here that he began to collaborate with Hans Gugelot. In 1965 he was appointed lecturer at the Folkwang College of Design in Essen, where he became Head of Industrial Design in 1969. In 1981 Lengyel was made professor at Essen University, a position he continues to hold. He has been a visiting professor in Canada, the United States, Hungary, and Finland.

Since 1961, Lengyel has worked as a freelance designer and design consultant for companies such as Aral, Miele, Liesegang, Rheinmetall, Ruhrgas Essen, and Mauser. Products he has designed include gasoline pumps, measuring instruments and regulators, light-switches, display systems, and furniture lines; his design work has received numerous awards.

Lengyel has written many articles, and continues to serve as a jury-member at design competitions inside and outside Germany and also as an expert consultant on questions of copyright. He is on the Board of Trustees of the German Design Council and a board member of other design institutions, and has been President of VDID, the Association of German Industrial Designers, since 1986. He lives in Essen.

Klaus Limberg was born in Giessen in 1936. From 1956 to 1963 he studied mechanical engineering and philosophy in Giessen and Stuttgart, where he worked from 1959–61 in the household appliance development department at the Bosch corporation. From 1962 to 1964 he devoted much effort to setting up and was the director of the DM Institute for Product Testing. In 1963 he took up teaching duties at the HfG Ulm, in the product design department. From 1967 to 1981 Klaus Limberg was head of product planning for Robert Krups in Solingen and simultaneously taught in the design department at Essen University. In 1981 he was appointed professor at the Pforzheim College of Design, where he has been rector since 1985. In 1986 he was made director of the new Transferzentrum Pforzheim Design-Innovation.

Alongside the design concepts he devised for all product areas at Krups, he has designed process control consoles for AEG and regional rapid-transit trains for the Federal German Railways, has worked for Daimler-Benz in the field of advanced design, and has been involved in German-Soviet joint ventures in automobile production. He also acts as an expert consultant and a jury member in various design competitions. He lives in Pforzheim.

Herbert Lindinger was born in Wels, Austria, in 1933. He studied graphic and exhibition design from 1949 to 1953 at Linz College of Commercial Art, and read visual communication and product design from 1954 to 1958 at the HfG Ulm. He then started to work with Otl Aicher and Hans Gugelot, setting up his own design development group in Ulm in 1962 and lecturing at the HfG from 1962 to 1968.

From 1968 to 1971 H. Lindinger played a substantial role in founding the Institute for Environmental Design in Frankfurt. In 1965 he was guest professor at Ohio State University and in 1970 at the Institute of Design, Ahmedabad, India. He has been a full professor and director of the Institute of Industrial Design at Hanover University since 1971, the year in which he founded the design consultancy Lindinger & Partner.

Among other things, Herbert Lindinger has devised rapid-transit systems for the cities of Hamburg, Hanover, Stuttgart, and Berlin, helicopters for MBB, road and rail vehicles for VW, MAN and the Federal German Railways, and hi-fi appliances for Braun; he has been active in the fields of graphic and corporate design for EBV and Olivetti. He was responsible for designing large squares and pedestrian zones in Hanover, Darmstadt, and Heidelberg.

Lindinger's projects have received numerous design and architectural awards and have been on public display in many exhibitions. He is a jury-member in various design competitions. He lives in Hanover.

Friedemann Lotsch was born on September 23, 1946. On leaving school in 1964 he embarked on an apprenticeship as an industrial fitter, qualifying as a skilled worker three years later. From 1969 to 1973 he studied at the Dortmund Technical College, taking a degree in industrial design. In 1973 he started studying design at the Brunswick Academy of Visual Arts, graduating in 1976. He founded the design studio Lotsch & Partner in Dortmund the same year. For the first two years the studio focussed mainly on interior planning and furnishing for youth vacation camps and rehabilitation centers.

In 1981 Lotsch & Partner was subdivided into a section for freelance work and a crafts department with a model workshop, authorized to train apprentices. A special license granted in 1986 permits toolmaking work.

Lotsch & Partner design capital and consumer goods predominantly of a technical nature, offering the full range of services from product conception via detail work and model and prototype construction to the development of comprehensive product ranges.

Lotsch & Partner have developed many different products, including loudspeaker systems, medical technology, measuring instruments, lamps, and computer equipment. The following is a brief selection of the studio's clients: ITT, Kettler, Linotype, Nixdorf, Philips, AEG, ERCO, Staff Leuchten, Stiebel-Eltron. Products developed by Lotsch & Partner have received various design awards.

Friedemann Lotsch is not only active in development and design work but also works on behalf of trainees at the Dortmund Chamber of Commerce and at the German Industrial and Trade Association, as well as being a jury-member for various design competitions. He lives in Dortmund.

Ernst Moeckl was born in 1931. In 1948 he began training as a technical draftsman and design engineer in the metal industry, a sector in which he worked until 1953. From 1954 to 1959 he studied at the HfG Ulm, in the product design department. While still studying, he began to collaborate with Max Bill.

In 1960 Moeckl founded his own development institute in Stuttgart, calling it *Gestaltung von Industrieprodukten* (Industrial Product Design).

The main focus of his product design work has always been furniture and technical equipment, including computers, measuring instruments, cameras, audio and television equipment, passenger and goods vehicles, and tools.

He has worked for companies such as Lübke, Drabert, Nixdorf, Braun, Tokyo Steel, Krauss-Maffei, and Bosch-Eisemann.

Since 1960, the designs produced by Moeckl and his development institute have received numerous awards, been on show in many exhibitions, and been incorporated into collections of design. Ernst Moeckl lives in Stuttgart.

Gerd A. Müller was born in Frankfurt/Main in 1932. After leaving school in 1948 he began training as a dental technician but gave this up a year later in order to take up an apprenticeship as a joiner, finally qualifying in 1952. From 1952 to 1955 he studied interior architecture at Wiesbaden College of Commercial Arts, graduating with a master's degree. On completion of his studies, Müller found employment as a product designer with the Max Braun company in Frankfurt (the presentday Braun AG of Kronberg). Here he was responsible for designing kitchen equipment and electric shavers. In 1960 Müller set up his own design studio in Eschborn, near Frankfurt; he has since worked freelance designing industrial products, trade fair displays, and advertising material. Among other things, he has designed typewriters, sewing-machines, writing utensils (biros, fountain pens, etc.), leather goods, packaging, displays, books, brochures, and advertising material for companies such as Lamy, Braun, etc. He has meanwhile become a specialist in corporate design. His industrial products have received many awards and he has won prizes in various competitions for logos. Besides product design, Müller has for a long time concerned himself with nature conservation and environmental problems, and has devised numerous exhibitions on the subject, concentrating particularly on the educational aspects of such exhibitions. He was artistic director involved in the planning work for the Bavarian Forest National Park.

He currently teaches a course on the methodology of museum and exhibition design at Wiesbaden Technical College. He lives in Eschborn.

Alexander Neumeister was born in Berlin on December 17, 1941. He studied product design at the HfG Ulm from 1963 to 1968. He was then awarded a one-year scholarship to study in the department of industrial design at Tokyo University of Arts. Since 1969 he has had his own design studio in Munich and has worked primarily for the capital goods sector. The main focus of his work hitherto has been on designs for new transportation systems, electronics, data-processing, and medical technology. He has worked for companies such as Messerschmitt-Bölkow-Blohm, Thyssen-Henschel, Krauss-Maffei, and German Federal Railways. On the strength of his submission to an invitation competition held by Deutsche Bank in 1974, the bank commissioned Neumeister to develop a nationwide interior design program for them.

Between 1975 and 1980 Neumeister taught in the industrial design department at Munich Polytechnic. In 1983, he was invited to take part in a competition for supplementary designs for the interior fittings of the ICE InterCity Experimental express train, which resulted in his being asked to supply detailed designs for an additional passenger car. From the initial design work involved in the first 1971 test vehicle, Neumeister Design have been responsible for designing the railcars for the Transrapid magnetic levitation rail system.

Neumeister's draft designs and designed products have received various awards in recognition of their qualities. Besides his design work, Neumeister has been active in the VDID (Association of German Industrial Designers) and in the ICSID (International Council of Societies of Industrial Design), taking a particular interest in questions of design for and in developing countries. He lives in Munich.

Dieter Rams was born in Wiesbaden in 1932. In 1947, he began studying architecture and interior design at the Wiesbaden College of Commercial Art, interrupting his studies between 1948 and 1951 in order to undergo an apprenticeship as a joiner. He then returned to the college, graduating with honors in 1953 and subsequently joining the Otto Apel architectural bureau, where he started work alongside architects Skidmore, Owings and Merrill on the consular wing of the US embassy in West Germany.

In 1955, Rams was employed by the Braun corporation as an architect and interior designer. He received his first assignments as product designer for Braun in 1956. In 1960 he was appointed deputy director and in 1968 director of Braun's design department. He has been an executive manager of Braun AG since 1988.

Rams' approach to design has been the hallmark of Braun products and the company's overall image up to the present day. Working together with Hans Gugelot in his first years at Braun, Rams created radios, audio equipment, and television sets that were regarded as pioneering in terms of their design. Rams and the Braun design team are now responsible for the design of the corporation's entire product range, which includes household appliances, alarm-clocks, pocket calculators, and hi-fi equipment.

In 1957, Rams turned his attention to another type of product. Working for Otto Zapf, a company which now operates as Wiese Vitsoe, he designed furniture, shelving systems, armchairs, and chairs, which still figure in Wiese Vitsoe's current catalogs; Rams continues to design new products for them.

Rams' product designs have been shown at countless exhibitions, included in design collections, and won numerous prizes and awards.

Since 1981 Rams has taught industrial design at the Hamburg Academy of Visual Fine Arts. He has been president of the Rat für Formgebung (German Design Council) since 1987. He lives in Kronberg.

Hans Roericht was born in 1932. From 1955–59 he studied product design at the HfG Ulm. For his master's project he devised the TC 100 stackable crockery, a novel idea at the time; it has been manufactured by the Porzellanfabrik Thomas (now part of Rosenthal) since 1961. After completing his studies he worked as an instructor at the HfG in visual communications and borderline zones of product design. In 1968 he founded the ProduktEntwicklung Roericht Ulm (PER) design studio, and the following year was visiting lecturer in industrial design at Ohio State University in Columbus. He has been professor of industrial design at the Berlin Academy of Fine Arts since 1973.

Hans Roericht was, together with Otl Aicher, responsible for designing the Lufthansa corporate image, and was in charge of product design for the 1972 Munich Olympics. He has worked for Wilkhahn, drawing up studies for workplaces and designing office and conference furniture.

PER, with the collaboration of Petra Kellner and Burckhardt Schmitz, now concentrate on design research and feasibility studies for companies such as Bosch/Siemens, Loewe Opta, and Nixdorf.

PER, with their subsidiary in New York and partners in London and Tokyo, see themselves as the cutting edge of an international network which, thanks to continual interchange of ideas via new communications technology, functions as the catalyst of potential new worlds of design. Here, alternative options are dreamed up and tried out; communicative processes impinge on the simulated inner life of products in an atmosphere of curiosity.

Hans Roericht lives and works in Ulm and Berlin.

Norbert Schlagheck was born in Wegberg-Beeck, Rhineland, in 1925. From 1940 to 1947 he learned the crafts of metalwork and beltmaking. He studied design at the Folkwang College of Design in Essen between 1949 and 1954. He subsequently worked for 13 years as a designer for the Siemens corporation, where he was in charge of the household appliance design group. From 1967 to 1970 Schlagheck was head of the industrial design department at the Cologne College of Crafts. He has been professor of industrial design at Munich Technical College since 1972. He lives in Grafrath, near Munich.

Herbert H. Schultes was born in Freiburg in 1938. He trained as an engineer and designer in Munich. From 1961 to 1967 he worked as a designer for Siemens, where he was assistant to the head designer. In 1967 he played a prominent role in setting up the industrial design course at Munich Technical College. He taught industrial design for several years at the Cologne College of Crafts and Munich Technical College. He has been head designer at Siemens since 1985. He lives in Fürstenfeldbruck, near Munich.

In 1967 Norbert Schlagheck and Herbert H. Schultes founded **Schlagheck & Schultes Design.** The partnership specializes in industrial design, corporate design, product graphics, and packaging design. In the field of product design they concentrate on radio, audio, office, and information equipment, on furniture, and on products for the sports goods industry. Companies include Agfa, Big Pack, BMW, Bulthaup, Gervais Danone, Kraft, Loewe Opta, Marker (ski bindings), Melitta, Metzler, Wilkens, and Wilkhahn.

Hans Schönfeld was born in Mügeln near Leipzig on April 3, 1933. After World War II he interrupted his schooling in order to undergo vocational training in various craft trades. He finished school in 1949 and embarked on a course in applied graphics at Bonndorf Commercial Arts College, which he completed three years later. He then found employment as a designer in the watch and clock industry, later working as an automobile designer at the Volkswagen plant in Wolfsburg from 1954 to 1961. Schönfeld regards himself as an autodidact in the field of industrial design.

He has been a freelance industrial designer in Wolfsburg since 1961. In 1962 he founded the **Interform** group, which since 1987 has operated as Interform Design-Studio Schönfeld. Interform and Schönfeld concentrate on creating designs for the technological and capital goods sectors. They have developed product designs for companies such as AEG, Braun, Bosch-Siemens, Heraeus, Melitta, Mitsubishi, Schott, Stiebel Eltron, Schuco, Volkswagen, Wega Radio, and Zeiss Ikon.

Besides product design and development, Interform are also engaged in other areas, providing engineering services, graphic design, design management, architectural design, and city planning design. Interform have drafted bridge constructions, designed public squares in Düsseldorf and Rotterdam, and developed design and construction forms for civic amenities in Berlin, Düsseldorf, Essen, Rotterdam, etc. In addition, Interform have for the past ten years been submitting artworks to competitions in the subject of "art and townscape."

Interform and Hans Schönfeld have received countless design awards, and their product designs have been on display at many an exhibition. Hans Schönfeld lives in Wolfsburg.

Hans Erich Slany was born in Wiesenthal in the Sudetenland (Czechoslovakia) in 1926. In 1941 he commenced studies at the Eger and Esslingen State Engineering Colleges, which were interrupted by a period of military service and internment as a POW. He graduated in engineering in 1948 and worked for the next eight years as a development engineer in industry, for example in the styling department at Daimler Benz. He set up Slany Design in 1956, while continuing to work freelance for Heinrich Löffelhardt until 1959. In 1956 Slany started designing for the Progress vacuum-cleaner company (which became Electrolux-Progress in 1980). Since 1958 he has worked for Robert Bosch and its subsidiaries designing power tools, industrial equipment, television equipment, and packaging machinery. In 1959 he was a founder-member of VDID, the Association of German Industrial Designers. He taught at the Berlin Academy of Arts from 1983 to 1988 and was awarded an honorary professorship there in 1985. A year later he was appointed professor at the State Academy of Visual Arts in Stuttgart, where he took charge of the newly created course in capital goods design. In 1987 Slany Design became a limited company.

Since 1959 Slany has developed products such as vacuum-cleaners, pressure-cookers, organizational filing systems, cleaning systems, and lathes for companies such as Leifheit, Silit, Leitz, Kärcher, and Traub. An important side of his work has always been capital goods and ergonomics; he has written articles on the design aspects of these subjects. In addition, he has been a member of juries in many German and international design competitions. Products developed by Slany Design have received countless awards, been shown at numerous exhibitions, and been included in many design collections. Hans Erich Slany lives in Esslingen.

Arno Votteler was born in Freudenstadt in the Black Forest in 1929. From 1948 to 1950 he studied at Bonndorf College of Commercial Arts in the Black Forest and then worked until 1954 as a designer for Walter Knoll, Herrenberg. In 1954–55 he studied interior design at the Stuttgart Academy of Arts. From 1956 to 1960 he worked freelance for Robert Gutmann in London; in 1961 he was appointed professor of industrial design at Brunswick College of Art, a position he held until 1975. He was head of a development group and consultant on home electronics for Bosch-Blaupunkt in Hildesheim from 1965 to 1975. In 1975, Votteler was made professor of interior and furniture design at the Stuttgart Academy of Arts, where in 1980 he founded the Institute of Interior and Furniture Design, which he still heads today. He has been a visiting professor on various occasions: in 1967 at the Rio de Janeiro College of Design; in 1970 at the National Design Institute in Ahmedabad, India; in 1971 at Ohio State, Columbus; and in 1987 at the Peking Academy of Arts.

Votteler has had his own design studio in Stuttgart since 1961, focussing on the design of furniture and workplace environments. His clients have included the following companies: Stoll/Giraflex, Martin Stoll, RTR Tritsch, Siechert, Bisterfeld und Weiss Objektmöbel, Linder Bankeinrichtungen, Hapag Lloyd (interior fittings for a cruise ship), German Federal Railways (fittings and seatings for rapid-transit trains).

In addition to product design and teaching, Votteler is active as a publicist and sits on numerous competition juries. His product designs have received many awards and often been shown in exhibitions. Arno Votteler lives in Stuttgart.

Wilhelm Wagenfeld was born in Bremen on April 15, 1900. He was an apprentice in the drawing office at Koch & Bergfeld, a Bremen silverware factory, from 1914 to 1918, simultaneously attending courses at the College of Arts and Crafts. In 1919 he was awarded the Bremen Scholarship for the State Academy of Drawing in Hanau, where he remained until 1922. In 1923, Wagenfeld went to the Bauhaus in Weimar, where he worked in the metals workshop under Laszlo Moholy-Nagy, passing apprentice examinations as a silversmith and engraver. In 1926 he was appointed assistant to the metal classes at the Weimar State College of Building, becoming director and teacher of the classes in 1929. After the dissolution of the college in 1930 Wagenfeld went freelance and started to accept commissions from industry; as from 1931, for example, he worked for Schott & Gen., the Jena glassworks, designing fire-

proof household glassware. In the same year, he became professor at Berlin State College of Art, resigning in 1935 to become manager of the Vereinigte Lausitzer glassworks in Weisswasser, where he remained until 1947. There, he modernized the production processes and created new designs for container glassware, drinking-glasses, and pressed glass products. Between 1942 and 1945 he saw active service and was taken prisoner. In 1946 Wagenfeld was appointed professor at Dresden Industrial Academy, which he helped to reorganize. A year later he accepted a post at the Institute for Building attached to the German Academy of Sciences in Berlin; at the same time, between 1947 and 1949, he taught industrial design at the Berlin College of Visual Arts. In 1949 he became departmental head at the Württemberg State Board of Trade in Stuttgart. From 1950 onwards he devoted himself to freelance work in the consumer goods sector. In 1954 he founded the Werkstatt Wagenfeld in Stuttgart, an experimental and developmental workshop for industrial models that existed until 1978.

Wilhelm Wagenfeld has designed and developed metal goods, ranges of glassware, crockery, cutlery, lamps, lighting fixtures, doorhandles, plastic products, etc., for companies such as WMF, Peill & Putzler, Rosenthal, Fürstenberg, and Hengstenberg. His work has received numerous awards and has been the subject of many exhibitions. Wilhelm Wagenfeld lives in Stuttgart.

Herta-Maria Witzemann was born in Dornbirn in Austria in 1918. She began studying at the Vienna College of Arts and Crafts in 1938, majoring in architecture. From 1940 to 1942 she continued her studies at the Academy of Applied Art in Munich. She re-

turned to Vienna the following year to work in Professor Haerdtl's studio and to act as an assistant in his architecture classes at the College of Applied Art. From 1945 onward she worked in various architects' bureaux, and from 1948 as freelance interior and furniture designer. In 1952 she was offered the chair of interior and furniture design at the Stuttgart Academy of Visual Arts.

Witzemann has created furniture for private homes and for administrative and commercial settings, working on behalf of companies like Bremshey, Behr, Interlübke, Knoll International Deutschland, Siematic Küchen, and Thonet.

As an interior designer she has designed private apartments and houses, government and administration buildings, banks, hotels and restaurants, exhibition halls, shops, libraries, and company cafeterias. Herta-Maria Witzemann lives in Stuttgart.

Walter Zeischegg was born in Vienna in 1917. After attending the College of Commercial Arts and Building in Graz he began studying sculpture at the Vienna Academy of Visual Arts in 1936. After leaving the academy, Zeischegg worked freelance as a sculptor and industrial designer. From 1951 to 1954 he was involved in the planning and inauguration of the HfG Ulm, where he was lecturer in product design until 1968.

Zeischegg was strongly committed to research work and registered numerous patents, e.g. for a current-carrying runner system for lighting fixtures and for a mixer tap for hot and cold water. The Helit ashtray, to be found the world over, is a spin-off of his research and development work in the field of spherical geometry. Walter Zeischegg died in 1983.

Design-Institutions	**Design-Center Hessen**	**DIHT Deutscher Industrie- und Handelstag**	**IFG Ulm.** Internationales Forum für Gestaltung Ulm

Design-Institutions

Design-Center Hessen
Eugen-Bracht-Weg 6
6100 Darmstadt
Design-Center Stuttgart
Landesgewerbeamt Baden Württemberg
Willi-Bleicher-Str. 19
7000 Stuttgart 1
Design Forum Nürnberg
IHK Industrie- und Handelskammer Nürnberg
Hauptmarkt 25/27
8500 Nürnberg
Design Initiative Nord e. V.
Transparent, Uwe Wagner
Fleethörn 23
2300 Kiel
Design Zentrum München
Geschäftsführung:
Dr. Arnica-Verena Langenmaier
Kaiserstr. 45
8000 München 40
Fax: (89) 39 66 36

DIHT Deutscher Industrie- und Handelstag
Arbeitskreis Produktform
Adenauerallee 148
5300 Bonn
Fax: (228) 10 41 58
Deutscher Werkbund
Weißadlergasse 4
6000 Frankfurt/Main 1
Deutsches Farbenzentrum e. V.
Bozener Str. 11–12
D-1000 Berlin 62
Haus Industrieform
Hindenburgstr. 25–27
4300 Essen 1
Fax: (201) 23 18 60
if Industrie Forum Design Hannover e. V.
Messegelände
3000 Hannover 82

IFG Ulm. Internationales Forum für Gestaltung Ulm
Am Hochsträß 8
Postfach 40 66
7900 Ulm
Fax: (731) 38 10 03
Institut für Neue Technische Formen e. V.
Eugen-Bracht-Weg 6
6100 Darmstadt
Internationales Designzentrum Berlin
Kurfürstendamm 66
1000 Berlin 15
Fax: (30) 8 82 52 28
Rat für Formgebung/German Design Council
Rat-Haus Messegelände
Postfach 97 02 87
6000 Frankfurt/Main 97
Fax: (69) 7 41 09 11

Design Associations

BDG Bund Deutscher Grafik-Designer e. V.
Altestadt 8
4000 Düsseldorf

BDIA Bund Deutscher Innenarchitekten
Königswinterer Str. 709
5300 Bonn 3

BFF Bund Freischaffender Foto-Designer
Tuttlinger Straße 68
Postfach 75 03 47
7000 Stuttgart 75

DT Deutscher Designertag e. V.
Dr. Wolfang Maaßen

Kreuzbergstr. 1
4000 Düsseldorf

VDID Verband Deutscher Industrie-Designer e. V.
Altestadt 8
4000 Düsseldorf

Design Awards

Bayerischer Staatspreis für Nachwuchs-Designer
Bayrisches Staatsministerium für Wirtschaft und Verkehr
Prinzregentenstr. 22
8000 München 22

Braun Preis
Braun AG
Informationsabteilung
Frankfurter Str. 145
6242 Kronberg/Ts.

Bundespreis Produktdesign
Rat für Formgebung
Postfach 97 02 87
6000 Frankfurt/Main 97

Design Auswahl
Design Center Stuttgart
Willi-Bleicher-Str. 19
7000 Stuttgart 10

Design Innovationen
Haus Industrieform Essen
Hindenburgstr. 25–27
4300 Essen 1

Design Plus
Initiative Form und Leben
c/o Rat für Formgebung
Postfach 97 02 87
6000 Frankfurt/Main 97

Deutscher Verpackungs-Wettbewerb
Rationalisierungs-Gemeinschaft Verpackung
Postfach 58 67
6236 Eschborn

frogjunor
frogdesign
Grenzweg 33
7272 Altensteig

if Designwettbewerb
Industrie Forum Design Hannover e. V.
Messegelände
3000 Hannover 82

Internationaler Farb-Design-Preis
Farb-Design-International e. V.
Danneckerstr. 52
7000 Stuttgart 1

Jugend formt
Mathildenhöhe-Preis
Rosenthal AG
Postfach 15 20
8672 Selb

Longlife Design Award
Busse Design Ulm GmbH
Nersinger Str. 18
7951 Elchingen 3

Marlboro Design Förderpreis
Philip Morris GmbH
c/o P. S. Promotion Service
Am Ginsterberg 31
4000 Düsseldorf 12

Produkte des Jahres
Fachverband Kunststoff-Konsumwaren
Am Hauptbahnhof 12
6000 Frankfurt/Main 1

Staatspreis des Landes Nordrhein-Westfalen für Design und Innovation
Ministerium für Wirtschaft, Mittelstand und Technologie
Postfach 11 44
4000 Düsseldorf 1

Design Periodicals

AIT-Architektur Innenarchitektur
Technischer Ausbau
Verlagsanstalt A. Koch GmbH
Postfach 10 27 41
7000 Stuttgart 10

architektur & wohnen
Jahreszeiten Verlag GmbH
Poßmoorweg 5
2000 Hamburg 60

Art Aurea
Ebner Verlag
Karlstr. 41
7900 Ulm

Braun + Design
Unabhängige Zeitschrift für Design-Sammler
Körnerstr. 5
2000 Hamburg 60

Design Report
Rat für Formgebung
Postfach 97 02 87
6000 Frankfurt/Main 1

DMK Die moderne Küche
Die Planung Verlagsgesellschaft mbH
Holzhofallee 25–31
6100 Darmstadt

form
Redaktion Karl Heinz Krug
Postfach 30 06 45
5090 Leverkusen

Licht
Richard Pflaum Verlag
Postfach 19 07 37
8000 München 19

Literatur-Hinweise
Editor-in-chief: Helge Aszomeit
Rat für Formgebung
Ludwig-Erhard Anlage 1
Postfach 97 02 87
6000 Frankfurt/Main 97

Mensch & Büro
Mensch & Büro Verlag
Postfach 22 47
Langestr. 94
7570 Baden-Baden

möbelkultur
Ferdinand Holzmann Verlag
Postfach 60 10 49
2000 Hamburg 60

Möbelmarkt
Mathias Ritthammer GmbH & Co. KG
Postfach 38 50
8500 Nürnberg

md
Konradin-Verlag
Postfach 10 02 52
7022 Leinfelden-Echterdingen

Office Design
FBO Fachverlag für Büro- und Organisations-technik GmbH
Hermannstr. 2
7570 Baden-Baden

Porzellan & Glas
futura verlag
Graf-Adolf-Str. 81
4000 Düsseldorf 1

VDID extra
Altestadt 8
4000 Düsseldorf 1

werk und zeit
Deutscher Werkbund
Weißadlergasse 4
6000 Frankfurt/Main 1

Selected Bibliography

General

Selle, Gert. *Design-Geschichte in Deutschland: Produktkultur als Entwurf und Erfahrung.* Cologne (DuMont) 1987.

Fuchs, Heinz/Burkhardt, François. *Produkt, Form, Geschichte: 150 Jahre deutsches Design.* Stuttgart (Institut für Auslandsbeziehungen) 1985.

Wichmann, Hans. *Industrial Design, Unikate, Serienerzeugnisse: Die Neue Sammlung; ein neuer Museumstyp des 20. Jahrhunderts.* Munich (Prestel) 1985.

if die gute Industrieform, ed. *Die gute Industrieform.* Hanover, since 1963 (annual).

Design-Center Stuttgart, ed. *Design-Auswahl.* Stuttgart, since 1967/68 (annual).

Haus Industrieform Essen, ed. *Design-Innovationen.* Essen, since 1985 (annual).

Hirdina, Heinz. *Gestalten für die Serie: Design in der DDR 1949–1985.* Dresden (VEB Verlag der Kunst) 1988.

Gsöllpointner, Helmuth et al., ed. *Design ist unsichtbar.* Vienna (Löcker) 1981.

Ulm (pages 21–46)

Lindinger, Herbert. *Ulm . . . die Moral der Gegenstände.* Berlin (Ernst & Sohn) 1987.

Seckendorf, Eva von. *Die Hochschule für Gestaltung Ulm: Gründung (1949–1953) und Ära Max Bill (1953–57).* Marburg (Jonas) 1989.

Rübenach, Bernhard. *Der rechte Winkel von Ulm: ein Bericht über die Hochschule für Gestaltung 1958/59.* Ed. Bernd Meurer. Darmstadt (Verlag der Georg Büchner Buchhandlung) 1987.

ProduktEntwicklung Roericht Ulm, ed. *hfg-synopse.* Ulm 1982.

The Fifties (pages 47–100)

Maenz, Paul. *Die 50er Jahre: Formen eines Jahrzehnts.* Cologne (DuMont) 1984.

fifty fifty: Formen und Farben der 50er Jahre. Stuttgart (Arnold'sche Verlagsanstalt) 1987.

Borngräber, Christian. *Stilnovo: Design in den 50er Jahren; Phantasie und Phantastik.* Frankfurt (Fricke) 1979.

Schulz, Bernhard, ed. *Grauzonen, Farbwelten: Kunst und Zeitbilder 1945–55.* Berlin (Medusa) 1983.

Braun-Feldweg, Wilhelm. *Beiträge zur Formgebung.* Essen (Heyer) 1960.

Jungwirth, Nikolaus/Kromschröder, Gerhard. *Die Pubertät der Republik.* Frankfurt (Fricke) 1978.

The Sixties (pages 101–144)

Blaser, Werner. *Element – System – Möbel: Wege von der Architektur zum Design.* Stuttgart (DVA) 1984.

Wichmann, Hans. *Made in Germany: Produktform, Industrial Design 1970.* Munich (Peter Winkler) 1970.

Wichmann, Hans. *Möbel und Geräte der Wohnung unserer Zeit.* Munich (Winkler Verlag) 1968

Rat für Formgebung. *Gute Form: An Exhibition of German Industrial Design.* London 1965.

Rat für Formgebung. *5 Jahre Bundespreis 'Gute Form.'* Darmstadt 1974.

Klöcker, Johann, ed. *Zeitgemäße Form: industrial design international.* Munich (Süddeutscher Verlag) 1967.

The Seventies (pages 145–188)

Colani, Luigi. *Ylem.* Gütersloh, Vienna (Bertelsmann) 1971.

Friedl, Friedrich/Ohlhauser, G. *Das gewöhnliche Design: Dokumentation einer Ausstellung des Fachbereichs Gestaltung der Fachhochschule Darmstadt 1976.* Cologne (Rheinland Verlag) 1979.

Internationales Design Zentrum Berlin. *Design? Umwelt wird in Frage gestellt.* Berlin, 1972.

Selle, Gert. *Ideologie und Utopie des Design: zur gesellschaftlichen Theorie der industriellen Formgebung.* Cologne (DuMont) 1973.

Löbach, Bernd. *Industrial Design: Grundlagen der Industrieproduktgestaltung.* Munich (Thiemig) 1976.

Burandt, Ulrich. *Ergonomie für Design und Entwicklung.* Cologne (O. Schmidt) 1978.

Corporate Identity (pages 189–206)

Brandes, Uta et al., ed. *Stammeskultur und Unternehmenskultur: metaphysische Aspekte eines Kalküls.* Darmstadt (Verlag der Georg Büchner Buchhandlung) 1988

Huber, Kurt. *Image: Global Image, Corporate Image, Marken-Image, Produkt-Image.* Landsberg (Verlag Moderne Industrie) 1987.

Birkigt, Klaus/Stadler, Marinus M. *Corporate Identity: Grundlagen, Funktionen, Fallbeispiele.* Munich (Verlag Moderne Industrie) 1980.

Antonoff, Roman. *Corporate Identity.* Frankfurt (Frankfurter Allgemeine Zeitung) 1983.

The Eighties (pages 207–243)

Albus, Volker et al., ed. *Gefühlscollagen: Wohnen von Sinnen.* Cologne (DuMont) 1986.

Borngräber, Christian. *Berliner Wege: Prototypen der Designwerkstatt.* Berlin (Ernst & Sohn) 1988.

Fischer, Volker, ed. *Design Now: Industry or Art?* Munich (Prestel) 1988.

"Deutsche Möbel: Unikate, Kleinserien, Prototypen." *Kunstforum 99/1989.* Cologne (Kunstforum International).

Projektgruppe Ökologische Wirtschaft. *Produktanalyse: Bedürfnisse, Produkte und ihre Folgen.* Cologne (Kölner Volksblatt Verlag) 1987.

Rat für Formgebung. *Designed in Germany: World Design Exposition Nagoya 1989.* Gießen (Anabas) 1989.

Picture Credits

AEG Aktiengesellschaft 610–622, 736, 752–755
Agfa Gaevert AG 526
Aicher, Florian 639
Albus, Volker 637, 640, 642, 643, 646, 648, 650, 651, 653, 655–658, 660, 685–688
Bader, Wolfgang 451, 513–515
BASF Aktiengesellschaft 511
Becker, Kurt, Daniel Ludig 635
Benz, Rolf GmbH 510
Benz & Hilgers GmbH 725
F. Biedermann GmbH & Co. KG 486
Blaupunkt-Werke GmbH 426, 529, 756–758
BMW Aktiengesellschaft 88, 631
Bodenseewerk Gerätetechnik GmbH 734
Bofinger 500–503
Bosch, Robert GmbH 476, 730
Brandolini, Andreas 691, 692
Braun AG 357, 363–366, 373, 374, 379, 460, 524, 531, 532, 759–761
BTS Broadcast Television Systems GmbH 735
bulthaup GmbH & Co 749
Cocktail 644
Commerzbank AG 573–576
Cullmann GmbH 745
Designwerkstatt Berlin 661–681
Deutsche Bank AG 598–602
Deutsche Bundesbahn 603–606
Deutsches Weininstitut GmbH 768
Drabert Söhne GmbH & Co 495
Drees, Holger 641, 705–708
ERCO Leuchten GmbH 717, 718, 762–764
Fröscher Sitform KG 506
frogdesign 533, 746, 748
FSB Franz Schneider Brakel GmbH & Co. 765–767
GARDENA Kress + Kastner GmbH 769–771
Geha-Werke GmbH 740
GINBANDE Design 682–684
Grohe, Hans GmbH & Co. KG 547
Gros, Jochen 507
Gruner + Jahr AG & Co. 553

HEAD acoustics GmbH 742
HEWI Heinrich Wilke GmbH 772–777
HfG-Archiv/Stadtarchiv Ulm 3, 4, 7–23, 25–32, 34, 36, 37, 55, 59, 66–75, 79–84
Hildmann, Simon, Rempen & Schmitz: SMS Werbeagentur GmbH 564–566
igus GmbH 743
Interform Design Studio Schönfeld 534, 733
interlübke Gebr. Lübke GmbH & Co. KG 512
Jacob, Heiner 5, 6
Keiper Dynavit GmbH & Co 558
Krupp Polysius AG 737
Krups, Robert Stiftung & Co. KG 541, 544, 778–780
König & Neurath KG 453
Kunstflug 702–704
LAMY C. Josef Lamy GmbH 781–784
Lecatsa, Rouli 645
Leitner GmbH 750
Leybold AG 726
Loewe Opta GmbH 785, 786
Lotsch & Partner 738
Lufthansa AG 623–630
MAHO Aktiengesellschaft 728
Mankau, Dieter 712–716
Mannesmann Kienzle GmbH 162
Mauser Waldeck AG 489
MBB Messerschmitt-Bölkow-Blohm GmbH 632
Mercedes Benz AG 790–793
MERO-Raumstruktur GmbH & Co 787–789
Messe Frankfurt GmbH 577–580
Meurer, Bernd 722–724, 739
Miele & Cie. GmbH & Co 794–796
Montanwerke Walter GmbH 729
Morphy Verlag Helga Kalversberg 456
Neumeister, Alexander 471
Nixdorf Computer AG 481
NSU GmbH 427
PAG Presswerk AG 545
Pentagon 689, 690, 693–696
Poggenpohl Möbelwerke GmbH & Co. 553

ProduktEntwicklung Roericht 720, 721
Rams, Dieter 375–378
Ritter GmbH 482
Rochelt, Günter 633
Rose & Krieger GmbH & Co. KG 744
Rosenthal AG 550, 559–563, 817–819
Rowenta Werke GmbH 536, 607–609, 797, 798
Siemens AG 567–572, 709–711, 805
Slany Design 334, 478, 525
Sommerlatte, Horst u. Marlies 421
Schlegel G. GmbH & Co 732
Schmid & Stemmann 649
Schmitz, Peter 654
Schott-Zwiesel-Glaswerke AG 799–801
Schulte-Elektrotechnik GmbH & Co. KG 802–804
Staff GmbH & Co. KG 520, 521
Stiletto Studios 638
Stoll H. GmbH & Co 727
Stoll, Martin GmbH 491
Stumpf, Axel 636
TA Triumph-Adler AG 741
Tecta 751
Trumpf GmbH & Co 477
Viessmann Werke 806
Villeroy & Boch AG 747
Volkswagen AG 423
Vorwerk & Co. Teppichwerke KG 588–594, 807–809
Wall, Monika 647
Weinand, Herbert Jakob 659
Wendtland, Thomas 652
Werner & Pfleiderer GmbH 480
Wilkhahn Wilkening + Hahne GmbH + Co 595–597, 810, 811
WMF AG 812–814
Yellow Design 697–701
Zeiss, Carl 173, 815, 816
Zintzmeyer & Lux AG 581–587

All other illustrations: Rat für Formgebung/German Design Council. The illustrations were chosen for their documentary value. In a few cases optimal reproduction quality was not possible.

Numerals in boldface indicate text pages, regular numerals refer to illustration numbers. Works designed by the manufacturers are listed under the name of the company followed by an (M).

Index of Designers

Abbé, Ernst **269**
Acella Benecke (M) 147
Ad Us 669
AEG (AEG Product Design, Industrial Design) (M) 86, 99, 110, 211, 303, 324, 354, 358–362, 435, 436, 610–622, 736, 754, 755
AEG-Telefunken (M) 283, 309, 474
Aicher, Florian 639
Aicher, Otl **11**, **21**, **23**, 71–73, 75–77, 79, 80, 626, 628
Alape Produktbau (M) 546
Albus, Volker 685–688
Albers **22**
Alpina Büromaschinenvertrieb (M) 168
Ambrozu, Stefan (→ Development Group TU Essen) 742
Arens, Gerd (→ Pentagon) 695
Arp, Jean **15**
Atv, Atelier C. W. Voltz 482, 484
Auerbach, Dieter 530
Bader, Wolfgang, bader – design – concept 451, 513–515
Bätzner, Helmut 500
Baginsky, Nicolas Anatol 637
Bahr, Frank 744
Bartels, Heiko (→ Kunstflug) 702–704
Bartlmae/Staudacher Design 479
Bauknecht (M) 112, 345
Baumann, Hans Th. 136
BBC Brown Boveri (M) 85, 86
Beck, Peter 59
Becker, Kurt 635
Beek, Bontjes van 371
Behrens, Peter **10**, **246**, 753
Bellini, Mario 762–764
Berger Fabrik elektrischer Meßgeräte (M) 302
Berghof, Landes and Rang 640
Bergmiller, Karl Heinz 35–37
Berke, Hubert 155
Berlinetta 661, 664
Bernadotte, Graf 223
Beuys, Joseph 503
Bill, Max **15**, **21**, **22**, 3, 5, 60
Billing, Peters & Ruff 606
Bitsch, Hans Ulrich, **266**
Bizerba Waagen (M) 175–177
Bjorn, Acton 223
Blaupunkt (M) **247**, 426, 529, 756–758
Blumenau, D. 165
BMW (M) 88, 90, 424, 580–87, 631
Boch, Helen von 549
Bode, Arnold 180
Bufinger Development Department (Mehnert, Valenta) (M) 496–499
Bohl, Rainer 486
Bohnet, Armin 548
Bonsiepe, Gui **22**, 1, 14–18, 23, 46, 47, 54
Bosch (M) 473, 542
Brand 485
Brandolini, Andreas 672, 678, 681, 691, 692
Braun-Feldweg, Wilhelm **47**, 160, 229, 230, 255, 257
Braun, Braun Product Design **47**, **48**, **102**, **103**, **132**, **248**, 355–357, 363–370, 372–374, 379–382, 460, 524, 531, 532, 537, 539, 759–761
Breger, C. A. 473
Breux, Schima le 285
Brevern, Renate von (→ Cocktail) 644
Breuhaus, Fritz August **268**
Buber, Martin **21**
Bulthaup (M) 555, 749
Burandt, Ulrich 21, 289

Busch, Fritz B. 69, 70
Busch Jaeger Dürener Metallwerke (M) 227
Busse, Rido 52, 351, 352
busse design ulm 538
Camaro, Alexander 154
Cavael, Rolf 151
Clittenhout, Cornelius 8
Clivio, Franco 516–519, 769–771
Cocktail 644
Colani, Luigi 405, 417, 550, 556
Conrad, Michael 69, 70
Croy, Peter 71–73
D-Team (Dorothee Hiller, Rainer Bohl) 486, 495
Daimler-Benz, Mercedes-Benz (M) **246**, 85, 91, 425, 752, 790–793
Danner, Alfred 114
Deckelmann, Reinhold 59
Delta-Design 470
DEMAG Baggerfabrik (M) 196
Design Bartlmae/Staudacher 479
Design Praxis Diener 459, 522, 523, 732
Designwerkstatt Berlin 661–681
Des–in **147**, 507
Dethleffs Wohnwagenwerk (M) 89
Dettinger, Ernst 135
Develop Dr. Eisbein (M) 159
Development Group for Design 555
Development Group of Technical University Essen 742
Diener, Theodor **267**
Dittert, Karl 116, 126, 439, 450
Dornauf, Helmut 249
Drees, Holger 641, 705–708
Dreistädter Group **147**
DWM-Automatenbau (M) 272
Ebert, W. 108
Eckart, Peter 731
Eckert und Ziegler (M) 190
Eckstein, Wil 510
Ehinger Jr., Adolf 170
Ehlert, Kai 62
Eiermann, Egon **15**, **47**, 134, 138, 253, 261
Eisemann (M) 321
Elektron (M) 96
Elektror Karl W. Müller (M) 183
Emmer, Peter 59
Engel, Hartmut S. 480
Engelhard, Peter 451, 513–515
Engels-Schwarzpaul, Anna Christina 579
Engle, Claude R., 717, 718
Engler, Heinz H. **47**, 204, 206, 207
ERCO (M) **249**, 717, 718, 762–764
Esslinger, Hartmut, Esslinger-Design (→ frogdesign) 442, 553, 734
Fabrini, Federigo 549
Federal German Railways Design Center 605, 606
Feith, Michel 651
Fiegl, Thomas 634
Firle, Otto 623
Fischer, Artur 199
Fischer, Hardy (→ Kunstflug) 702–704
Fischer, Richard 355, 357, 371, 558
Fischer, Uwe (→ GINBANDE Design) 682–684
Fissler (M) 221
Flachglas DELOG-DEFAG (M) 447
Flacke, Jochen 819
Fleischmann, Klaus 330
Flesche, Klaus 191, 192, 271
form technik international fti (Louis L. Lepoix) 297, 343
Francis, Sam 592
Frank, Rudolf 254

Franz, Christian 15, 16
frogdesign 453, 533, 547, 734, 746–748
Fröshaug, Anthony **22**
FSB 765–767
Fuchs, Günter 338, 339
Garnich, Rolf 535
Geha Product Design (M) 740
Gehrmann, Hasso 554
German Federal Railways Central Office 85, 271
Geyer, Johannes 722, 723
Ghia 95
GINBANDE Design 682–684
GIRA Gustav Giersiepen (M) 226
Giugiaro, Giorgio 423
Glasenapp, Werner 305
Göhling, Klaus 418
Goepfert, H. 278
Goertz, Graf 215
Golka, W. A. 195.
Gonda, Tomás 75–77, 79, 80
Gossen (M) 244, 327
Graessner Getriebe- und Maschinenfabrik (M) 308
Greiser, Hans 241, 242
Gretsch, Herrmann 125
Greubel, Jürgen 374
Griemert, Hubert 119
Gröbli, Karl 78
Gropius, Walter **10**, **21**, 561
Gros, Jochen 507
Grote, H. 470
Grundig (M) 248
Gugelot, Hans **13**, **22**, **23**, **47**, **103**, **131**, 12, 33, 34, 38–43, 52, 57, 63–65, 71–74, 369, 370, 412–414
gugelot design 57, 65, 412–414, 455, 457
Gustedt, Hanno von 493
Hadid, Zaha M. 590
Häfner 485
Haesler, Otto **10**
Haller Maschinenbau (M) 292
Hartl, Hans 252
Hartmann, Horst 293, 294, 301
Hasenauer, Wolfgang 724
Haubold, E. 158
Hausmann, Raoul **10**
Heine, Klaus-Achim (→ GINBANDE Design) 682–684
Heisenberg, Werner **21**
Hempel, Klaus 401
Hengstler (M) 325
Henke Jr., E. 101
Henkels, Jochen 731
Henschel (M) 271
Hentschel, Harry 805
Herkenrath, Peter 148
Herold, Willy 174
HEWI (M) 772–777
Hildebrand, Margret 152
Hildmann, Simon, Rempen & Schmitz: SMS 564–566
Hileebrand Leuchtenfabrik (M) 239
Hiller, Dorothee (→ D-Team) 486
Hilsmann, Georg 23
Hilti (M) 473
Himmelwerk (M) 306
Hirche, Herbert 140, 145, 415, 416, 545
hircheteam 489, 512
Hochberger, Heinz 268
Hödicke, K. H. 502
Hölsken, Jürgen K. 520, 521
Hölzinger, J. P. 278
Hoffmann-Lederer 231
Hofmeister, Peter 25, 26
Holland-Letz, Horst 473
Holthöfer, Ulrike 646

Horntrich, Günter (→ Yellow Design) 729
Hosenfeld, Michael (→ Development Group TU Essen) 742
Hüskes, Charly (→ Kunstflug) 648, 702–704
Hullmann, Harald (→ Kunstflug) 702–704
Hundertpfund, Jörg 662, 677
Hundertwasser, Friedensreich 560
Hutschenreuther Arzberg Porzellan (M) 264
IGL-Design, Ernst Igl 454
igus-Team (M) 743
Interform Design Studio Schönfeld 534, 733
Interform Wolfsburg 92, 342, 344
Jablonski, Bernhard 103, 111, 245, 337, 350
Jens, Walter **21**
Joseph, G. 274
Junkers (M) 106
Käo, Tönis 709
Kammermeier, A. 659
Kantner, Liselotte 104, 120
Kapitzki, Herbert W. 81, 84
Karpf, Nikolaus 385
Kerting, Walter M. 188
Keysselitz 607
Kiehlneker, Walter 31
Kienzle Apparate (M) 162, 443
Kirchhoff, Ernst 146
Klar, Michael 84
Klier, Hans von 58
Klöckner-Humboldt-Deutz (M) 87
Klose, Odo (Klose & Partner) 197, 275, 291, 449
Kluge, Alexander **22**
Knauff, Volker (Development Group TU Essen) 742
Koch-Weser, Elke 8
Kövari, Peter 62
Kohen, Mosche 202
Kolloch, Hardy 473
Kornreich, Gabriel 676
Kraatz, Günter 167
Kramer, Friso 270
Kramer, Wolfgang 291
Kranz, Kurt 153
Krause, K. D. 741
Kremendahl, Daniel 473
Kronberger Werkstatt für Gestaltung 249–251
Krüger, Rolf 402, 799
Krupp, Friedrich, Central Institute for Research and Development (M) 298
Krups (M) 353, 540, 541, 544, 778–780
Kufus, Axel 646
Kuhles, Martin 705–708
Kunstflug 648, 702–704
Kupetz, Günter 557
LAMY (M) 781–784
Landes, Heinz H. 658
Lang, Julia 2
Lange, Gerd 404
Lange, Jürgen 506
Langenmayr, Albert 663, 675
Lannoch, Hans-Jürgen 62
Lanz (M) 194
Laubersheimer, Wolfgang (→ Pentagon) 694
Lecatsa, Rouli (→ Möbel Perdu) 645
Leitner, Burkhardt 750
Leitz (M) 172, 243, 247, 387
Leonhard & Kern 597
Leowald, Georg 157, 403
Leutner, Karl 121, 132
LeWitt, Sol 593
Lichtenstein, Roy 594

Liebe, Albert 246
Lindinger, Herbert **22**, **131**, 63, 71–74, 78
Linhof Kamera Werke (M) 388
Linke-Hofmann-Busch (M) 85
Lintener, Axel 14
Löffelhardt, Heinrich **15**, **47**, 118, 122, 128, 130, 131, 203, 205, 224, 225, 256, 801
Loewe (M) 785, 786
Lorenz, Franz-Wolfgang 666
Loritz, Axel 709
Lotsch & Partner 725, 738
Lubs, Dietrich 460
Ludi, Jean-Claude 78
Ludig, Daniel 635
Ludwig, Eduard 137
Lufthansa (M) 624, 625, 627, 629, 630
Luthe, Klaus 427
Magg, Helmut 142
MAHO (M) 728
Maibach (M) 85
Maldonado, Tomás **22**, **23**, 1, 9, 21, 46, 47, 54, 61, 62
MAN (M) 85
Mankau, Dieter 712–716
Manzoni, Pio 69, 70
Mauder, Bruno 102
McCloy, General **21**
Mengeringhausen, Max 787–789
Mentzel, Thomas 25, 26
Meurer, Bernd 739
Meyer-Voggenreiter (→ Pentagon) 690
Michel, Kurt 332
Miele (M) 794–796
Möbel Perdu 645
Möbius, Walter 187
Moeckl, Ernst, Atelier Ernst Moeckl 35–37, 51, 53, 60, 133, 299, 300, 383, 384, 406–411, 444, 448, 473
Moeckl, design team moeckl 444, 452
Möllenberg, Günter 553
Moll, Reiner, Moll-Design 477, 494
Moles, Abraham **22**
Moore, Henry 15
Morandini, Marcello 559, 818
Morgenstern, G. 287
MTU (M) 85
Muche, Georg 149
Mühlhaus, Heike 644
Müller, Gerd A. 369, 370
Müller, Reinhard (→ Pentagon) 690, 693
Müller, Walter 509
Müller-Deisig, Wolfgang 487, 488
Müller-Kühn, Helmut 63, 71–74
Muhr & Bender (M) 189
Nadkarni, Sudhakar 62
Nagel, Erwin 817
Neumeister, Alexander, Neumeister Design 422, 471, 632
Niggemann, F. 275
Nixdorf (M) 481
Nocon, Günter 527
Nonné-Schmidt, Helene **21**

Oberheim, Robert 371, 380, 381, 531
Obitz, Friedbert (Development Group TU Essen) 742
Oestreich, Dieter 276, 326, 348, 349
Oestreich, Herbert 274
Offelsmeyer 100
Ohl, Herbert **23**, 28–30, 32
Olympia-Werke (M) 438, 440, 461, 462
Otto, Frei 810
Paladino, Mimmo 591
Pappritz, Frau von **12**
Patschull, Rainer 346
Pelzel & Zaliukas 745
Pentagon 689, 690, 693–696
PER ProduktEntwicklung Roericht 504, 719–721
Perrine, Meruyu W. 11
Petri-Raben, Trude 123, 260
Picard, Johann Hermann 473
Piene, Otto 559
Poggenpohl Möbelwerke (M) 97
Pohl, Achim 634
Pohlig-Heckel-Bleichert (M) 193
Porsche (M) 277
Pott, Carl 127
Product Design Working Group (Hartmut S. Engel) 480
Prometheus (M) 216
Punzmann, Q. 144
Querengässer, Fritz 75–77
Raacke, Peter 164, 166, 169, 419
Raffler, Dieter 44, 45, 516–519
Rams, Dieter **47**, **103**, **131 ff.**, **250**, 42, 43, 355, 357, 363–366, 371, 373–379, 382, 460, 531, 532, 765–767
Rasch, Bodo 139
Ratzlaff, Jörg 656
Reich, Dieter 59
Reif, U. 275
Reif, Ulrich 705–708
Reinhold, Dieter J. 552
Reitz, Edgar **22**
Richter, Gerhard 589
Richter, Hans Werner **21**
Ritter Werk F. Ritter & Sohn (M) 222
Ritz, Wilhelm 490
Robeck, Sylvia 662, 677
Rochelt, Günter 633
Roehrer, Gerhard 736, 755
Roericht, Hans (→ PER ProduktEntwicklung Roericht) 48–50, 75–77, 504, 719–721
Rohde & Schwarz (M) 198
Rollei-Werke (M) 383, 384
Rosenstand, G. 287
Rosenthal (M) 560
Roth, Harald 143
Rowenta Design Department (M) 536, 607–609, 797, 798
Ruf, Sep 98
Saltus Werk Max Forst (M) 319
Sauer, Francke 811
Schack, Hans Ulrich 18
Schaerer, Rudolf 78
Scharfenberg, Rudolf 46, 47, 54

Schiedrum, Rolf-Dieter 340
Schlagheck, Norbert 389
Schlagheck Schultes Design 443, 526, 737
Schmauser, Dirk 17
Schmid, Jens Peter 657
Schmid & Stemmann 649
Schmitz, Peter 654
Schnaidt, Claude **22**, 78
Schneider, Peter 524
Schneider, U. 274
Schneider-Esleben, Paul **47**, 141
Schnüll, Herbert 286
Scholl, Hans **21**
Scholl, Inge **11**, **21**, **23**
Scholl, Sophie **21**
Scholz, Helmut 472
Schroff Development Group (M) 466
Schulte, Siegfried 802–804
Schultes, Herbert (→ Schlagheck Schultes Design) 330
Schultze, Hans Uwe 653
Schulze, Wolfgang 653
Schumacher, Emil 150
Schwitters, Kurt **10**
Schwagenscheidt, Walter 249–251
Schwann, Bernhard 316
Schwuchow, Anette 711
Seeliger, Klaus 240
Sennheiser electronic (M) 528
Sieber, Peter 109, 182, 186, 228, 754
Siemens, Siemens-Design (M) 113, 208, 213, 214, 217, 219, 304, 307, 310, 317, 318, 322, 328, 389, 420, 428–434, 437, 441, 445, 446, 458, 463–465, 467–469, 483, 567–572, 709–711, 805
Siemens & Halske (M) 163, 179, 269
Siemens-Schuckert-Werke (M) 86, 220
Siol, Wolfgang 79, 80
Sittmann, Tassilo 249
Slany, Hans Erich 105, 210, 212, 290, 311–315, 320, 323, 333–335, 341, 472, 475, 476
Slany Design Team 472, 473, 478, 525, 730, 735
Sommer, Ralph (→ Pentagon) 689
Sommerlatte, Horst 421
Sommerlatte, Marlies 421
Staatliche Prozellanmanufaktur Berlin (M) 178
Staff & Schwarz Leuchtenwerk (M) 391–393
Stanitzek, Joachim B. 665, 670, 680
Stankowski, Anton 601
Stankowski + Duschek 577, 579, 600
Stark, Günther 456
Staubert (→ PER ProduktEntwicklung Roericht) 504
Stiletto 638, 667
Stolz, Walter 580
Stolzenberg, F. 741
Strassl, Peter 643
Studer (M) 284
Stützer, Franz Alban 543
Stumpf, Axel 636, 642, 668
Stumpf, Jörg 444

Sukopp, Hans 64
Sulz, Günter 508
Syniuga, Siegfried Michail 650
TA-Design (Triumph-Adler) (M) 741
teamform design 551
Theiss, K. 101
Time and Motion Institute 473
Trippel, Hans 273
Uecker, Günther 501
Ullmann, Karl 296
Ulm Development Group 5 75–77
Ulm Development Group 6 46, 47, 54
Ungers, Oswald Mathias 578
Vahlenbreder, Aribert 55, 56
Viessmann (M) 806
Vogtherr, Burkhard 288, 492, 495
VOKO development team (M) 439
Volkswagen (M) 93
Völker, H. 281, 282
Voltz, C. W. (→ Atv, Atelier C. W. Voltz) 329, 347, 473, 482, 484
Vordemberge-Gildewart, Friedrich **22**
Vorwerk (M) 807–809
Votteler, Arno 491, 511
Wachsmann, Konrad 27
Wagenfeld, Wilhelm **15**, **47**, **262**, 107, 117, 124, 125, 129, 161, 218, 232–238, 258, 259, 262, 263, 800
Wahl, Eberhard 67, 68
Waldenburg, Hermann 660, 673
Wall, Monika 647
Warneke, Helmut 115
WEGA (M) 279–282
Wegmann (M) 85
Weidler, Fritz 126
Weinand, Herbert Jakob 659, 671, 674, 679
Weishaupt (M) 336
Weiss, Michael 78
Weiss, Reinhold 66, 356, 371, 372
Wendtland, Thomas 652
Wenz, Diethard 726
Werner, Peter 655
Wewerka, Stefan 751
Wieland, Rudolf M. 727
Wiese Förderanlagen (M) 184
Wilms, K. H. 331
Winter, Fritz 156
Wirgin Kamerawerk (M) 386
Witte, Dieter 394–400
WMF (M) 812–814
Wolf-Design (M) 473
Woyak, W. 295
Yellow Design 697–701
Zapf, Otto 505
Zapfmöbel InDesign (M) 390
Zarges-Leichtmetallbau (M) 200, 201
Zeischegg, Walter **22**, **23**, 22, 24–26, 31, 44, 45, 55, 56, 59
Zeiss (M) 171, 173, 181, 815, 816
Zemp, Werner 25, 26, 61
Zerver, Hermann J. 473
Zimmermann (M) 185
Zimmermann, Hubert 276
Zuckmayr, Karl **11**, **21**